Walking the Antonine Wall

A Journey from East to West Scotland

Alan Montgomery

Illustrations by Rob Hands

Walking the Antonine Wall – Alan Montgomery
Copyright © 2022. All rights reserved.

The right of Alan Montgomery to be identified as the author of the Work has been asserted in accordance with the Copyright, Designs & Patents Act 1988. First Edition published and copyright 2022 by Tippermuir Books Ltd, Perth, Scotland.

Second Edition 2023

mail@tippermuirbooks.co.uk – www.tippermuirbooks.co.uk.

No part of this publication may be reproduced or used in any form or by any means without written permission from the Publisher except for review purposes.

All rights whatsoever in this book are reserved.

ISBN 978-1-913836-12-2 (paperback).

A CIP catalogue record for this book is available from the British Library.

Project coordination and editorial by Dr Paul S Philippou.
Cover design by Matthew Mackie.
Illustrations by Rob Hands.
Editorial support: Ajay Close, Steve Zajda and Jean Hands.
Text design, layout, and artwork by Bernard Chandler [graffik].
Text set in Dante MT Std Regular 10.5/14pt with Dante MT Std Bold titling.

Printed and bound by Ashford Colour Press.

Walking the Antonine Wall charts a voyage on foot along one of Scotland's most fascinating ancient monuments, a 38-mile rampart constructed in the second century AD by the Romans to mark what would briefly become the northernmost limit of their vast empire. It is a personal account of historian Dr Alan Montgomery's encounters with the enigmatic remains of this Roman frontier which have inspired myths and legends and intrigued and baffled generations of chroniclers, antiquarians and archaeologists. Leading through wild open spaces and along city streets, past curiosities man-made and natural, ancient and modern, it records a journey across central Scotland and through 2,000 years of captivating Scottish history.

PRAISE FOR
WALKING THE ANTONINE WALL (2022)

'*Walking the Antonine Wall* is a personal exploration of one of Scotland's oldest monuments, and the author really makes you feel that you're walking alongside him, seeing and experiencing history with him. It is a beautifully written, illustrated, and presented love letter to the Antonine Wall, which should find itself on the bookshelf of anyone who is interested in Scotland's Roman past.'

Andrew Tibbs
Author of *Beyond the Empire: A Guide to the Roman Remains in Scotland*
and *A Short Guide to Hadrian's Wall*

'A pleasure to read, charming and engaging…I certainly learned from it.'
Professor Lawrence Keppie,
Author of *The Legacy of Rome: Scotland's Roman Remains*

ACKNOWLEDGEMENTS

A huge thanks to Paul Philippou of Tippermuir Books, whose input and advice made the writing and editing of this book a real pleasure. I am grateful to Rob Hands for his beautiful illustrations, which bring back happy memories of my walk along the Wall, and also to Matthew Mackie, who created the stunning cover. Thanks to Derek Hall for reading the book and offering helpful feedback; and to Ajay Close, Jean Hands and Steve Zajda for their proof-reading and editorial support.

One of the most enjoyable aspects of my journey along the Roman frontier was the people that I met and spoke to along the way, and I am indebted to all of them for sharing their time and their expertise: Dr Fraser Hunter, Ian Shearer, Dr Gaele Macfarlane, Professor Lawrence Keppie, Jim Mearns, Kevin McAleer, Dr Louisa Campbell, Josephine Crossland and Svetlana Kondakova.

Thanks to Susan, Graeme and Gail for offering me food and lodgings on my journey, and most of all thanks to James, for his continual support and encouragement.

ABOUT THE AUTHOR

Alan Montgomery was born in Glasgow and raised in Edinburgh, and his lifelong love of history was largely inspired by regular childhood visits to Scotland's historical monuments. After studying History of Art at the University of Glasgow, he moved to London and spent many years working in the art world. He returned to academia in 2010, achieving an MA in Classical Civilisation at Birkbeck, University of London, that included a thesis focusing on the post-Roman history of the Antonine Wall. Next, he completed a PhD at the same institution which investigated eighteenth-century attitudes towards Scotland's Roman past. He was elected a fellow of the Society of Antiquaries of Scotland in 2018. He is the author of *Classical Caledonia: Roman history and myth in eighteenth-century Scotland* (EUP, 2020).

CONTENTS

Preface 1

Chapter One   Carriden to Falkirk 15

Chapter Two   Callendar to Bonnybridge 51

Chapter Three   In Search of Arthur's O'on 83

Chapter Four   Bonnybridge to Kirkintilloch 111

Chapter Five   Croy Hill to Kirkintilloch 141

Chapter Six   Kirkintilloch to Bearsden 173

Chapter Seven   Bearsden to Old Kilpatrick 203

Epilogue 231

Select Bibliography 237

PREFACE

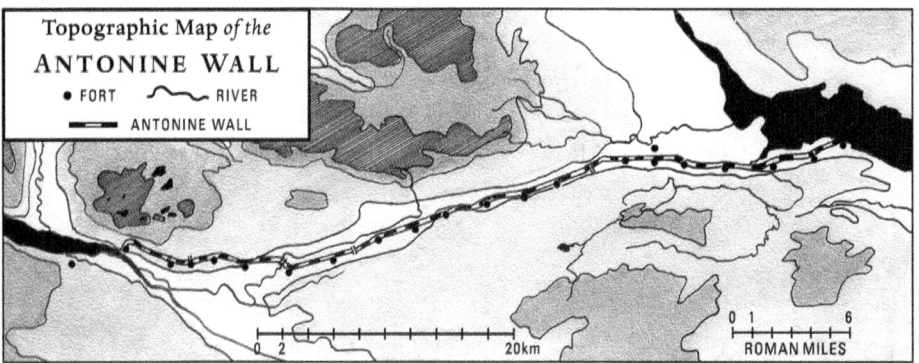

My Antonine Wall journey began in Chambers Street, Edinburgh, in the National Museum of Scotland. I grew up in this city and know the museum well – in fact, I spent an inordinate amount of my childhood there, wandering through its echoey rooms, gawping at the whale skeleton suspended from the ceiling in its natural history gallery, marvelling at its dioramas of ancient Egypt, pressing the button that sent the wheels of a model steam train into furious motion. I live in London now, and have done for over two decades, but whenever I am back in my home town, I try to make time to visit Chambers Street, to see how the old place has evolved, expanded and improved over the years.

That day, I was at the museum to see something specific. I was in the basement surrounded by an unrivalled collection of precious ancient artefacts, including some of the oldest objects discovered in the land that we now call Scotland. It's quiet down there, this part of the museum apparently off the radar of most visitors, so I had it pretty much to myself. In front of me, set into a wall just above eye level, was a huge block of rich red sandstone covered in intricate carvings.

I was looking at a Roman sculptured panel, more than 1,800 years old, rediscovered over 150 years ago at Bridgeness, in Bo'ness, a spot roughly 15 miles west of Edinburgh. Often referred to today as the Bridgeness Distance Slab, it is the largest (and arguably the finest) of several such carved stones that have been found across central Scotland.

After a moment of contemplation, I was joined by Dr Fraser Hunter, the museum's Principal Curator of Prehistoric and Roman Archaeology, who had kindly agreed to talk to me about this incredible sculpture. Fraser has been working at the museum for over 30 years, and this basement dedicated to Scotland's Early People is very much his domain. 'It's the only part of the museum worth visiting', he joked as we surveyed the glass cases that surrounded us, filled with everything from simple terracotta pots and cooking implements to luxury bronze vessels and piles of shiny silver coins.

The Bridgeness Distance Slab

We began by discussing the composition of the Bridgeness Distance Slab. At its centre sits a carved Latin inscription. Dedicated to the Emperor Antoninus Pius, the incised text records that the Second Legion Augusta constructed 4,652 paces (around 6,884 m) of a frontier, hence the term 'distance slab'.

More eye-catching are the figural scenes on either side of the inscription. The scene on the left is easy to interpret. A Roman cavalryman, resplendent in his armour and crested helmet, spear in one hand and shield in the other, gallops relentlessly over his defeated enemies. Four 'barbarians', naked and vulnerable, scatter and cower under the horse's hooves. One has a spear stuck in his back; another has quite literally lost his head. Its brutal depiction of Roman military might is uncompromising and, to our eyes at least, rather horrifying.

The scene on the right, however, requires explanation. It features a tight group of figures standing around a bull, a pig and a sheep. Four soldiers, one carrying the *vexillum* (a military standard), stand in line around a figure in a toga who is pouring a liquid offering onto an altar. Before them is a musician playing the pipes, his cheeks puffed with air. This is a Roman religious ritual known as the *suovetaurilia*, during which beasts were slaughtered and prayers made to the god Mars, music and chanting drowning out the cries and groans of the sacrificial victims.

A more elaborate rendering of the *suovetaurilia* can be found on Trajan's Column, the 38-metre-tall, heavily carved monument erected in Rome to celebrate victory in Dacia (a territory that covered parts of modern Romania and Serbia) 35 years before this Scottish slab was erected. One of the most important rituals in the Roman religion, *suovetaurilia* was a process of purification, cleansing the land and inaugurating new beginnings.

The Bridgeness Distance Slab commemorated the start of a new era for the region we know as southern Scotland – an era of Roman rule. It once decorated a frontier built on the order of the Emperor Antoninus Pius, a substantial rampart that stretched across the narrowest part of mainland Britain between the estuaries of Forth and Clyde. The supposed 'barbarians' carved on the stone are in fact the people sometimes referred to by the Romans as 'Caledonians', inhabitants of this part of the world long before the nation of Scotland was born.[1] For a while at least, this would become a small, rather insignificant part of the mighty Roman Empire, a realm that extended all the way across Europe and beyond, as far east as Syria and south to the deserts of Egypt.

This distance sculpture is an extremely compelling object and one of my favourite things in the entire museum collection. To modern viewers, its carved figures, with their chubby, cartoonish faces and bulging almond eyes, may appear simplistic. But what they lack in finesse they more than make up for in drama. As Dr Hunter pointed out, Roman sculpture in this part of the world was vastly different to the sophisticated marbles found in the city of Rome, but that does not mean that the carvings from the frontier

---

1 The Caledonians were just one tribe amongst several mentioned by the Romans in this part of the world, but for clarity and simplicity 'Caledonia' and 'Caledonians' will be used here as cover-all terms for the region now known as Scotland and its ancient inhabitants.

lands should be viewed as inferior. Rather, he explained, they belong to a local tradition which focused more on 'line and pattern' than form, as can be seen in the sinuous folds of the cloaks and robes worn by the Romans portrayed on the Bridgeness Distance Slab.

The sculpture would have been even more stunning when first made. Dr Hunter revealed that its carved details were originally covered with brightly coloured pigments, vivid reds highlighting both the letters and the blood pouring from the wounds of the injured and dying Caledonians. We are still not sure how it was positioned on the Roman frontier, but no doubt it would have been highly visible, unmissable for anyone passing by. There are sockets for metal clamps on the sides of the panel, and Dr Hunter proffered a theory that it may have been inserted into some sort of stone structure or support, adding that the wall in which it is currently framed was specially constructed to give the museum visitors a sense of how it might have been displayed in ancient times.

We stood for a minute and considered the imposing carved stone, pondering why it was erected. The inscription records the hard work of the legionaries who built the new Roman Wall and Dr Hunter believes that this and the numerous other similar stone panels that originally decorated the ancient frontier were made for their benefit. Ancient graffiti indicates that many in the Roman legions were literate, so this conspicuous commemoration of their achievements would have been understood and appreciated by the soldiers themselves.

As for the carved scenes, their message would have been clear not only to the Roman soldiers, but also to the illiterate natives. Roman conquest will be ruthless and unforgiving, they seem to say, but afterwards there will be peace and harmony. Defy us at your peril but reap the rewards if you submit. Then I remembered that the Bridgeness Distance Slab was found smashed to pieces, buried face down in the Scottish dirt. Suddenly, this imperialistic bombast seemed like nothing more than empty hubris.

Exactly why Titus Aelius Hadrianus Antoninus Augustus Pius, better known as Antoninus Pius, chose to conquer what is now southern Scotland, a land so distant from Rome, situated at the very edge of the known world, remains a mystery. Following a successful political career, Antoninus had been adopted by the Emperor Hadrian, who then declared him his successor, a common procedure at the time that helped to ensure a smooth succession from one generation to the next. Succeeding Hadrian as emperor of Rome in AD 138, Antoninus would become known as a man who ruled calmly and carefully, a good administrator whose long reign is widely regarded as a time of peace and prosperity.

Current thinking is that Antoninus ordered the conquest of (part of) Caledonia to prove his military prowess, to demonstrate to his subjects that, as well as being a safe pair of hands, he was also a man with bold ideas and imperialist ambitions. So it was that, in or around AD 142 (as is often the case with ancient history, the exact date remains uncertain), the famous Wall built by his predecessor Hadrian was abandoned and the Roman governor of Britain, Quintus Lollius Urbicus, led his troops into the lands that lay beyond it. A new frontier was established 100 miles further north and Antoninus was declared *Imperator* (Conqueror) for the only time in his long career. Coins were minted in Rome in AD 143 bearing the emperor's portrait on one side and the goddess Victory next to the letters 'BRITAN' on the other.

This was not the first or indeed the last Roman expedition into this part of the world. The Roman author Tacitus documented an invasion of northern Britain led by the general Gnaeus Julius Agricola (who happened to be Tacitus' father-in-law) way back in the early 80s. Tacitus recorded that Agricola built a line of forts between the firths of Forth and Clyde to keep out the barbarians to the north, with, as he described it, 'the enemy pushed back into a separate island, so to speak'. Despite the success of further campaigns in Caledonia which concluded with him winning a decisive victory against the northern tribes at the battle of Mons Graupius in AD 83 or 84, Agricola did not hang around to consolidate his conquests.

The Emperor Septimius Severus, known as a ruthless warrior, marched north with his son Marcus Aurelius Antoninus (better known today by his nickname Caracalla) and an enormous army in the early third century, but this invasion was also short-lived. According to the Roman author Cassius Dio, Severus withdrew after forcing the northern tribes to make terms and give up much of their territory. So, while the Romans were clearly interested in conquering Caledonia, Antoninus Pius was the only emperor who seemed intent on securing the region long term, on adding it to the

Roman Empire and keeping it there.

No doubt taking inspiration from his late adopted father, Antoninus decided that the best way to control and protect his newly acquired territory was to build a secure barrier along its northern edge. A single sentence in a Latin text, the *Historia Augusta (Augustan History)*, an undated and unattributed collection of biographies of the Roman emperors, is the only ancient written record of the construction of this enormous boundary marker:

> *nam et Brittanos per Lollium Urbicum vicit legatum alio muro cespiticio summotis barbaris ducto*
> for his Legate Lollius Urbicus defeated the Britons and having driven back the barbarians, built another wall of turf.

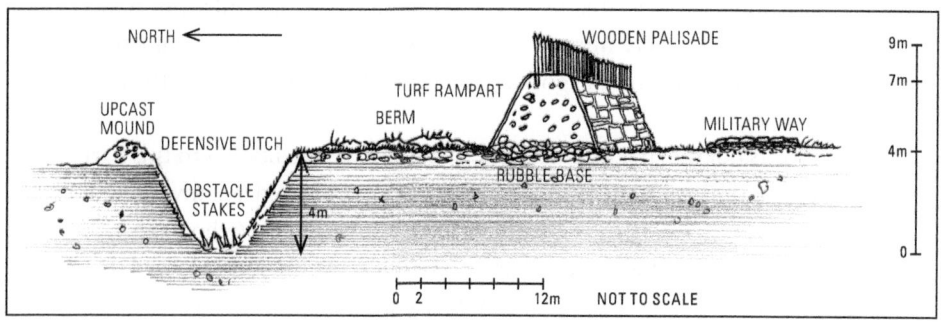

Cross-section Of The Antonine Wall

It is worth pointing out at this stage that the frontier built by Antoninus, the monument referred to today as the Antonine Wall, is not a 'wall' at all, or at least, not a wall in the strictest sense. It was a linear defence system that consisted of various elements, all of them working together to create a fearsome barrier. Rather than building a stone fortification like the one constructed by Hadrian two decades previously, Antoninus (or whoever it was that took such decisions for him) opted for a tall rampart built mostly from blocks of cut turf, a huge banking with sloped sides that could have reached around 3 m in height.

It seems likely that this earthwork would have been topped with a walkway and wooden palisade, although no evidence of this has been found to date. If it was, then the whole structure could have been up to 5 m tall. The massive rampart was supported by a solid stone base, a wide platform of rubble with neatly chiselled kerb stones at the outer edges. While the *Historia Augusta* calls it a *murus*, a Latin word translated as 'wall', the inscriptions found along the Antonine Wall refer to it as a *vallum*, meaning 'rampart' or 'fortification'. Many modern archaeologists describe the frontiers of the Roman Empire using the Latin term *limes*, meaning 'limit'.

Running along the north side of this turf rampart was a vast V-shaped ditch, typically around 12 m wide and 4 m deep. Between the two was a flat area, between 6 m and 9 m wide, known as the berm. The earth dug out of the ditch was piled along the north side of the frontier, creating another barrier and increasing the depth of the ditch in the process. To the south of this ran a road, often referred to as the 'Military Way', which allowed speedy travel along the entire frontier. Up to 8m wide, the surface of the road was cambered, allowing rainwater to run off into the drains at either side.

All along the frontier were forts, large permanent installations built to house the units of auxiliaries who garrisoned the frontier. Seventeen of them have so far been identified, and it seems likely that there were more – each one is located roughly two miles from the next, some much bigger than others. Several of them have 'annexes', fortified areas outside the walls of the fort that seem to have been used for industrial activity and sometimes contained a bath house, but whose primary purpose is still not fully understood.

It has been suggested that six of the larger forts were built first, with more added later in a major change to the design of the frontier, although theories about how the Antonine Wall was planned and built are constantly evolving. Its various elements – the rampart, the ditch, the road and the forts – were all constructed by the Roman legions, their work recorded in the elaborately decorated 'distance slabs' as well as other commemorative stone panels.

And then, for reasons that remain unclear, the whole thing was completely abandoned only a few years after it was built. The Roman army retreated southwards and Hadrian's Wall was reinstated as the northerly frontier of the Roman province of Britannia. Although the date of the withdrawal is much debated, some historians have proposed that the Antonine Wall was already out of use by the time Antoninus Pius died in AD 161.

Early archaeologists noticed signs of burning and demolition at sites along the Scottish frontier and interpreted these as evidence of a brutal Caledonian attack. Today, it is widely agreed that this intentional destruction indicates an orderly withdrawal, the frontier's forts decommissioned by the Roman troops as they departed. As it stands, the abandonment of the Antonine Wall is just one of the mysteries that surround this enigmatic ancient monument, yet another tantalising conundrum that I suspect will never be fully solved.

The Antonine Wall has inevitably suffered in the centuries since its abandonment – much of it has been lost to erosion, agriculture and urban sprawl. But many sections survive as a testament to its immense strength and a tangible reminder of its fleeting glories. The reason that I was in the National Museum of Scotland, looking at the Bridgeness Distance Slab, was that I was about to set off on a journey along the ancient frontier, a walk along all 38 or so miles to search out its remains and find out more about its current state.

I first discovered the Antonine Wall when I was still a (rather swotty) Edinburgh schoolboy. My interest in ancient Rome piqued by Latin lessons, a weekend exploring Hadrian's Wall had further fired my imagination. When I found out that there was another Roman frontier much closer to home, I was over the moon. Visits were made to several of its sites, and I was not disappointed. I loved both the history and the atmosphere of those places and was particularly enchanted by their magical air of antiquity.

More recently, a return to academia as an adult led me into studying the Antonine Wall in a more scholarly way, investigating both its Roman history and its fate after it was abandoned. As my research has revealed, this enormous monument became a source of immense interest over the centuries, inspiring all sorts of myths and legends, intriguing and baffling the generations of historians and archaeologists who have tried to unravel its secrets.

I regard the Antonine Wall as one of Britain's greatest historical monuments, but also one of its most overlooked and underappreciated. While Hadrian's Wall has become world famous and instantly recognisable, the Antonine Wall is less well-known. Perhaps due to the common belief that Hadrian's Wall formed the ultimate boundary of Roman power in Britain, many people are still surprised to hear that the Romans made it into Scotland at all.

I wanted others to get to know this incredible monument but realised that I first needed to get to know it better myself. Although I had visited most of its better-known sites, some of them on numerous occasions, I had never examined the Antonine Wall in its entirety. I decided that now was the time, and on foot was the best way to do it.

In exploring and writing about the Antonine Wall, I would follow in the footsteps of countless people across the centuries. Early reports of it are confused and inaccurate. Writing only about a century after the Romans left Britain, Gildas, a monk who later became a saint, described two Roman Walls in his *De excidio et conquestu Britanniae* (*On the Ruin and Conquest of Britain*).

The first is a wall of turf that sounds like our Antonine Wall. Gildas, however, dated the building of this turf frontier to the early fifth century, and stated that it was completely ineffectual due to its construction, requiring another stone wall to be built not long after. As has been pointed out, the turf wall that he mentioned could be the so-called 'vallum' of Hadrian's Wall, a sizeable earthwork that runs along its south side that is now recognised as contemporary to the stone rampart but was long thought to predate it.

The eighth-century monk and historian Bede, who spent most of his life in Jarrow, also mentioned a turf wall built towards the end of the Roman occupation of Britain in his *Historia ecclesiastica gentis Anglorum* (*Ecclesiastical History of the English People*), but he helpfully added some geographical details that show beyond doubt that he was referring to Scotland's Roman frontier.

Bede proposed that it was built by the Britons to keep out the rampaging northern hordes and claimed that they used sods of turf instead of stone due to their ignorance and lack of skill. He noted that much of the frontier could still be seen during his lifetime, although this information must have been second-hand, since Bede almost certainly never saw the Antonine

Wall himself. Just as damning as Gildas and Bede in their judgement of the Antonine Wall is the *Historia Brittonum* (*History of the Britons*) attributed to the ninth-century monk Nennius, which described it as *'rusticus'*, meaning 'unsophisticated' or 'crude'.

Scotland's first home-grown historian, John of Fordun, who was writing in the late fourteenth century, had much to say about Roman exploits in Caledonia in his *Chronica gentis Scotorum* (*Chronicles of the Scottish People*). He sometimes cited Gildas and Bede amongst other sources, but much of his 'history' was in fact complete fiction, bombastic tales of Caledonian bravery against fearsome foreign foes.

Things had not improved 200 years later, when George Buchanan, a renowned Latinist, poet and tutor to the boy who would become King James VI and I, wrote the *Rerum Scoticarum historia* (*History of the Scots*) which was published in 1582 soon after its author's demise. Although his description of the Antonine Wall was the most accurate to date, he was clearly flummoxed by the confusing ancient sources and as a result incorrectly named it the *'vallum Severi'*, the Wall of Severus.

Like Fordun before him, Buchanan was more concerned with patriotic tales of Scottish exceptionalism than historical accuracy. The idea that Scotland was one of the few nations to have resisted Roman conquest, its inhabitants so fierce that the Romans had been forced to keep them out with high walls, appears in all sorts of Scottish medieval and Renaissance writing, as a sort of David and Goliath tale of heroic resistance to foreign rule. As many Scots liked to repeatedly point out, resisting Rome was something that their old enemy, the feeble English, had notably failed to do.

The eighteenth century was a period of intense interest in Scotland's Roman heritage, particularly the Antonine Wall. Although there was still debate as to who had built the stone wall in the north of England (the Emperor Severus was then seen as the most likely candidate), the numerous inscriptions found along the Scottish Wall had finally proved beyond doubt that this was the frontier constructed by Antoninus Pius and Lollius Urbicus.

This was a time when ancient Rome was widely admired, particularly by the educated elite, and held up as a paradigm of high culture, military strength and imperial power. It was also the age of the antiquarians, men (and it was almost exclusively men) who loved to visit historical monuments and discover, collect and study ancient artefacts.

In 1707, Scotland gave up her sovereignty to become part of Great Britain. Many Scots, particularly those who disapproved of the Act of Union, turned to their ancient history in search of stories of Caledonian glory, memories of a time when the inhabitants of the north were brave and free. As a result, eighteenth-century discussions on Roman Scotland were often clearly influenced as much by the politics, prejudices and tastes of the period as they were by historical evidence or the latest antiquarian discoveries.

As well as being a physician, natural historian and geographer, Edinburgh-born scholar Sir Robert Sibbald also developed a passion for Scotland's Roman past. Something of a Romanist obsessive who held the Romans in high regard, he travelled along the Antonine Wall (or at least the eastern stretches of it) and wrote down what he found in his *Historical Inquiries Concerning the Roman Monuments and Antiquities in the North Part of Britain Called Scotland* of 1707. In 1723, Alexander Gordon took proper surveying equipment as he trekked around Scotland in search of Roman sites, and the book he published three years later, *Itinerarium Septentrionale (Northern Journey)* contains maps, charts and plans of the Antonine Wall and its forts.

English scholars took an interest too. William Stukeley published a detailed description of the Roman monuments on and near the Antonine Wall in 1720 without ever actually visiting it, while John Horsley made a long and laborious journey all around Britain (Scotland and the Antonine Wall included) while researching his *Britannia Romana*, which appeared in 1732 soon after its author's untimely death.

When it came to the Antonine Wall, this was an age of discovery, but also an age of intense disagreement as to what the Romans had achieved (or failed to achieve) in the north, as the old traditions of Caledonian valour conflicted with the widespread admiration for ancient Rome.

The most accurate early modern record of the Antonine Wall was made in 1755 by William Roy, a cartographer in the employ of the Hanoverian army who developed an interest in Roman remains as he mapped Scotland's topography. His work was finally published posthumously in 1793 in a lavish volume entitled *The Military Antiquities of the Romans in North Britain*, which includes maps and plans of sites along the frontier. Although his text is a garbled affair that does not stand up to modern analysis, Roy's carefully drawn plans are still admired today, and are particularly useful for understanding sites that have since been lost or damaged.

The later eighteenth century and much of the nineteenth century were an age of destruction. As the passion for Scotland's Roman past faded, replaced by a fashion for ruined castles, windswept moors and tartan, so large chunks of the Antonine Wall were lost, erased by intensive farming techniques, swept away by a canal and a railway, disappearing under rapidly expanding towns. Its location near to both Edinburgh and Glasgow had previously meant that it was easy to access and study, much more so than the remote Hadrian's Wall. Now, the Antonine Wall found itself in the very epicentre of Scotland's industrial heartlands, and its fragile remains suffered as a result.

Things have improved in the last 130 years. The 1890s witnessed renewed interest in the Antonine Wall, with advances in archaeology allowing late-Victorian scholars to understand its subtle remains more fully. The decades that followed saw large scale excavations of several of its forts directed by the eminent archaeologist Sir George Macdonald, who published his book *The Roman Wall in Scotland* in 1911, following it up with a longer revised edition in 1934. While today's experts may not always agree with his conclusions, his findings have been fundamental in our modern understanding of the frontier.

The first woman to publish a description of a journey along the Antonine Wall was Jessie Mothersole, an artist with a special interest in archaeology. Born in Essex, she trained at the Slade School of Art in the 1890s. Her first archaeological drawings were made in Egypt in the first decade of the twentieth century, after that she concentrated on British (particularly Roman) sites. Mothersole's experiences on the Roman frontier are recorded in her evocative (and beautifully illustrated) *In Roman Scotland*, published in 1927.

Since then, two names have dominated the excavation and study of the Antonine Wall: Professors Anne Robertson and Lawrence Keppie. A native Glaswegian, Robertson spent 40 years teaching Roman archaeology at the University of Glasgow. She was also a prolific excavator who dug at many sites along the Antonine Wall. In 1960, she published the first edition of *The Antonine Wall: A Handbook to the Roman Wall Between Forth and Clyde and a Guide to its Surviving Remains*.

PREFACE

Several editions have appeared since and the latest, entitled *The Antonine Wall: A Handbook to Scotland's Roman Frontier* is an invaluable little tome for anyone wishing to explore the Wall. For the last 30 years, the *Handbook* has been edited and revised by Lawrence Keppie, now Emeritus Professor of Roman History and Archaeology at the University of Glasgow who worked for three decades as a curator at the university's Hunterian Museum.

Today's academics are more impressed by the Antonine Wall than those early medieval monks – indeed, Professor David Breeze (who knows more than most about the Wall's history and archaeology) has described it as 'the most complex and highly developed of all frontiers constructed by the Roman Army'. In 2008, the Antonine Wall was inscribed as a UNESCO World Heritage Site, one of only six in Scotland. Its international importance was finally acknowledged, and a pledge was made to protect and preserve it for future generations.

When it came to planning my own journey along the Antonine Wall, the first major decision that I had to make was the direction of travel. The written descriptions of the frontier left by my predecessors, such as Sir Robert Sibbald, Alexander Gordon, John Horsley and George Macdonald, mainly start in the west and finish in the east. In the end, mainly because it is the direction followed by Anne Robertson and Lawrence Keppie in *The Antonine Wall: A Handbook to Scotland's Roman Frontier*, I decided to walk east to west – hence my visit to the National Museum in Edinburgh and my inspiring meeting with Dr Hunter to kick off the whole endeavour.

That meeting was at an end, but just as we were about to leave the Bridgeness Distance Slab, that captivating record of a key moment in Scottish history, Dr Hunter shared a final fascinating fact. It is possible to tentatively identify the figure at the centre of the *suovetaurilia* ritual who is shown pouring the offerings onto the altar. The man responsible for such a task would have been the legion's legate, and in the case of the Second Legion Augusta we know that the legate at the time of the Antonine Wall's construction was a certain Aulus Claudius Charax.

Surprisingly, Charax had no military experience before the invasion of Caledonia, but he may have been a friend or acquaintance of the emperor. He originally hailed from Pergamum in the Roman province of Asia, so the two could have met when Antoninus served as proconsul there in the mid-130s. So, while the (heavily restored) cartoon-like face that we see on the stone could hardly be described as a portrait in the modern sense, it could well be the earliest image of an identifiable person that we have in Scotland.

After a coffee in the museum café during which we chatted about my forthcoming walk, I said goodbye to Dr Hunter and left the National Museum of Scotland. I headed back towards my accommodation, all the while thinking about the challenge that lay ahead.

As I had worked out the best route, charting a path over three Ordnance Survey maps that linked the places already familiar to me with those yet unknown, I had realised that my walk would be much more than an exercise in identifying and exploring Roman archaeology. In fact, the journey led me through almost 2,000 years of Scottish history, across open fields and woodland and over high hills, through towns and city suburbs. In following the line of the ancient frontier, I passed by medieval tower houses and concrete tower blocks, historical stately homes and wonders of modern engineering.

A walk along the Antonine Wall offers not only a thick slice of Scottish history, but also a snapshot of modern Scotland, a chance to see some of the country's most beautiful landscapes and visit some of its most interesting places. My route included a detour, as I ventured into the lands north of the Wall to investigate the southern edges of unconquered Caledonia which, although not fully subdued by Rome, were not completely outside its far-reaching iron grip.

This book is a record of my journey, a history of the Antonine Wall and the places that it passes by and through, a guidebook of sorts, as well as a memoir of my own experiences as I travelled along it. It features the people that I met along the way, the people who have excavated the Roman frontier, studied it and worked to promote and preserve it. As we shall see, these journeys through Scotland past and present turned out to be mostly enjoyable and enlightening, sometimes unpredictable, occasionally frustrating, on one occasion even terrifying, but certainly never dull.

Chapter One

CARRIDEN TO FALKIRK

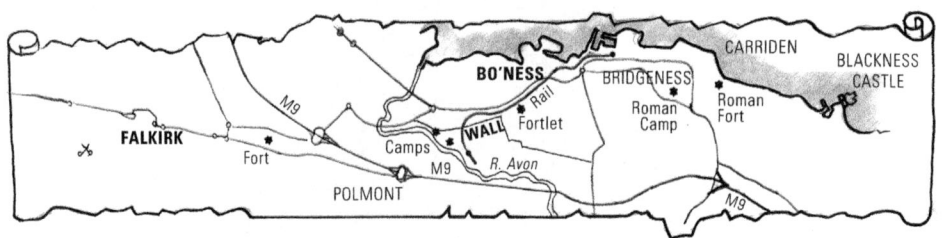

From Carriden To Falkirk

Having decided to walk the Antonine Wall from east to west, I was immediately faced with an important question. Where was I to set off? Although previous generations of cartographers and archaeologists have recorded much of the course of the Roman frontier allowing us to accurately map it even in places where no physical signs of it now remain above ground, the exact location of its eastern end has long been a mystery. The distance sculpture dug up at Bridgeness in the nineteenth century is still the most easterly relic of the rampart to have been discovered – beyond that its route becomes completely untraceable. I realised that I needed to do some (metaphorical) digging and look at the writings of my predecessors, the historians and antiquarians who studied and explored the Antonine Wall in centuries past, in the hope that they might provide an answer.

I soon discovered that several potential locations have been proposed for the east end of the Roman frontier, some more convincing than others. Bede's eighth-century *Historia ecclesiastica Gentis Anglorum* placed it two miles west of Abercorn, which would mean somewhere near the picturesque medieval castle at Blackness. Bede's muddled references to the Antonine Wall's history and geography, however, are full of inaccuracies, and it is likely that he never visited the monument in person. The name of

Walton, a small village to the south-west of Blackness (somewhere, I assume, close to the modern Walton Farm), led some antiquarians to claim that this supposed 'Wall-town' must have been the spot where the frontier ended, but to me it was too far south to be a viable option.

Blackness Castle

Sir Robert Sibbald, the eighteenth-century antiquarian who spent much of his time hunting for Roman antiquities in this part of the world, believed that the frontier extended further east beyond Abercorn, but then he was convinced that a long earthwork in East Lothian was the famous Wall built by the Emperor Hadrian, so we should certainly treat his conjectures with caution. The modern Ordnance Survey map shows the Antonine Wall as a dotted line which hits the coast of the Firth of Forth on the eastern edge of the town of Bo'ness, but this is purely conjectural, and since a scruffy industrial estate next to a noisy road did not seem like the best place to start my walk, I quickly discounted that possibility.

So far, so confusing. There was, however, one other place name that I noticed in medieval and early modern accounts of the Antonine Wall. The vague and confused descriptions of the Roman frontiers in Gildas' original *De excidio et conquestu Britanniae* contain no specific geographical detail, but an early thirteenth-century manuscript copy of it, written at Sawley Abbey in Lancashire, noted that the Antonine Wall ran westwards from 'Kair Eden'. This idea was repeated by fourteenth-century Scottish chronicler John of Fordun, who wrote that its eastern terminus could be found '*juxta villam Karedin*', meaning 'next to the village of Karedin'.

The discovery of Roman artefacts in the following centuries in the place now known as Carriden demonstrated to eighteenth-century antiquarians that there had certainly been extensive Roman activity in the area. The village may be gone, but Carriden House and its grounds survive, loitering just beyond the eastern outskirts of Bo'ness, near to Bridgeness. Modern archaeology has confirmed that this was once the site of an important Roman military installation located at, or more probably a short distance from, the end the Antonine Wall. I knew that it was a spot with an interesting story to tell, so it was there that I chose to begin my journey.

Carriden House

The next question I faced was how to get there. Few people visit Carriden nowadays, I suspect, because it is not an easy place to find. The journey from Edinburgh, only 15 miles as the crow flies, would take over an hour on public transport, hopping on and off trains and buses before finishing on foot. You can drive it in half the time, but there are no signposts to point the way, and nowhere to leave your car when you get there. I ended up taking the easiest but most expensive option, catching a train from

Edinburgh to Linlithgow and then calling for a taxi at the station.

The taxi driver was a friendly sort and interested to hear of my plans. He was aware of the Roman frontier, but not particularly impressed by what he had seen of it: 'The thing is, it's really just a ditch', he told me, as if to prepare me for disappointment. For a moment I felt the urge to correct him, to explain the unique qualities of this ancient wonder, but in the end, too polite or maybe too lazy, I simply nodded, smiled and changed the subject.

The taxi dropped me off on Carriden Brae, north of a cluster of cottages known as Muirhouses, where a lodge house sits at the end of a long, straight drive. I walked down this drive, past an abandoned eighteenth-century kitchen garden, once filled with fruit trees and vegetables, its worn and fractured brick walls now offering shelter to nothing more than long grass and weeds. Carrying on through woods, I passed a group of outbuildings, an old stable block recently converted into houses by the look of it, catching glimpses of a larger building hidden further back in the trees to my left before I emerged into an open field.

The harvest had recently been gathered, leaving behind only a rough stubble of straw poking out of the broken earth, a soil that the *Ordnance Gazetteer of Scotland* of 1884 described as 'generally light and early, capable of producing good crops'. I stepped off the tarmacked road and onto the field, through a dark, soggy patch where lines of tyre tracks ended their sinuous routes through the golden stalks. My walking boots, worn in on London streets, finally got a taste of Scottish mud.

My arrival clearly came as something of a shock to the local wildlife. A small brown bird, a female pheasant perhaps, instantly took fright and tottered anxiously across the open ground towards the safety of nearby bushes. Seconds later a rabbit sprang to life, briefly breaking its camouflage as it hopped into a clump of long grass. And then, well nothing much, just the soft sound of the wind in the trees and light clouds sailing across the late summer sky, some darker outliers to the north sliding ominously towards me, bringing with them the threat of summer showers.

Today it looks like an unassuming, unremarkable corner of rural Scotland, one that continues to hold out against the industrialisation and urban sprawl that has swallowed up so much of the surrounding countryside. But Carriden has not always been so quiet. In past centuries, it has seen plenty of dramatic history. The physical remains of that history lay all around, particularly beneath my feet, lying layer upon layer like igneous strata, some layers visible, some buried, levels of the past overlapping and folding into one another. Occasionally the top layers rupture and allow others, long hidden, to briefly reappear.

Standing there, it was hard to imagine that, for a short while around the middle of the second century, this field was the location of a significant Roman military installation which played a key part in the expansion of the greatest empire that the world had ever seen. There is nothing Roman to see above ground now, nor has there been for centuries, but that does not mean that nothing survives. In fact, the fascinating antiquities that have been unearthed at Carriden over the years, most of them dug up accidently by workers or turned up by the plough, give some clues as to what lies beneath.

With thoughts of buried treasure filling my head, I began to stroll along the grassy edge of the field, down towards the shore of the Firth of Forth. I cast my eyes to the ground, searching for any little fragments of Roman terracotta or the glitter of half-buried gold. Nothing of course, and it turned out I don't really have the patience for this kind of search – known as 'fieldwalking' – which requires a steady gaze and a slow, diligent pace.[1] Soon I was distracted by a break in the trees to my left that revealed Carriden House, a hulk of caramel-coloured masonry surmounted by pepperpot turrets and surrounded by neat lawns.

The oldest (and tallest) part of Carriden House bears the date 1602, but there may be the remains of an earlier castle hidden in its solid mass of antique stonework. In England at that time, they were building elegant mansions, their oak-panelled, tapestry-lined rooms bright with sunlight. Although, by then, Scotland was becoming a more settled nation, high, fortified towers with tiny windows and iron yetts were still preferred. Centuries of rebellion, civil war and invasion made the Scottish nobility reluctant to give up their high-security homes.

Carriden House's thick walls were later pierced by oriel windows installed to brighten its gloomy vaults, but it still has an austere air about

---

1 Unauthorised digging or metal detecting on any part of the Antonine Wall is illegal and, moreover, undermining of this internationally important historical site. Any chance finds should immediately be reported to the landowner and the Treasure Trove Unit at the National Museum of Scotland (treasuretrovescotland.co.uk).

it, as well as gunloops, tiny round holes designed for taking pot shots at potential attackers who, in the end, never materialised. It is interesting to wonder if the people who built the tower chose this location in the knowledge that it had long been a place of strength and safety, if they had heard tales of a Roman fortress built on the same spot or even found traces of its crumbling ramparts. The name Carriden certainly seems to be partly derived from the Celtic word 'caer', meaning 'a stronghold' or 'citadel'.

Antiquarians flocked to Carriden in the eighteenth century, several of them proposing that there must have been a major Roman site thereabouts. Sir Robert Sibbald visited 'the House of Cariddin' in the early 1700s and was shown a locally found gold coin of the emperor Vespasian by the house's owner, Alexander Milne, as well as a 'Stone with the Head of an Eagl [sic] graven upon it' that Milne had dug up by chance and inserted into the wall of his new, more spacious west wing.

For Sibbald, such artefacts were proof that Roman civility had permeated the region, demonstrating that his homeland had once formed part of the classical world that he so admired. He had no hesitation in declaring Carriden the location of a Roman *municipium*, a town with an adjoining port, one of many Roman settlements that he imagined had been established across what is now southern Scotland.

Following in Sibbald's footsteps, Alexander Gordon came to Carriden in the early 1720s in search of Roman antiquities. In *Itinerarium Septentrionale*, the book that resulted from his extensive research into Scotland's Roman past, Gordon described the carved eagle, illustrating it with a clumsy line drawing. He also mentioned Milne's gold coin as well as a stone altar and what he alleged was a Roman (but was more likely a Bronze Age) sword found nearby that had recently been donated to the Advocates Library in Edinburgh.

To Gordon, however, this was all evidence not of Roman conquest, but of brief and unsuccessful attempts to subdue the tribes of ancient Caledonia. He roundly dismissed Sibbald's claims of Roman civility and instead presented Roman Scotland as a blood-soaked war zone. Like others unhappy with the Acts of Union, Gordon found nostalgic solace in the mythical courage of his ancient ancestors, indomitable warriors who had, it seemed, been better at resisting subjugation than his contemporary Scots.

English antiquarian John Horsley headed to 'Caër-ridden' soon after Gordon to inspect and record the eagle stone while researching his iconic *Britannia Romana*, a book that still commands respect in archaeological circles today. He agreed with Gordon that Scotland had not been conquered by Rome but did not accept that this was all down to the courage of the indigenous Caledonians. Instead, Horsley suggested that the Romans were simply 'indifferent' to the territory that would later become Scotland, seeing no gain in conquering such a cold, miserable wasteland, a theory that found predictably few adherents north of the border.

As for that carved stone, Sibbald had underplayed it by describing it as the head of an eagle. The illustrations of the stone panel published by Gordon and Horsley (whose drawing skills were thankfully better than those of his Scottish counterpart) both show a full eagle with wings outstretched and a wreath grasped in its beak. Next to it were carved letters.

Gordon claimed these were too worn to decipher but thought they might be read as 'COH IVLIA'. Horsley recognised the sculpture as a centurial stone, a carved panel inserted into a structure by one of the Roman soldiers who had laboured to build it. More confident, also more scholarly than Gordon, he interpreted the inscription as follows:

COH

VIII

STA

TELES

To literate Romans, such texts were no doubt instantly legible. I have a decent grasp of Latin, having studied it at school and as a mature student, but I still find Roman inscriptions difficult to translate – with all their obscure terms and cryptic abbreviations, they are a language unto themselves.

Modern scholars of such carved texts (epigraphists, to give them their proper title) have filled in the gaps and read this inscription as *'cohortis VIII centuria Statili Telesphori'*: 'From the eighth cohort, the century of Statilius [or possibly Statius] Telesphorus (built this)'. Who Statilius Telesphorus was, or what he helped to build, we will never know, but he obviously identified strongly with the eagle, *aquila* in Latin, that potent symbol of Roman military power.

Carriden has changed hands many times over the centuries, from the Cockburns, who owned it long before the present house was even begun, to the Abercrombies, from Sir John Hamilton of Letterick, who completed the old tower around 1602, to the Setons, the Cornwalls and the Hopes. By the mid-twentieth century, the building had fallen into disrepair, and it was almost demolished in the 1960s when (thankfully aborted) plans were drawn up to replace it with a power station.

Back in those days, stately piles like this – too big, too expensive to run and maintain – were being dynamited and demolished all over Scotland. Carriden thankfully escaped the massacre. Successive owners have lovingly restored it since then, and it is now a family home once more. Unfortunately, that carved eagle has disappeared at some point (antiquarian Robert Stuart found no trace of it when he visited in the early 1840s), presumably lost as the house was repeatedly remodelled and extended. It may well have been destroyed, but I like to think that is has just been covered up and is still lurking in there somewhere, waiting patiently to be rediscovered yet again.

Carriden's role as a vital part of the Roman frontier was finally confirmed at the end of the Second World War. This time the discovery was made not under the ground, but from the air, by pioneering archaeologist and aerial photographer Kenneth St Joseph. He took black and white photographs while flying over the site in 1945, images that revealed shadowy parallel lines in the field close to where I had walked. These are what are known as 'cropmarks' – most apparent in hot summers, they appear as the grass thrives in the deep, moist earth that has filled ancient trenches or holes but grows less well in the shallow, drier soil covering buried walls or earthworks.

Featuring a distinctive rounded corner, the ghostly cropmarks at Carriden were instantly recognisable as the defences of a Roman fort. St Joseph's photographs show the fort's eastern side, revealing three ditches and a causeway leading across them to a gated entrance, while its western side remains invisible under the lawns of the house. Excavations in 1946 uncovered not only these once formidable ditches, but also pottery from the Antonine period. Carriden's location by the coast would have provided the perfect dropping off point for supplies arriving by sea, and it could be that the rampart of the Antonine Wall extended as far as the fort, although no remains of it have been found in the vicinity.

Another chance discovery shed light on Carriden's Roman history in 1956, when a ploughman uncovered a sandstone altar at the northern edge of this same field. An inscription was carved into the front of the block of soft stone, its letters weathered but still legible. It opens, as such altars often do, with the letters 'I O M', an abbreviation of *Iovi Optimo Maximo*, 'Jupiter the Best and Greatest', a dedication to the chief deity in the Roman pantheon. Amazingly, the inscription mentions the place it was set up – Velunia, or possibly Veluniate – making Carriden one of the few Roman sites in Scotland to which we can confidently assign an ancient name.

It also refers to *'vicani'*, meaning 'villagers', showing that there was a Roman civil settlement adjoining the military fortress. But forget any grand ideas that you might have of classical civilisation – rather than paved streets lined with marble-columned temples and centrally heated houses furnished with elaborate mosaics, Velunia was probably just a huddle of simple wooden huts and workshops, home to wives, children, traders and the numerous hangers-on who tended to follow the Roman army on its seemingly endless campaigns.

Reaching the northern edge of the field, I stepped through the trees to find a narrow coastal path running along the top of a steep bank. This was the John Muir Way, a 134-mile walking and cycling route that I encountered repeatedly during my travels along the Antonine Wall. It is a challenging trail named in honour of a Scot who became one of the first great American conservationists. Plonking myself on a rudimentary wooden bench by the path, I took time to enjoy the splendid view north across the Firth of Forth.

The tide was well out that morning, revealing extensive sandy flats riddled with a network of silvery streams. The Forth was still wide, bigger than a river here, but nothing like the broad, open estuary that it becomes further east. Recent research suggests that the firth may have been even wider and deeper in Roman times due to higher sea levels, although opinions on this vary.

On the other side was Fife, a patchwork of fields and trees with a hazy chain of blueish hills beyond. My OS map did not extend that far, but I later worked out that these were the Ochils, a range that runs for over 25 miles from the River Tay down to Stirling, acting like a sort of primordial north/south divide between Lowlands and Highlands.

Of everything I had seen so far, it is only this horizon, this distant line of cloud-grazing peaks and slopes that would look familiar to the Romans. I wondered how a soldier based at Velunia would have reacted to this view. A shiver of fear as he considered the unconquered (even unconquerable, depending on who you believe) Caledonians who inhabited the north? A sense of relief or satisfaction that he was on the civilised side of the frontier and not in the barbaric (as the Romans saw it) wastelands beyond?

On that fresh August morning, the rugged open spaces of Caledonia looked inviting, that is until I again spied those dark, menacing clouds, still far in the distance, but moving towards me at some speed. I realised that it was time to head off on my trek and cover as many miles as I could before the weather took a turn for the worse.

Back on Carriden Brae, I turned right and walked along the side of the road, heading once again towards the shoreline. Down there, the Forth was hidden from view behind an ugly industrial estate, a muddle of featureless buildings, car parks and high fences. The OS map shows that the Antonine Wall took a sharp dogleg turn towards the north and ended by the waterfront close to the industrial estate. If it did, then any physical remains of it are surely lost forever, swept away by a tide of concrete and tarmac.

I was entering the town of Bo'ness, or Borrowstounness to give it its official name, although I don't think anyone has called it that for many years. The fortunes of Bo'ness were built on two activities – the mining of coal and the shipping of that coal from the town's harbour. Both industries are now defunct, and today Bo'ness is a commuter town for Edinburgh and Glasgow.

After a few minutes' walk I took a left turn into Harbour Road, its name a memory of former glories. Here I found not one, but two memorials to a valuable discovery made nearby in 1868 – it was in these parts that the Bridgeness Distance Slab, that hefty slice of carved sandstone that I had admired in the National Museum of Scotland the day before, was found.

The first of these memorials, erected not long after the initial excavation, would be easy to miss if you did not know it was there. Walking up Harbour Road, I spotted a flaking, soot-stained stone panel built into a garden wall. On it was a worn inscription, many of the words carved into it now virtually illegible.

I could still make out the date of the ancient slab's discovery, 29 April 1868, while below it in a different font was carved the abbreviated Latin inscription found on the Roman stone that commemorates the hard work of the Second Legion. Although this inscription survives as a testimony to the fact that local pride in Bo'ness's links with ancient Rome is not a new phenomenon, it seems ironic that the original distance marker is in better condition than this Victorian memorial to it – but then the nineteenth-century panel has spent a significantly longer time exposed to the temperamental Scottish weather than its Roman predecessor.

A little further up the hill on the other side of the road can be found a newer and more worthy reminder of this important find. A full-size replica of the carved Roman panel was erected here in 2012, created using a combination of modern technology (laser scanning, buzz saws and router machines) and more traditional techniques (old-fashioned hammers and chisels) at a cost of £70,000.

It certainly looks spectacular, set into a stone plinth and accompanied by panels explaining its history and its context as part of the Roman frontier. Seeing it again, that time out in the real world, the scene of a Roman cavalryman riding over his vanquished Caledonian enemies seemed even more terrible. A piece of imperial propaganda no doubt, but such things could have happened around here, to real people – Roman conquest was a bloody, violent affair. What this reproduction lacks are the bright colours that enhanced the original carving, as was to become apparent at the other end of the Antonine Wall.

Reports of its excavation and the results of late twentieth-century digs in the area have led some experts to conclude that the so-called Bridgeness Distance Slab may not have originated here in Bridgeness at all, and that it was moved in more recent times, maybe during the construction of the unusual eighteenth-century castellated structure known as Bridgeness Tower (originally a windmill, now a private house) that sits on top of a rise not far away. Where and how the sculpture was displayed on the Antonine Wall we can only guess, although, as local archaeologist Geoff Bailey

Bridgeness Tower

pointed out in an essay that he wrote on the possible locations of the eastern end of the frontier, such an unwieldy lump of stone would not have travelled far.

Reaching the brow of the hill, I was surrounded by twentieth-century housing and soon came to a wide road, buzzing with traffic. Ahead of me I could see more of the same stretching far into the distance. Standing on the grass verge, bombarded by the constant roar of cars, vans and lorries, it might appear that any signs of the Roman frontier have been completely erased here, but that is far from the truth – as is often the case with the Antonine Wall, hints of its presence persist even when all visible remains are lost.

In fact, this street runs along the exact line of the ancient rampart and ditch, while its very name, Grahamsdyke Road, recalls the name by which the monument was commonly known for centuries. The term 'Grahams Dyke' (sometimes written as Grim's, Grime's or Grymis Dyke) was first mentioned by John of Fordun back in the fourteenth century and still appeared regularly on nineteenth-century maps, but its origins are lost in the mists of time and have been much discussed by academics.

Could it, as has been argued for the earthworks in England with a similar nickname, be something to do with Grimr, the Anglo-Saxon alias for the Norse god Wodin? Or is there a link with the Scots word 'grym', meaning 'fierce' or 'stern'? One convoluted and completely implausible seventeenth-century theory was presented by poet Michael Livingston who, believing that the Antonine Wall had been built by third-century Roman emperor Septimius Severus, proposed that 'grym' was the Scots translation of the Latin 'Severus', which also means 'severe'. My favourite explanation involves a truly fantastical tale told by Fordun, the legend of a courageous Caledonian prince named Gryme, but that is a story that can wait until the next chapter, in which I will pass the alleged site of Gryme's heroic endeavours.

The walk along this road was not one of the most picturesque legs of my journey, although the views to my right out across the water to Fife were breathtaking, no doubt the reason this has long been the poshest part of Bo'ness. As I progressed, grandiose stone villas, the former homes of the rich families who made their fortunes in the Victorian and Edwardian boom, eventually gave way to an estate of council houses, a rapid fall in social status that effectively mirrors the fate of Bo'ness itself. Like similar communities throughout central Scotland, the town suffered in the post-industrial age. Luckily, it was not too long before I was able to step away from the road and escape the noise of the traffic as I walked into the relative peace of the Kinneil Estate.

The Kinneil Estate is a 200-acre public park, formerly the private grounds of a great mansion that I have always known as Kinneil Palace, although it has apparently been relegated to the slightly less regal Kinneil House by its current guardians, Historic Environment Scotland. The name Kinneil derives from the Gaelic '*Ceann Fhàil*', meaning 'head (or end) of the wall', and while this was certainly not the location of the end of the Roman frontier, it was here that I finally encountered tangible evidence of it.

The mansion was the first thing I saw as I passed through a thick band of trees and found myself at the end of another long, straight drive. From a distance it looked suitably grand, a square central block surmounted by a balustrade and flanked by tall, pointy-roofed pavilions, its classical proportions accentuated by large, regularly placed windows.

Walking towards it down the avenue, I looked out for the barely perceptible hollow in the bank of the burn to my left that Robertson and Keppie's *Handbook* identifies as the most easterly trace of the Antonine Wall's ditch – it is there, but only just. I passed through a pair of handsome gate posts, now conspicuously gateless, which flank the drive.

As I got nearer, I noticed signs that the house was not as palatial as it had at first appeared. Those big windows were dull and dusty, some replaced with painted wooden boards. The main entrance was behind boards too, a door in the shabby panels secured by a hefty padlock. A web of delicate cracks and fissures ran across the façade above. The building's north-easterly wing was roofless, virtually a ruin. Kinneil House was obviously uninhabited and had certainly seen better days.

Like Carriden, Kinneil House started life as a thick-walled tower, but it too has been extensively altered and expanded over the years. Much of it

Kinneil House, Bo'ness

was built in the mid-sixteenth century by James Hamilton, 2nd Earl of Arran, whose family had been granted these lands centuries before by King Robert I (better known today as Robert the Bruce), but its present design is mostly a result of late seventeenth-century improvements made by Anne, Duchess of Hamilton.

In its heyday, Kinneil was home to a large part of the 4th Duke of Hamilton's incredible art collection, which included works attributed to Rubens, Rembrandt, Van Dyke, Tintoretto and Titian. In the eighteenth century, the Hamiltons rented out the house. One of its most significant tenants was Dr John Roebuck, an inventor and industrialist who became a co-founder of the Carron Company Iron Works (more of which later) in 1759.

Like Carriden, Kinneil later fell on tough times – it lay empty for years and was in a poor state of repair by the early twentieth century. It was bought by the local council in the 1920s and in 1936 work began to strip it back to a shell. The floors and interior fittings of the central block were ripped out, the roof partly removed from the north-east wing, but then, amazingly and fortuitously, a cycle of rare sixteenth and seventeenth-century wall paintings was uncovered. Such was their importance that demolition was immediately halted. Kinneil House was saved in the nick of time. The precious painted rooms were preserved, the roof of the central block was restored in the 1970s, but since then little has been done to the house, hence its current, slightly melancholy aspect.

In a small orchard close to the house, I met Ian Shearer, chair of the Friends of Kinneil, a band of local volunteers who have been working hard to improve and promote this place since 2006. He had generously agreed to give me a tour of Kinneil and tell me more about its illustrious past. Ian's enthusiasm for the park and its story was immediately infectious, but I also sensed his frustration that it has not received the attention, or indeed the public funding, that it deserves.

He first came to Kinneil Park in 2007, having recently moved to the area, and could not understand why such as wonderful asset was so little known. 'There is more history here than almost any other place in Scotland I can think of', he said, his love for it evident. 'You've got so much of the story of Scotland all in one place. Where else has a Roman Wall, a twelfth-century church, a sixteenth-and seventeenth-century palace, a great local museum and played a role in one of the world's most important inventions?' He had a point, and I was intrigued to find out more.

As we sauntered back towards the house, Ian pointed out the museum (currently only open in the afternoon, so I was not able to visit), which was situated in one of the old outbuildings behind us and contains all sorts of artefacts from across the ages, including a beautiful bronze fixture from a Roman horse harness found nearby. A sculpture based on the harness's timeless design of interlocking circles and squares had recently been commissioned to stand by the entrance to the park.

We admired the fine façade of Kinneil House but talked too about what improvements were needed. Ian told me that it used to have a custodian who opened it up to visitors daily, but since the 1980s it has been mostly locked up. A limited schedule of regular 'open days' organised by the Friends and Historic Environment Scotland has proved a tremendous success, each event attracting hundreds of people and demonstrating that there is abundant interest in the building and its long history.

Bronze Roman Harness Loop, Kinneil

As we rounded the corner of the house, we came to the roofless ruin of what looked like a tiny cottage – this, Ian explained, was a workshop used by inventor James Watt as he developed his prototype steam engine in 1769-70. Watt had been provided with the workshop by John Roebuck, who needed a method of pumping water out of his coal mines and had sponsored Watt's research.

This secluded little building, hidden in the trees in the shadow of the old mansion, was chosen as the perfect spot to conduct top-secret experiments. When his work came to commercial fruition in Birmingham a few years later, Watt's steam engine would prove fundamental in the development of the Industrial Revolution – this was an invention that changed the world.

Next, Ian and I crossed a gully behind the house and soon came upon the ruins of Old Kinneil Kirk, built in the twelfth century on the site of an earlier place of worship. All that remains now are low foundations and an impressive gable end with a belfry at the top, which stood for centuries as

James Watt Workshop, Kinneil (Reconstruction)

a helpful landmark for sailors on the Firth of Forth. There used to be a village here too, but it was swept away in the late seventeenth century by the Hamiltons, a brutal piece of landscaping designed to open up the views to their elegantly landscaped park.

    I could have happily spent the rest of the morning exploring the Kinneil estate with Ian, but it was the Antonine Wall that I was really there to see. As we walked further west, leaving the house and church behind us, Ian led me to a plaque that records the Antonine Wall's 2008 inclusion on the list of UNESCO World Heritage Sites, as part of a group of monuments known as 'The Frontiers of the Roman Empire'. Beyond it, I could see a slight hollow in the grass, more faint remains of the Roman ditch. Given the regular spacing between each of the Antonine Wall's forts, common sense decrees that there should be one around here somewhere, but to date no signs of it have been detected.

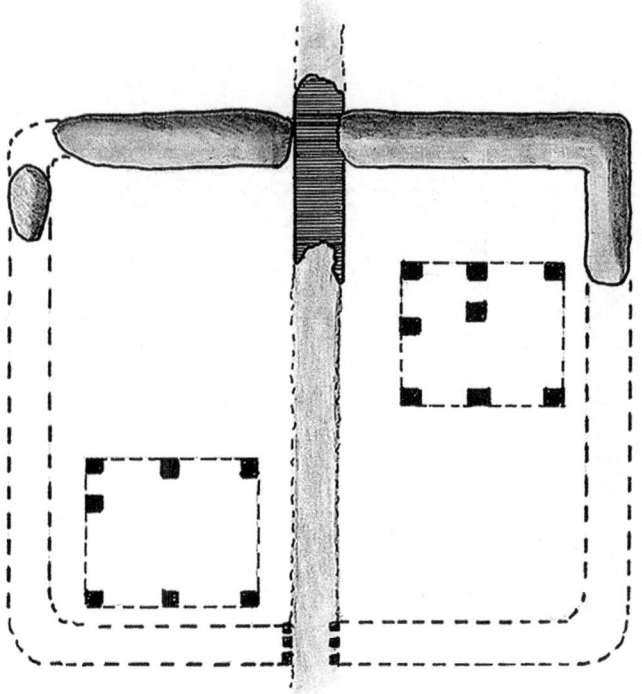

Kinneil Fortlet

After a short stroll on from there, however, we arrived at the site of a Roman fortlet, a mini fort of which there were several dotted along the frontier. Discovered in 1978 and excavated over the following three years, its remains have been partially preserved for public display. The fortlet measured 18.5 m by 21.5 m, the Antonine Wall forming its northern defence, with two wooden buildings inside flanking a metalled road which ran right through the middle of the enclosure.

A gate led through the frontier here, an exit from or entrance to the Roman Empire that was guarded by a small resident garrison, although no firm evidence of a causeway across the ditch has been identified. Today the stone kerb of the fortlet's ramparts can be seen, while modern timber stakes mark the post holes of the lost wooden structures. Part of the road that led through the gate is exposed, giving the opportunity to walk in the footsteps of the Roman auxiliaries who were stationed here and stand on what was once the threshold between Rome and unconquered Caledonia.

Kinneil Fortlet (Reconstruction)

Would this gate have seen much traffic, or was this in effect a 'closed border', built to keep out those troublesome Caledonian tribes? The purpose of the Antonine Wall is very much open to interpretation, with some scholars favouring the idea that it was purely defensive, others proposing that it was designed to control the movement of people and goods between the Roman Empire and the north. Both this frontier and the one built previously by Hadrian are pierced by numerous gateways. This raises the obvious question, if the Roman Walls were intended to keep people out, then why put so many gates in them?

It seems probable to me that the Antonine Wall was intended to provide a combination of both defence and control. The forts along it are much closer together than those on Hadrian's Wall, implying that its builders felt the need for a stronger military presence here. Its role as a piece of propaganda should also not be overlooked. In its heyday, this high turf rampart would have made a bold and explicit statement about Roman power. Today, faded and ambiguous, it could, like the broken Bridgeness Distance Slab, be viewed more as a symbol of overarching ambition.

Kinneil is a marvellous place, and it is easy to see why Ian and his colleagues in the Friends are so committed to preserving and publicising it. We both agreed that it would be the perfect spot for an Antonine Wall visitor centre, an idea that has been proposed in the past, but which has so far come to nothing.

A Roman museum here would be an ideal starting point for anyone wanting to explore the frontier and would attract more visitors to the park and house as well. It was great to hear from Ian how much the community cherishes its local heritage. 'The people of Bo'ness, and people all along the Wall, are very proud of their history', he told me. All Kinneil needs now is some serious cash to bring it fully back to life and put it firmly on the tourist trail.

Ian and I said our goodbyes and I decided to take a short break before heading onwards. Sitting myself down next to the remains of the fortlet, I relaxed with a snack from my backpack and a drink from my water bottle while taking in the bucolic surroundings.

The sky above me was by then blanketed in grey, and I realised that I had seen the last of the day's sunshine. With thoughts of the grim weather predictions for the afternoon playing on my mind, I pushed myself up and headed on towards the western end of the Kinneil Estate as my journey along the Antonine Wall continued in earnest.

Striding past a body of water known locally as the Curling Pond and out of the park, I found myself on another road that exactly follows the course of the Roman frontier. Unlike Grahamsdyke Road in Bo'ness, however, this was a pretty country lane bordered by bramble-filled hedges and surrounded by rolling farmland.

There were no visible remains of the Antonine Wall here, all of it wiped out by agriculture. In most places we have no knowledge of how or when it was destroyed, but at Nether Kinneil Farm its loss was recorded in vivid (or indeed heart-breaking) detail by archaeologist Sir George Macdonald.

In his book *The Roman Wall in Scotland*, first published in 1911, Macdonald cited a letter that he had received from the tenant farmer at Nether Kinneil, one Mr Learmonth, which explained how he had come across 'a causeway of rough stone, varying in size from about one to two feet' buried just below the surface of one of his fields back in 1861. Whether this was the remains of the Roman Military Way, or the stone base of the rampart is unclear.

What we do know for sure is that Mr Learmonth then proceeded to remove the stones to avoid them damaging his plough. His uncles, the previous tenants of the farm, had done the same thing many times before at various locations. Learmonth recalled that his predecessors had filled in a long length of the Roman ditch, which he reckoned had survived to a depth of up to 8 ft in some places on their land, to make it easier to get carts and ploughs across the fields.

Such things happened all along the Antonine Wall across the centuries. As I had already learned at both Carriden and Kinneil, the belief that historical monuments should be preserved for posterity is a relatively modern one. Although I cannot blame those farmers for what they did – their lives were tough and preserving inconvenient ancient earthworks did not put food on the table – it is still impossible not to lament such deliberate destruction of our priceless national heritage.

Nowadays, the locals are more respectful of the Antonine Wall, as I was about to find out. By happy chance, one of the current residents of Nether Kinneil, a woman named Gaele, had contacted me on social media a couple of days previously, after reading a post about my upcoming walk. She had found some interesting stones on her property and wondered if I would drop by to take a look, an offer I could hardly refuse.

It turned out that Gaele and I have led remarkably parallel lives. Both of a similar vintage and both Glaswegian by birth, we grew up in the same suburb of Edinburgh, we both went to the University of Glasgow, and both subsequently lived in London, although she then moved to more exotic climes before returning to Scotland.

Like me, she is passionate about history and an inveterate treasure hunter, always on the lookout for ancient artefacts. Since her home and smallholding lie in proximity to the Antonine Wall, she has more chance than most of finding them.

Gaele led me through her garden, stopping in front of a collection of sizeable lumps of sandstone that she had recently dug up across her property. We speculated that they may have formed part of the stone base of the Roman rampart, and it seems likely that many of the stones used to build her cottage in the early 1900s could have come from the same source.

One of the stones that Gaele had recently discovered was worth a closer look – on a flattened surface on one side was what looked to me like a worn inscription. It was not neatly carved like the words on the Bridgeness Distance Slab, and most of it was lost, but I could see letters – an 'A' near the top, then below that what looked like 'IP'. And was that 'IAT' further along?

It was impossible to make it out for sure. A bit of Roman graffiti carved by a bored soldier perhaps? Its poor condition was a problem, but it was an intriguing find, worthy of further research. I took some photos and promised to look into it after my walk was completed, while Gaele promised to keep me updated on any future discoveries.

Bidding farewell, I set off again on my journey. Memories of that busy Bo'ness road were fading, and it was good to be back in the open countryside. The views of Fife to my right were only getting better, and although the clouds heading from that direction were becoming even darker and more foreboding, I felt like I was making considerable progress.

But then, as I reached a break in the hedge that opened an outlook to the north-west, one of the most arresting sights that I would meet on my journey along the Antonine Wall stopped me in my tracks. Not a characterful stately home this time, nor a range of distant hills, nor even a relic of ancient Rome. What had caught my attention was the Grangemouth oil refinery, a sprawling 1,700-acre complex of pipes, chimneys and towers that stretched out below me along the south coast of the Firth of Forth.

Not what might first spring to mind if you were asked to picture an eye-catching snapshot of Scotland, but there was something magnificent about it all the same, something captivating about its ostentatious scale. The landscape before me was littered with stout cooling towers, countless metal tubes snaking around featureless buildings and vast tanks. A few tall, skinny chimneys had orange flames leaping from their high tops, the sky above rippling with intense heat. On the other side of the Forth I could see the even taller chimney of Longannet, formerly one of the biggest (and most polluting) power stations in Europe, closed since 2016. The view, with all its ugly grandeur, was reminiscent of an enormous film set, the location for some dystopian sci-fi fantasy.

Mid-nineteenth-century maps of the area show Grangemouth as a small town on the banks of the River Avon, close to where it runs into the Forth, the area surrounding it dotted with farmsteads and clusters of houses. Things changed fast in the following decades. A map from the turn of the twentieth century shows the mouth of the Avon transformed into a harbour, a busy port that was already taking business away from the docks at Bo'ness. The operation then known as Scottish Oils (owned by Anglo-Persian Oil, a forerunner of BP) arrived in 1924, drawn here by the port and the large areas of cheap reclaimed land around it.

The refinery expanded massively in the last quarter of the twentieth century as North Sea oil poured in, becoming a source not only of vast income, but also of Scottish national pride. In 2019, Grangemouth supplied 70% of the fuel to Scotland's filling stations and it also provides power to the Forties pipeline, which carries oil and gas from the North Sea.

But things are changing yet again, as the problems associated with extracting and burning fossil fuels become more widely recognised. Long the saviour of the Scottish economy, oil is now seen as a threat to our environment, even to our very existence. Parts of the refinery were closed a few months after my walk, with significant job losses. Looking to the future, I have to wonder whether this massive complex will soon become as redundant as the ancient frontier that I was following.

Who knows what the Roman soldiers who used to garrison the Antonine Wall where I stood, or indeed Mr Learmonth and his uncles who farmed this land a century and a half ago, would have made of this incredible sight? In Roman days, long before the land was drained, it was all shimmering grey water. I am sure plenty of people view the Grangemouth refinery as nothing more than a giant blot on the landscape. As a combine harvester noisily collected up the wheat in the field below me, the refinery spreading out into the distance beyond it, the scene neatly summed up the modern state of central Scotland, the rural and the industrial sitting cheek by jowl as traditional ways increasingly yield to the pressures of modernity.

The next farm along this road is called Inveravon, meaning 'the place at the mouth of the River Avon'. Before the river came into view, I passed farm buildings, old cottages sitting by the roadside close to modern barns closely followed by twentieth-century houses. It was in the garden of one of these houses that I caught sight of a substantial chunk of broken masonry, the remains of a semi-circular tower that had obviously once formed part of a much larger structure. What it was, or indeed how old it might be was difficult to tell, particularly at that time of year when it was hidden amongst the summer foliage.

I was not the first Antonine Wall explorer to spot this shattered old tower. It also caught the eye of Sir Robert Sibbald just over 300 years ago. He noted that the 'Ruines of Ancient Buildings' could be found here at Inveravon, his use of the plural implying that the remains were more extensive then than they are today. Sibbald, as he tended to do, decided that these ruins were the vestiges of a Roman fort and port, which he proposed had been positioned to take advantage of the river in the valley below. The more discerning Alexander Gordon, on the other hand, wrote that he could find 'no clear Vestiges' of any Roman fort, and John Horsley, for once, agreed with him.

The *Statistical Account* of 1845, a fascinating 15-volume work that contains descriptions of every parish in Scotland, reveals the truth. This was the site of an enormous castle. Ironically, it was only due to a description of the castle's destruction at the hands of King James II in an old manuscript known as the 'Auchinleck Chronicle' that its existence was ever recorded at all.

This tower, then, was not Roman, but the paltry remains of what had been an important but short-lived 'Castell of Inveravyne'. The castle's fall came about in 1455 as a result of King James' campaign to bring down its owner, the over-powerful Earl of Douglas, and it was never rebuilt. It has been speculated that more of the castle's masonry survives in the walls of the farm buildings far behind me, meaning that it must have been a truly massive fortress.

Given the fact that the king ordered its demolition over 500 years ago, it is not surprising that we know almost nothing about its history or its architecture. This single ruined tower, a fragile, crumbling stack of sandstone with hints of a vault in its interior, is all that we currently have, but no doubt much more lies beneath the earth, the castle's buried foundations awaiting the trowels of future archaeologists to uncover their many secrets.

It turned out that Sibbald was not wrong to suppose that there was a Roman fort near here. The empty road that I was following took a turn to the right and headed gently downwards, but, as a result of excavations conducted by Professor Anne Robertson in the 1960s, we know that the Roman frontier continued straight on towards the Avon.

Further investigations in 1991 produced the scant remains of a fort on the southern side of the Antonine Wall close to the river, with finds including coins, pottery and an incised gaming board. The discovery on the riverbank of hollow box-flue tiles, designed to allow warm air to circulate through the walls of a building, strongly indicates the presence of a Roman bath house in the vicinity.

As I followed the road downhill, I prepared myself for another spectacular view. Having driven through this area before, I knew that I was about to see my first well-preserved stretch of the Antonine Wall, a short but deep section of ditch gouged out of the side of Polmonthill that now lies, incongruously, beside a dry ski slope. So I was disappointed, and a little confused when I looked across the fields to see the ski slope and nothing else. Where the ditch should be was a mass of green scrub.

I consulted my map and surveyed the landscape around me. Far in the distance, sparkling white amongst the grey haze of a summer shower, were the tower blocks that mark the eastern edge of the town of Falkirk, as expected. To my right was the A905, a busy route that runs from Grangemouth to Stirling, right where it should be. And there was the dry ski slope. This was definitely Polmonthill.

I carried on down to the main road, then continued past the edge of the oil refinery, turning left and then quickly left again, finally crossing the Avon via a modern metal bridge. Instead of continuing my journey by turning right into Polmont Woods, however, I decided to take a short detour southward to take a closer look at the hillside and search for the missing Roman ditch.

It took only a couple of minutes to get there. Next to the roadside I spotted one of the old signposts erected at historic sites decades ago by the now defunct Scottish Development Department, or even further back by the Ministry of Works. These metal panels bearing a simple but informative text in a classic font always stir up a sense of nostalgia for me, evoking childhood memories of happy hours spent exploring ruined castles, romantic abbeys, prehistoric burial mounds and, of course, the Antonine Wall. This sign revealed that this was indeed the Polmonthill section of the Roman frontier. The metal panel was almost lost in the bushes and the post that supported it was engulfed by leaves.

And then the penny dropped. The ditch was in there somewhere, it was just completely hidden by the greenery, smothered by a summer's burst of grass and hogweed, brambles and bracken. Most eye-catching were the soft pink flowers of the Himalayan balsam, an appealing plant that I have since discovered is an unwelcome invasive species.

The hillside was undoubtedly pretty, but it was all extremely frustrating for someone on the lookout for Roman archaeology. I had chosen to walk the frontier in August because I had assumed that I would be guaranteed weather that was, if not glorious, then at least dry. It was becoming increasingly clear that I had been over-optimistic in that respect, and to add insult to injury, it turned out that this was the worst time of the year to inspect the Antonine Wall's less manicured sections.

Lesson learned, I headed back to Polmont Woods. For the first time since Bo'ness, I had to leave the route of the Roman frontier here, as it runs through private property along the side of Polmonthill. Instead, I took a footpath through the lower reaches of the forest that covers much of this area, an oasis of calm rich in flora and fauna.

Although the path was clear and well-kept, the shadowy woodland around me felt thrillingly wild. All sorts of trees flourish there, including oak, alder, beech and rowan, as well as the native ash and elm that were once the most common species in this part of Scotland. I could not see any birds, but I could certainly hear them, chirping and fluttering in the canopy above me. The ground was muddy in places and, after days of intermittent showers, the air smelt loamy and moist.

My map showed that a sharp left turn somewhere along this path would take me up the hill, through the trees to the line of the Antonine Wall. Happening upon an unexpected flight of concrete stairs leading me in that very direction, I naturally took it. But instead of finding the ancient frontier, I ended up wandering onto Grangemouth Golf Course, the habitat not of Roman auxiliaries or cavalry, but of pastel-clad men in motorised buggies.

I consulted my map again, trying and failing to work out where I had gone wrong. I tentatively began to head onwards across the course, but, with thoughts of flying golf balls filling (and potentially hitting) my head, I soon had second thoughts.

If the golfers were surprised to see a confused-looking figure wearing walking boots and a backpack in their midst, then they were too polite to show it. Still trying to make sense of the map while self-consciously working my way around the edges of the greens and fairways, it took me a while to work out that the only sure way to get off the golf course was to go back the way that I had come, down the stairs to the path that I had just left and continue on my walk through the woods.

Not long after this little detour I arrived at a car park, next to which I found the trail leading up the hillside that I had been looking for all along. The forest changed from deciduous to conifer, Scots pine and larch, the trees much taller and the undergrowth thinning out, replaced by a crackling carpet of fallen cones and needles.

The path was steep, but at the summit I soon reached my goal, or I should say almost fell into it. I suddenly found myself teetering on the edge of a large ditch, choked in places with fallen tree trunks and bursts of bracken, but deep and broad and unmistakable nonetheless.

Now at last I was able to get an idea of the true scale of the Roman frontier. The rampart of the Antonine Wall may have disappeared here, but the massive V-shaped gulley dug almost 2,000 years ago along its north side was still clear for all to see as it plunged down the slope to my right. To my left, a fenced-in strip of long grass indicated the route of the frontier in the other direction, back towards Bo'ness.

I was standing on the Caledonian side, where the earth removed from the ditch was piled up to form an additional barrier, often referred to by archaeologists as the 'upcast mound'. It was amazing to think that this had all been built by hand, hollowed out by Roman legionaries using picks and shovels, and that it had run right across the Scottish mainland, the ditch up to 12 m wide in places. The amount of manual labour involved is quite astounding.

Evidence of the temporary accommodation provided for these frontier builders has been found near to Polmont Woods – thanks to more of those cropmarks, the signs of a Roman camp have been identified under the fairways of the Grangemouth Golf Course. The camp comprised a rectangular area of at least 3.2 hectares, protected by a low mound of earth topped with a robust palisade of sharpened stakes. Inside stood orderly rows of leather tents, home to the men working on the construction of the frontier. As well as being skilled in the art of war, some of the soldiers were trained surveyors, masons, carpenters and builders, their skills vital for a huge army that was often on the move.

Another similar camp has been discovered about half a kilometre to the west, and many more were erected all along the Forth-Clyde isthmus as the Antonine Wall worked its way across the landscape. There is, for example, another at Muirhouses where I had started my journey, and three around Inveravon. The camp under Grangemouth Golf Course has yet to be excavated, and given its location, may not be for a long time, but it has been designated a scheduled monument because of its historical and archaeological importance.

Intriguingly, crop marks close to the camp have been interpreted as evidence of an Iron Age settlement, while others close by are thought to be trenches excavated by the Home Guard during the Second World War as a training exercise or as defences for an airfield at Grangemouth. With the enigmatic remains of two momentous military endeavours lying right next to one another, one ancient and the other modern, as well as potential evidence regarding relations between the Romans and the indigenous Iron Age tribes that they were attempting to subdue and control, this is a site that will have much to reveal, if and when it is ever fully investigated.

My descent along the lip of the ditch was challenging, the path, such as it was, slippery and uneven, clogged with bracken and knotted tree roots, so it was a relief to arrive back at the car park where I had picked up the trail just a few minutes before. Looking at my map, it was obvious that another detour from the Roman frontier was required here, unless I fancied taking my life into my hands by picking my way around the edge of a major roundabout, crossing slip roads and passing under the M9 motorway in the process.

To avoid that, I turned left past the solid Victorian bulk of Polmont Old Parish Church and crossed over the thundering motorway on a high bridge that led me into the village of Polmont. After a short walk I was by the Polmont Burn, with a narrow path next to it leading north down a wooded glen and away (if only briefly) from the noise and fumes.

As I emerged by the side of the A9, I was able to see one of the more controversial recent developments near to the Antonine Wall. Still a work in progress over a decade after it was initially proposed, the Falkirk Distillery is a striking white structure topped by two pagoda roofs. It had been established not only to bring back whisky production to Scotland's central belt, but also to attract tens of thousands of tourists every year, with the original plans for the distillery including a visitors' centre, retail complex and restaurant. While the building looked complete on the day that I passed, there was no sign of it being open, and no evidence that whisky making had begun.

Part of the reason for the project's long, slow development were the objections raised way back in 2009, when Historic Scotland (a previous incarnation of what is now Historic Environment Scotland) opposed its location within the so-called 'Buffer Zone', the protected area on either side of the Antonine Wall that had been laid out when the frontier was registered as a World Heritage Site only a year before. Many saw the ensuing public enquiry as a test case, with the local council in favour of the development, but the archaeological community very much against it, pointing out that although the location of the new distillery was not directly on the line of the Wall, its construction would inevitably have an impact on the frontier's wider environment and context.

It was the economic argument, the lure of jobs and visitors that won out in the end. Looking on the bright side, maybe the visitors who come to the distillery will search out the nearby Antonine Wall, leading to an increased awareness of this undervalued monument. Only time will tell.

My journey next led me onwards and (quite literally) upwards along Mumrills Road, an old single-track lane now closed to traffic. I was back on the route of the Roman frontier. Ahead, I spotted a man leading a hefty horse along the lane, a timeless sight and a pleasant reminder that I was back in the countryside. For a moment, the modern world, with all its stresses and strains, seemed far away.

The man nodded politely as I went to overtake, the narrow path forcing me to sidle warily past the animal's enormous hind legs. Not much further on I emerged onto a broad and breezy plateau with good views across the landscape, particularly to the east and the north, over the rooftops of Grangemouth to the hills of Fife. An ideal place, you might think, for a Roman fort.

Eighteenth-century antiquarians thought so, and the evidence backed them up. Alexander Gordon confidently stated that a fort had stood here, although he noted after his visit in the early 1720s that 'no Vestiges of it can now be traced'. He based his conjecture on the fact that 'some quantities of Roman vessels made of red earth are found here'. These vessels were presumably the common pottery we now call Samian ware that was mass-produced in Gaul (modern-day France) and exported around the Roman world.

William Maitland's *History and Antiquities of Scotland* of 1757 contains some decidedly outlandish ideas, but its author correctly identified the historical importance of Mumrills (or 'Numerills', as he called it) thanks to the discovery of 'many Roman chequered stones' thereabouts, by which he surely meant the squared masonry blocks with cross-hatched incisions often used by Roman builders. In 1834, the tombstone of a Roman soldier, Nectovelius, was unearthed nearby, the neatly carved letters of its inscription (some of which retain traces of red pigment) revealing that he was of British origin, and that he died, aged only 29, after nine years of loyal service in the Second Cohort of Thracians.

Proper excavations were finally carried out at Mumrills Farm between 1923-8, directed by Sir George Macdonald and lawyer-turned-archaeologist Alexander Ormiston Curle on behalf of the Society of Antiquaries of Scotland. Their investigations uncovered parts of the largest known fort on the Antonine Wall, with an internal area of some 2.6 hectares.

While the digs initially only took place in winter to avoid disrupting the planting of crops, they continued uninterrupted for the last 15 months of the project. Instead of complaining at the inconvenience, the tenant farmers, two brothers named Smith, followed the discoveries with enthusiasm, helping out and offering hospitality to the members of the Society of Antiquaries' supervising committee whenever they could.

The second edition of Macdonald's *The Roman Wall in Scotland*, published in 1934, includes detailed descriptions of the finds at Mumrills, as well as some wonderful photographs of the work in progress. My favourite is a shot of one of Macdonald's colleagues from the supervising committee who sports shiny shoes, a natty tweed cap and a bushy moustache typical of the day. He is sitting down in the depths of one of the fort's freshly re-dug ditches.

A photograph in Curle's personal album (now in the collection of the Society of Antiquaries of Scotland) shows Macdonald himself, bearded and grand in his fedora hat, half hidden in the junction of two other Roman ditches. Both men are dwarfed by the high banks of the ancient earthworks. Neither, in their smart coats, collars and ties, are dressed for digging. Another image from the same album shows an open-shirted worker with spade in hand, mucky boots, staring intensely at the camera, surrounded by the muddy remains of a Roman hypocaust, a raised floor which allowed warm air to circulate below.

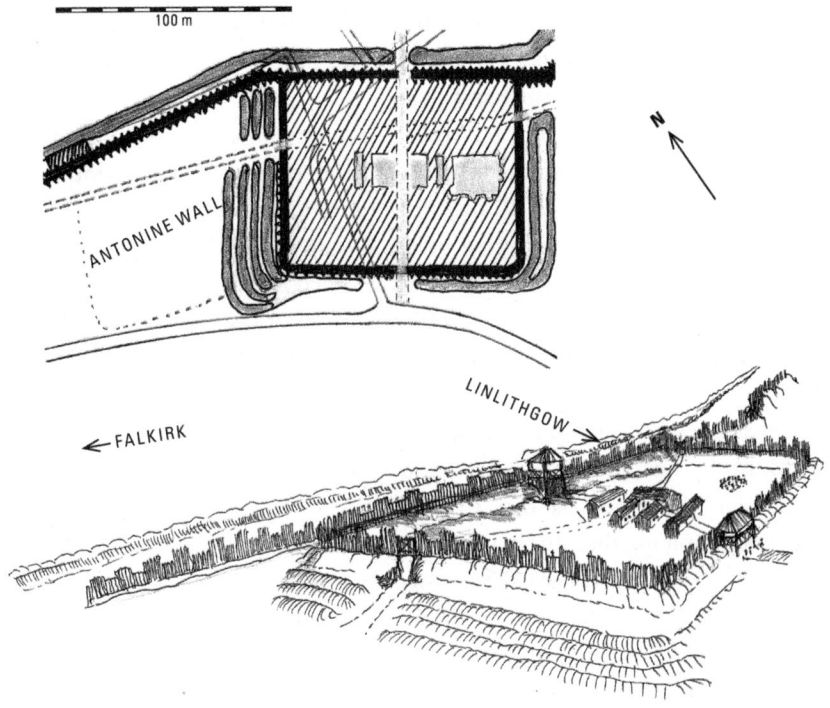

Mumrills Roman Fort (Plan And Reconstruction)

As well as recording the extensive remains of the Roman fort, these photos capture the hierarchy of the archaeological site: gentlemen scholars like Macdonald, Curle and their committee colleagues were there to supervise, direct, inspect and analyse, while it was hired labourers, local farmhands or builder's mates no doubt, their names now long forgotten, who got on with all the hard, dirty work. Even more shocking for modern archaeologists is the complete lack of concern for what might today be termed 'health and safety' – those high banks of mud, liable to collapse at any moment, would now be shored up to protect the workers toiling in their gloomy depths.

The remains that these men found were confused and confusing, a mess of fallen buildings on top of older foundations and post holes, leading

Macdonald to speculate that this fort had been rebuilt, abandoned and dismantled by the Romans on more than one occasion. I had already discovered that much of the Antonine Wall had been destroyed by recent human activity, but there are also signs that the Romans demolished parts of the frontier themselves as they retreated, probably to avoid valuable resources falling into enemy hands.

Macdonald noted signs of burning and saw this as evidence of a successful Caledonian attack, or the remnants of a terrible accident. He believed that Agricola, the Roman general who ventured north a good six decades before the Antonine invasion, had established the first fort here, as mentioned in Tacitus' biography. Macdonald identified what he thought to be at least four layers of Roman activity, some more evident than others, resulting in an archaeological site that was, and still is, difficult to fully understand.

Despite all this apparent destruction and dismantling, the unusual scale of Mumrills fort was still apparent to its excavators. The building that Macdonald identified as the 'Commandant's House' was particularly splendid, implying that this may have been a fort with special significance, potentially even the frontier's centre of operations. The fort's commanding officer lived here in some style, possibly with a wife and family, along with a staff of slaves to see to his needs.

The commandant of Mumrills, clearly a man of exceptional importance, was also granted a rare luxury – a private bath house attached to his spacious residence. A large stone headquarters building was unearthed at the heart of the fort, as well as a communal bath house towards the north rampart. Also found were the postholes of what might have been timber barracks and two storehouses where the copious amounts of grain (mostly imported barley and wheat)required to keep the troops in bread and porridge would have been stockpiled.

Macdonald's report on the dig listed the quantity of smaller finds made in the fields of Mumrills, including pottery fragments (many of them prettily decorated shards of Samian as described by Alexander Gordon), terracotta oil lamps, coins, bronze jewellery and plenty of weapons in the form of rusty iron spearheads and knives.

Archaeological artist and writer Jessie Mothersole was lucky enough to see some of the buildings still uncovered when she visited Mumrills in early

1927. She noted in her book *In Roman Scotland* that she inspected the foundations of 'the baths belonging to the commandant's house, built partly of old red sandstone' and recorded the remarkable size of both house and baths. She was, like me, quite taken with the vistas here, describing the 'splendid situation, overlooking the Carse to the north, while north-east is seen the Firth of Forth, and beyond it the Fife hills'. Bravely walking in the depths of winter, she even spied snow on the distant Airngath Hill above Bo'ness.

Further small-scale excavations were conducted at Mumrills in 1958-60, 1996 and 2000, and chance finds have been made in the gardens of the modern houses that border the farm. For now, however, the considerable remains of this important site have been covered up, and much of it remains completely unexamined.

The theory proposed by George Macdonald in the 1930s that the fort could have been deserted and then rebuilt and regarrisoned on several occasions is now generally dismissed, with modern archaeologists believing that Mumrills was simply adapted and updated over time as requirements changed. As for who pulled down and burned the fort, that is a subject that is still open to debate. Was it rampaging Caledonians or retreating Romans? Macdonald's findings had proved inconclusive, but, as I would later discover, more evidence of how the Roman frontier met its end was to be found further along the Wall.

As at Carriden, no signs of Mumrills' extraordinary past can be seen above ground today, but Jessie Mothersole suggested that the ruined cow shed that still sits at the edge of the field next to the lane could have been built from salvaged Roman masonry, so I decided to take a closer look. I walked through the open gate and picked my way along the fringes of the straw-scattered field, gazing down as I went because, well, you never know what you might spot in the disturbed soil.

The old shed was roofless and overgrown, its floor a mass of nettles and its walls cracked and collapsing, pushed apart by the branches of the trees that had sprouted up inside. In those broken walls, however, I could see a few well-shaped blocks displaying faded traces of those tell-tale hatched lines, evidence of expertly-handled ancient chisels – William Maitland's 'Roman chequered stones'.

Carefully cut by trained masons who were building an enormous fortress designed to control the edge of a world-dominating empire, these stones have ended up in the walls of a lowly byre. A bit of a comedown and another example of how things change round here, but at least all that hard work did not entirely go to waste. Recycling, it seems, is nothing new.

By that point, I had reached the edge of the town of Falkirk. Leaving the farmland behind, I walked along Sandy Loan into Laurieston, originally a village, now a suburb. Alexander Gordon found fading traces of the frontier here in the 1720s, describing a length of ditch that was 'very visible, though not near its ordinary Breadth and Depth'. The *New Statistical Account* of 1845 noted that the earthwork was still 'particularly conspicuous' hereabouts, but by the early twentieth century it was gone. George Macdonald saw the few cracked walls and subsiding gables on several of Laurieston's houses as the only evidence that the Antonine Wall once stood here, a reminder that building on top of buried ancient ditches and ramparts is never wise.

Further west, Sandy Loan becomes Grahamsdyke Street. There was that old name for the Antonine Wall again, used for centuries but now largely forgotten, a subtle sign that the road I was following had been built directly on top of the Roman frontier.

This quiet residential road in turn led me to a busy roundabout. I was in Falkirk with all its noise and bustle. A rumbling stomach reminded me that it was time to eat. Ever conscious of my school motto, 'Never Unprepared', I had sensibly packed an adequate lunch in my rucksack. But then something unexpected came into view – a fish and chip shop with restaurant attached named 'Benny T's', which I have since learnt is something of a local institution. The luscious smell of frying fat called to me like a siren's song and, soggy sandwiches quickly forgotten, I headed inside.

Sitting down to enjoy the dish that I consider to be the pinnacle of Scotland's rich and varied national cuisine (an enormous portion of haddock and chips all washed down with a long glass of Irn-Bru), I considered my morning's progress. The walk had proved as varied and interesting as I had hoped, taking me through towns and villages, farms and parks, past remarkable buildings both old and new.

Even though so much of the Roman frontier in this part of the world has been destroyed over the years, sometimes on purpose, sometimes unawares, I had detected evidence of a century and a half of pride in the area's Roman heritage. Having met a couple of the locals, I got the impression that this pride is stronger today than it has ever been.

My encounters with the archaeological remains of the Roman frontier had been fleeting – its remains had so far proved relatively insubstantial and picturing the Antonine Wall's ancient strength had as yet required no small amount of imagination. But I knew that would soon change, with some of its most impressive sections lying not far ahead of me. Amazingly, despite the appalling weather forecasts and darkening skies, I was still dry, although I strongly suspected that was about to change too.

I had started to get a picture of how the Roman surveyors and builders had made use of the terrain, picking a route for their Wall that took advantage of the natural rises and plateaus in the landscape. These high places offered the widest, longest views across the supposedly savage lands that lay beyond the frontier, making it easier to keep an eye out for any potential threats that Caledonia might harbour.

That the locations of most of the forts on this eastern end of the frontier would remain seats of power for centuries, long after the departure of the Romans, is also noteworthy. Roman enthusiast Sir Robert Sibbald saw this as proof of the ancient empire's enduring legacy in Scotland, imagining an unbroken link between modern Scotland and its classical past. The real reasons, now lost in time, are no doubt more complex than that.

So far, I had seen only slight remnants of Rome's conquest of Caledonia, but I had nevertheless been struck by the way that the Antonine Wall has left an indelible mark on the topography of modern Scotland. Even in places where the ditch and rampart are long gone, their route is echoed in roads and farm boundaries, memories of the Wall surviving in centuries-old place names, even in the names of the modern streets that follow its line. While its lifetime as a Roman frontier may have been brief, the brooding presence of such an imposing monument, this immense barrier designed to control, separate and intimidate, was clearly hard to erase.

Chapter Two

CALLENDAR TO BONNYBRIDGE

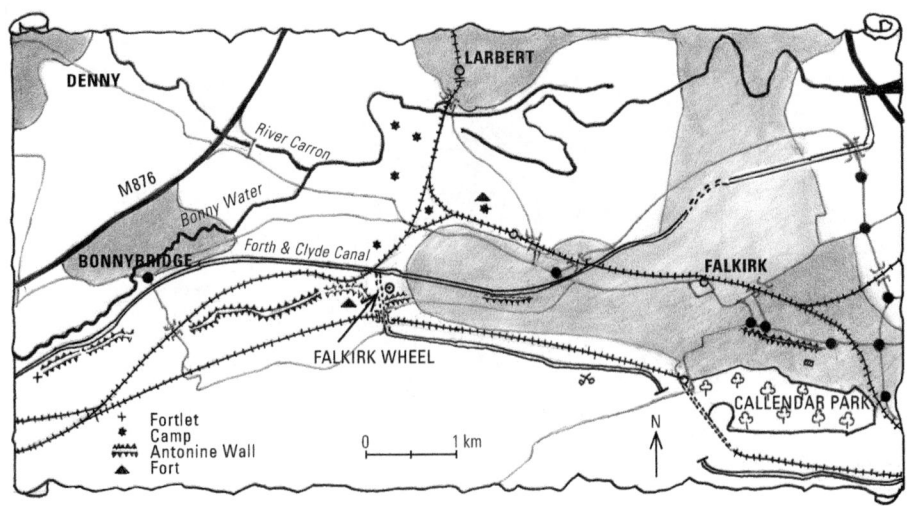

From Callendar To Bonnybridge

I emerged from Benny T's feeling completely satisfied, my legs rested and my belly full, ready for the second half of my walk along the eastern end of the Antonine Wall. I was in Falkirk, a decent-sized place with a population in the region of 40,000. As the unrelenting noise and exhaust-fume aroma of the town rose to meet me, I was already missing the fresh breeze of Mumrills and the shady calm of Polmont Woods. It was becoming clear that I would never escape the modern world for long on this leg of the journey. The good news was that I did not have to travel far before I came across a long stretch of the Roman frontier.

To reach it, I walked out of the restaurant car park, under a grimy railway bridge and past the entrance to the Callendar Business Park, a cluster of characterless office blocks. I stepped off the pavement and onto a strip of grass before carrying on westwards up a low rise. Cars and lorries whizzed past. The environment was carefully controlled, tarmac and concrete, neatly trimmed lawn under my feet, even the trees and conifers planted in strict rows. It seemed like unpromising territory for anyone hunting the remains of Scotland's ancient past.

Callendar House, Falkirk

Presently, a subtle dip appeared in the grass to my left, getting deeper and deeper as it progressed. It was the Roman ditch, a sign that I was now back on the frontier. Although it lies next to one of the main roads into the town centre and is surrounded by twentieth-century streets and buildings, a kilometre-long section of the Antonine Wall has survived because of its location inside the limits of Callendar Park, a historic private estate that is now a much-loved public park

This ditch was by far the most conspicuous length of the Antonine Wall that I had seen during my walk. Having said that, it was not too long before I came to a sizeable gap in the Roman earthworks with a road running right through the middle. To my left stood the magnificent Callendar House, long home to the rich and influential Livingston family who owned the estate for almost four centuries. The road which has sliced its way through the Roman frontier is its driveway.

An oft-told tale claims that this breach, which has eradicated a large chunk of the Antonine Wall's base and ditch, was created in 1842 in preparation for a visit to Falkirk by Queen Victoria. The story goes that the ancient earthworks were levelled so that Her Majesty would be sure to spot and admire Callendar House's fancy façade as she entered the town. After all that effort, just as her carriage rattled past, it is said that the queen turned to glance in the other direction, completely missing the view. A delightful story for sure, but it is sadly not entirely true.

Queen Victoria did come to Falkirk in 1842. The gap, however, was already in existence by the late seventeenth century as can be deduced from a poem published by Michael Livingston (a neighbour and relative of the Livingstons of Callendar) in 1682. Entitled *'Patronus Redux*' ('The Patron Restored'), the 176-verse epic celebrated the virtues of Alexander, the 2nd Earl of Callendar, lamented his long absence from his 'palace' at Falkirk due to ill health and celebrated his glorious return – hence the title of the poem.

A footnote to verse 133 of *'Patronus Redux*' not only included the poet's previously mentioned idea that the Antonine Wall's nickname, Graham's Dyke, was derived from the Emperor Severus, but also recorded that 'the Earl made this Dyke level with the ground, upon which his Palace is built'.

Rather than being saddened by this act of archaeological vandalism, Livingston the poet was delighted that the Earl's recently refashioned mansion now outshone the fading remains of Roman glory:

> His Palace, bord'ring with the common Rode,
> Seems, hospitably, for its guests to call;
> And, by his pains, repaired alamode,
> Outbraves the Shadow of the Roman wall.

The latest incarnation of Callendar House is strongly reminiscent of a fairy-tale castle. Its aspect, long and symmetrical, is a romantic vision of towers and turrets, its roofline bursting with an array of tall chimneys and spires. Like the two previous country houses that I had passed on my journey, Callendar began life as an austere medieval castle. Hidden at its core is a fourteenth century tower. The 2nd Earl's desire to render it more *à la mode* was just one example of the various improvements made over the years as the Livingstons extended and updated their home.

Great historical events have taken place at Callendar House. Alexander, 5th Lord Livingston was guardian to Mary Queen of Scots during her childhood. As a result, a proposed marriage between the young queen and Prince Edward of England was rejected at a meeting of nobles at Callendar in 1543. This audacious decision provoked the fury of Henry VIII and led to the infamous 'Rough Wooing', a war between the two nations that lasted for almost eight years. Remaining close to the Livingston family all her life, Mary was a regular visitor during her short, ill-fated reign.

Oliver Cromwell besieged the house in 1651, with scores of the men defending it killed during the bombardment. A century and a half later, their bones were discovered in a mass grave during landscaping work in the park. In 1715, the Livingstons, ever loyal to the Stuarts, backed the wrong horse during the Jacobite rebellion, when James Stuart, the so-called Old Pretender, unsuccessfully attempted to regain the British throne. Callendar was seized by the Crown and, after being leased back to the Livingstons for over 60 years, was eventually sold in 1783 to William Forbes, a wealthy coppersmith.

The house's fancy façade is the result of major remodelling undertaken by Forbes' descendants in the 1860s and 70s that took inspiration from the chateaux of France. It is a fantastical mishmash of diverse architectural elements, Scots Baronial meets the Loire Valley, gaudy and gothic.

The Forbes sold up in 1963, at which time Callendar House fell into the hands of the local council, who had their eyes not on the beautiful mansion, but on the land surrounding it. Over 500 new homes were built in the grounds, and the house, like Carriden and Kinneil before it, was allowed to fall into disrepair. Its future looked bleak. A reprieve came in the 1990s, when it was restored and repurposed as a museum. Today Callendar House is a vibrant and popular local resource, part museum, part stately home, with a renowned tearoom.

Despite having many more miles to cover, I decided to make a detour inside, specifically to visit the small but informative exhibit dedicated to the Antonine Wall. I received a warm welcome at the front desk inside the main door and was directed up the stairs to the Roman gallery. Here I got the chance to see a scale model of Mumrills fort, as well as several artefacts that had been uncovered at or near the fort.

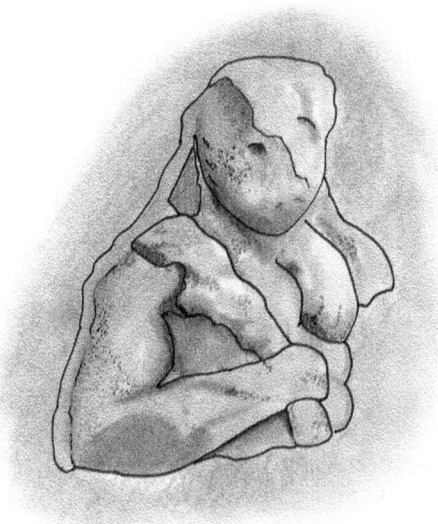
Statue Of Hercules

A small sandstone sculpture of Hercules was the object that really caught my attention. He may be shattered, legless and time-worn now, but he was well carved, his signature club resting on his right shoulder, a bushy beard sprouting from his lantern jaw. His ripped torso, a mass of solid muscle, is truly heroic.

Given his unrivalled bravery and determination in the face of seemingly impossible tasks, it is understandable that Hercules was popular amongst Roman soldiers posted to Britain, particularly those garrisoned in the northern regions. He pops up on an inscription found at the fort of High Rochester in Northumberland, also on a panel from Corbridge in which he might be battling the monstrous Lernaean Hydra, a terrifying many-headed beast with poisonous blood and toxic breath, although only a fragment of the hydra's tentacles survives.

An altar from Housesteads, the most famous fort on Hadrian's Wall, features our hero alongside the Hydra, the Nemean Lion and the Apple of the Hesperides. Closer to home, an altar dedicated to Hercules, unearthed at Brightons, a village just south of the Antonine Wall, has led to speculation that a Roman temple may have been built in the vicinity of Mumrills.

Lying in the glass case next to Hercules was a broken stone panel decorated with a more stylised relief figure that the museum label politely describes as 'naïve'. Almost childlike in its simplicity, it consisted of a triangle that sprouts a featureless head at one end, two stick legs at the other and a pair of rudimentary wings emerging from its back.

This has been interpreted as a winged Victory, its style identified as 'typical of Romano-British sculpture'. Notably provincial, it is likely the work of a soldier who, if no great artistic genius, was at least handy with a hammer and chisel. More accomplished Victories appear on four of the distance slabs found along the course of frontier – a goddess bestowing honours upon the all-conquering legions, her appeal as a glamorous symbol of Roman imperial success is obvious.

While perusing a downstairs gallery that explains the history of Callendar House and its estate, I discovered that a much older residence once stood right by the stretch of Roman frontier that I had inspected on the north edge of the park. Dating from the ninth century, it is often referred to today as the 'Thane's Hall', home to the powerful Thanes of Callendar.

Excavations in 1990 uncovered the remains of a large timber structure, 25 m long and 7 m wide with rounded ends, a line of internal wooden posts supporting the roof and a paved stone floor below. The old Roman Wall was probably repaired to form the north side of the hall's defensive enclosure. Its builders presumably chose this spot to take advantage of the Roman Military Way, which was in use as a highway from east to west for many centuries after the Romans left.

The hall might seem basic to us, even barbaric compared to the luxurious nineteenth-century mansion of Callendar House, but in its day this aristocratic home would have been something special, a symbol of elite power in the earliest days of the Scottish nation.

Still fully fortified by my enormous lunch, I resisted the temptation to visit the museum's tearoom and sample its famous scones. Time was getting on, and there was more of the Antonine Wall to see. Back at the front door, I paused inside the porch to look out over the extensive lawns. The rain had finally started. Only a light drizzle, but the sky was darkening, and the temperature was dropping. Hood raised, I gritted my teeth and headed out into the Scottish summer.

Back near the main road the Roman ditch was deep but overgrown, its bottom hidden under a thick layer of nettles, dock and broom with here and there the pink flowers of a plant that I later identified as rosebay willowherb. Turning left towards the west, I was able to follow the earthwork through a park. An intriguing line of raised earth could be seen on the south edge of the ditch, not, as I at first suspected, the remains of the Roman rampart, but the faint traces of an eighteenth-century estate road.

As the ditch became progressively shallower, the bushes and flowers in its dip gave way to tidily mown grass.

With a line of trees to the north, then a road and row of low industrial buildings beyond, it was hard to get an idea of how this part of the Antonine Wall interacted with the landscape when it was first constructed. It seems like something of a miracle that this section of the ancient frontier has survived at all, given the developments that have taken place around it in the last few decades.

The land along the south side of the ditch, about where the Roman Military Way would have run, was the spot that the Falkirk Council chose to build new housing in the second half of the 1960s in the form of four lofty towers named, from east to west, Symon, Paterson, Marshall and Leishman. Another high block, Maxwell, stands right behind them.

The towers had recently been refaced and reroofed, their lofty exteriors a dazzling white. Love them or hate them, they are certainly conspicuous landmarks in their own way – these were the tall, shiny structures that I had seen in the distance way back at Inveravon. Each tower is named after a local councillor, although whether that would now be seen as an honour is open to question. The original plan was to build low-rise homes, but the fact that much of the Callendar estate is riddled with old mines quickly put paid to that idea.

While they may seem at odds with one another, there are surely similarities between these high modernist towers and the ancient frontier that lies in their not insignificant shadow. After all, both were ambitious engineering projects that failed to live up to the initial hype.

The construction of the flats must have caused untold damage to the fragile archaeology of the Roman frontier and its wider setting. It would be reassuring to think that such developments would no longer happen thanks to the Antonine Wall's Buffer Zone, but given the recent work carried out at the Falkirk Distillery, who knows? Despite such impertinent encroachments, the Roman ditch continues unperturbed, forging onwards past these 16-storey concrete monoliths before finally disappearing under a shabby block of lock-up garages.

At the bottom of a gentle slope, I came to a street named Kemper Avenue. To my right, on a patch of grass next to the road, I found a tatty interpretation panel that detailed discoveries made here in 1980, when a

Roman building with a stone floor and hypocaust underneath was uncovered during the construction of a car park. The text on the board was mostly illegible and the Roman floor had long since been covered up, but my trusty *Handbook* gave more information on what had been unearthed.

Excavations revealed that the walls of the ancient building were almost completely gone, but its rectangular floor gave some clues as to its original purpose. Archaeologists identified it as part of a bath house – possibly associated with the fort that stood further to the west, the baths maybe built here to make use of a natural water supply. Another theory, that it could have been a *mansio* or travellers' inn, has also been proposed. Either way, it was located right alongside the rampart of the Antonine Wall.

This unexpected discovery forced the developers to curtail the size of their car park. The line of a short stretch of the ancient rampart was marked out with kerb stones and the area of the hypocaust highlighted with gravel. Today it is hard to decipher, all messy and weedy, not much to look at for those who do manage to find it. Feeling despondent at such neglect of our national heritage, I headed onwards through the rain.

The ditch in Callendar Park was the last section of the Antonine Wall that I saw for a while, as I was passing beyond the eastern limits of the estate and entering the heart of Falkirk. Signs of the Roman frontier pop up from time to time during building work or in private gardens, but its course has been largely lost under the town's streets and houses. That has been the case for centuries. Way back in the 1720s, both Alexander Gordon and John Horsley found no traces of Roman rampart or ditch in the area.

The town of Falkirk has ancient roots, its name derived from the 'Faw Kirk', literally the 'speckled church', that has long stood at its centre. The building's strange moniker was presumably inspired by the type of spotty stone used to construct it. A newer church, parts of which dates from the fifteenth century, stands on the same spot and is still in use today. It is speckled too, in case you were wondering, its stones stained black from the soot and smoke of heavy industry.

By the 1700s, the town was playing host to the famous 'Falkirk Trysts', some of the largest cattle markets in Scotland, with farmers coming from every corner of the land to sell their livestock. Industrial manufacture, particularly ironwork, took over in the following century, and then inevitably declined. Today, Falkirk, like Bo'ness, is finding a new life as a commuter town, with two train stations linking it to Edinburgh and Glasgow, its roomy Victorian houses cheap compared to those in Scotland's two biggest (and most overcrowded and overpriced) cities.

Falkirk town centre was bustling, despite the persistent mizzle. Folk dashed past under their umbrellas and cars hissed by over the wet tarmac. Numerous empty shops, many optimistically advertised as 'TO LET', stood as a reminder of the ongoing struggle to keep such places alive. Past an eye-catching gilded sign above a music shop which proclaimed that 'ROBERT BURNS, POET, SLEPT HERE AUGUST 25TH 1787', I turned off the pedestrianised high street into a part of town known as the Pleasance.

In his 1757 *History and Antiquities of Scotland*, William Maitland recorded the unearthing of a section of Roman road here (he called this area 'THE PLEASANTS') and guessed that a fort had stood in the vicinity. Late twentieth-century archaeologists proved him right. A more sedate bowling green now sits on the location of the fort, beautifully tended but empty on such a damp and miserable afternoon. A Scout hall next door is home to a unit known as the Antonine Explorers.

I came across a bright blue metal sign on a garden wall nearby that highlighted the site's ancient past and described the discoveries made here during excavations in the early 1990s, which included evidence of wooden structures in an annexe adjacent to the fort. The remains of Roman kilns, along with charcoal and iron slag, demonstrated that iron production was taking place here 1700 years before Falkirk's industrial heyday.

Heading onwards, I soon came to Arnothill, a quiet side street that runs along the crest of an east-west ridge, which is lined with handsome baronial mansions, remnants of that Victorian industrial boom. Their architectural importance is now widely recognised – several are listed, and Arnothill was designated a conservation area in 1988.

Today these stately sandstone villas are in all sorts of conditions, a couple recently restored, several converted into flats. One dilapidated example in overgrown grounds had the eerie air of a haunted house. Many of their owners have obviously sold off land from their gardens over the years, with more recent houses shoehorned in wherever possible.

The street itself also runs right along the route of the Antonine Wall. At its western end I entered a development of 1970s homes, its streets a maze of turns, loops and cul-de-sacs that were almost impossible to decipher on my OS map. This is Bantaskin, the modern houses built on what used to be a private estate adorned with a grand mansion and gardens.

In the late 1600s, Bantaskin (sometimes spelt Bantaskine) was the home of Michael Livingston, author of *'Patronus Redux'*. A big house is mentioned here in eighteenth-century accounts of the Antonine Wall. Little is known about the building's history, but it must have been remodelled at some point, since the few grainy photos that survive show a tasteful classical structure surrounded by lawns, its architecture dating it to the late eighteenth or early nineteenth centuries.

It was owned by several generations of the Hagart family who made a fortune from trade, shipping and plantations in the West Indies, then was purchased in 1879 by James Wilson who was about to retire from the role of Provost of Govan. By the early twentieth century, the Wilson family no longer resided there but they struggled to get rid of it, even at a knockdown price. The estate was gradually sold off piece by piece and the house was abandoned. Unlike Callendar and Kinneil, Bantaskin House's decline ended in its ultimate loss. After sitting uninhabited for several years, its roof lead was plundered in 1947 and the house was demolished soon after. Nothing now remains.

The lost gardens of Bantaskin, famous for their flower-filled greenhouse and fine fruit trees, included one unusual feature that has, however, inexplicably survived – a 200 m stretch of Roman ditch. Perhaps the residents of the house were interested enough to protect and preserve it, or perhaps they were simply indifferent and completely ignored it. Either way, it has endured through endless change, all the gardening and landscaping, the urban planning, the road laying and housebuilding that have taken place over the last century.

Nowadays, this precious fragment of the Antonine Wall is marooned at the very centre of the modern housing estate that has replaced the old house and gardens. The Roman frontier runs along another pronounced ridge here, a position that would have provided expansive views both north and south, before, that is, it was hemmed in and hidden. To get to it, I ended up walking parallel to the Antonine Wall along Anson Avenue, finally finding an entry point at its western end. Stepping through the gate, I entered a little pocket of calm.

This was undoubtedly the most atmospheric piece of the Roman frontier that I had yet encountered. The ditch may not be as deep as it was in ancient times – at Bantaskin it has now softened from its original steep-sided V-shape into a flat-bottomed hollow – but it is long, the southern side where the rampart stood now significantly higher than the northern edge. Bordered by old beeches and oaks, remnants of Bantaskin House's gardens, the ditch cuts a lengthy line through the earth like a wide, grassy avenue.

I had the place to myself, not a single tourist, not even any dog walkers on a dank, wet afternoon like this. Drizzle pattered lightly through the leaves, the grass below a rich green in the wake of all this summer moisture. I stood quiet and still for a moment, taking in the tranquillity of the ancient landmark, protected in its little green sanctuary.

It was easy to forget that I was surrounded by the hustle and bustle of a twenty-first century town. To think that this peaceful place was once the hectic, heavily-garrisoned border of a mighty empire, that this country-spanning barrier, constructed on the command of an emperor, briefly constituted the border between Rome and Caledonia, is impressive enough. That it is still here 2,000 years later, seemingly against all the odds, is truly astounding.

Things were about to get even better. The Roman ditch gets lost under the western loop of Anson Avenue, reappearing briefly as two shallow dips in the grassed verges either side of the B8080 before it disappears again under a post-war housing estate. Most of what remained of the Antonine Wall in these parts was destroyed in the early nineteenth century during the construction of a huge canal basin.

This pool was known as Port Downie, named in honour of Robert Downie of Appin, a Scot of modest origins who made a fortune in India and ended up a local MP and landowner. It marked the conjunction of the Union Canal, which runs eastwards toward Edinburgh, and the Forth & Clyde Canal, which reaches from Grangemouth right across to the west coast.

Linking these two important waterways, the first sitting 30 m higher than the second, meant building a lofty flight of 11 docks that worked their way up the hill and apparently took the best part of a day to navigate. This mammoth construction was infilled in 1933 as canals fell out of favour and transport moved onto the roads, but the Forth & Clyde Canal survived, just in view at the bottom of the slope to my right. The stark white façade of the Union Inn, which has stood next to the waterway since the 1820s, was also visible beyond the gaunt steel panels of the New Camelon War Memorial.

When the Antonine Wall reappeared not far away, past the junction of Glenfuir Road and Tamfourhill Road, it was on a different scale to anything that I had previously seen. This section of Roman ditch, commonly known as Watling Lodge, is undoubtedly the best-preserved on the whole frontier, surviving close to its original dimensions. A forbidding chasm which is still around 4.5 m deep and 12 m wide, its steep sides remind us why, in its day, the Antonine Wall would have been virtually impossible to breach. To its north lies a sharp downward slope, a natural feature this time, and yet another obstacle to any Caledonian force intent on attack.

Today, tall trees line the ditch at Watling Lodge, thick trunked oaks that offered me much-needed shelter from the rain. Robertson and Keppie's *Handbook* promised long views out towards Camelon to the north and the Kilsyth Hill to the west, but on the day that I visited both were hidden behind the thick foliage of the woods that have sprung up on the northern side of the frontier.

I walked along the line of the rampart, still perceptible in places as a long, low mound, while marvelling at the scale of the ditch, its muddy depths filled in places with drifts of fallen leaves and broken branches. And then, quite suddenly, the frontier ended abruptly. Sitting right in the middle of the ditch was a brick building. Next to it, a wooden fence halted my progress.

I later found out that this building is the former stable block of the large sandstone house that lies hidden in the bushes beyond. The house is called Watling Lodge, and in recent years this stretch of the Roman frontier has taken its name. Watling Street, one of the most important roads in the Roman province of Britannia, ran from Dover up to Wroxeter via London and St Albans and the word 'Watling' is derived from Wætlingaceaster, the Saxon name for the last of these towns.

More recently, the term Watling Street has been incorrectly applied to other Roman roads in Britain, including the one that ran from York up to what is now central Scotland (more correctly referred to as Dere Street). The fact that the house built here in 1894 is named after a famous Roman highway implies that its original owners had a knowledge of classical history and were interested in their property's historic associations – although they were not interested enough, it seems, to stop them from building their Arts & Crafts villa right on top of the Antonine Wall.

Luckily for us, local antiquarian Mungo Buchanan was on hand as the house at Watling Lodge was being erected and its grounds planted and landscaped. He was thus able to investigate the site as the ancient remains were eradicated in front of his eyes.

Watling Lodge (Reconstruction)

Buchanan noted the existence of a gap in the Wall enclosed by what he described as a 'guard house' – this was the first fortlet to be rediscovered. Its importance as part of a broader scheme of such installations along the length of the Antonine Wall would only be recognised decades later when archaeologists identified other similar structures including those at Duntocher to the west and Kinneil to the east.

In the case of the Watling Lodge fortlet, a metalled road ran right through the middle of it, over the ditch and across the frontier. The fortlet protected and controlled this exit from the Roman province, and further excavations in the 1970s uncovered the remains of its ramparts, severely damaged by garden landscaping, which enclosed an internal space measuring 18.5 m by 15.5 m. Traces of a hearth and fragments of Roman cooking pots were found inside, and there would have been wooden barracks too, home to the men charged with policing this vital gateway into unconquered Caledonia.

As the only known location where a major road traversed the frontier, this was undoubtedly an important spot in Roman times. The ancient road led to isolated outposts in the north, a route that I would soon follow myself. The Antonine Wall may have been an unambiguous signifier of the edge of empire, but that did not mean that the Roman presence did not permeate further into the Caledonian territories.

Buchanan also noticed that the construction of the house at Watling Lodge necessitated the flattening of a sizeable artificial mound, a mysterious earthwork known locally, for reasons that are now long forgotten, as Maiden Castle. Although little evidence of it survives, modern archaeologists believe that it was a medieval motte that may have been topped by a wooden fortalice, yet another example of canny medieval builders making use of ready-made Roman defences.

The inconvenient position of the Watling Lodge house and grounds, now the property of children's charity Barnardo's, required that I stumble down some perilously steep steps, each one slick and slippery due to the drizzle, back to the level of Tamfourhill Road where I could safely get around this brief interruption to the course of the frontier.

When I reached the other side of Watling Lodge, I found the Antonine Wall re-emerging from under its garden fence, the eaves of the house visible behind. The ditch was shallower now, but it still displayed a certain air of stateliness as it swept down the brae towards me. Above ground it looked little different to what I had already seen, but excavations carried out by Sir George Macdonald early last century revealed that the materials used to construct the Roman rampart changed there.

By cutting sections into the earthwork, Macdonald established that the superstructure of the rampart east of Watling Lodge was built of earth with clay facings. It is partly because of this that so little of it survives. To the west, the direction in which I was heading, it was constructed from blocks of cut turf, the more typical *muro caespiticio* mentioned in the *Historia Augusta*, around 20 layers being required to reach the rampart's original height of 3 m.

Scholars have proposed several possible reasons for this change in the composition of the rampart. Is it evidence that the Antonine Wall was originally intended to end at this fortlet and road junction, with everything else to the east right up to Bridgeness or Carriden a later extension? Or could it be down to more mundane reasons, such as the fact that usable turf was scarcer at the eastern end of the frontier? Did the soldiers simply refine their building techniques as the project progressed? The question so far remains unanswered, yet another of the many enigmas that swirl around this captivating and complex monument, but one that might be solved one day after further excavation and analysis.

On the other side of the road, I spotted an old wooden sign pointing into woodland that bore the words 'Antonine Wall'. Following it, I was soon able to see the ditch again. In places it was very deep, but the fact that it was cluttered up with trees and undergrowth made it difficult to inspect properly.

These woods had none of the charm of Polmonthill. They felt sad and neglected, their floor strewn with all manner of litter, the trees broken and bent, their trunks thick with ivy. Within a couple of minutes, the muddy footpath veered away from the Antonine Wall in a southward direction, and I could advance no further, my way blocked by fallen trees and scrub. Frustrated, I retraced my steps out of the woods and continued along the pavement, the shadowy trench of the Roman frontier occasionally discernible in the bushes to my right. The houses became sparser as I approached Falkirk's outer limits.

My mood lifted not much later when I spotted a large sign advertising one of the town's best-known tourist attractions, the Falkirk Wheel. It opened in 2002, billing itself as the world's first and only rotating boat lift. Designed to attract sightseers to a region searching for a new purpose and new sources of income, the Wheel has certainly succeeded in putting Falkirk on the tourist map.

Although I had long been aware of it, and had passed this signpost many times, I had never actually visited the Falkirk Wheel. I knew that it had an indoor visitor centre and café, an opportunity to escape from the increasingly inclement weather, dry myself off and grab something to eat.

I couldn't have timed it better. During the short walk from the road to the Wheel, the weather took a turn for the worse. The rain, previously an irritating drizzle, suddenly tipped over into a full-scale downpour. I sprinted the final few metres as the heavens opened, letting out an audible

The Falkirk Wheel

sigh of relief as the doors closed behind me and I found myself in a dry and warm interior. Crowds of similarly soaked visitors crammed in around me, shaking the water from their coats and umbrellas, a few sorry souls staring in disbelief through the glass doors at the grey, misty world outside.

It was obvious that I could not continue, for a while at least. Even in my waterproofs, walking in this weather would be no fun, and exploring Roman remains almost masochistic. Some rest and refreshment were required, time to check my map, dry out my cagoule and rest my (not particularly weary) legs. This was also an opportunity to look at the Falkirk Wheel itself, perfectly located right beside the café, from where it can be viewed through an enormous sloping glass wall.

By the time I had sat down with a cup of tea and a slice of cake, the glass wall had become a virtual cascade, the rain simultaneously hammering onto it and pouring down it in gushing, gargling streams. Behind this noisy deluge loomed the metallic bulk of the Wheel, a vast, futuristic structure that was designed as a faster equivalent to the Port Downie canal basin and its time-consuming system of locks.

Nowadays, instead of spending hours navigating their way up or down from lock to lock, it is possible for boats to move between the Forth & Clyde and Union Canals in a matter of minutes. The construction of the Falkirk Wheel was part of an £84.5 million scheme to revitalise and reconnect the two neglected waterways. Christened the Millennium Link, work began in 1999 and involved clearing and consolidating almost 70 miles of run-down canal and restoring 121 associated structures such as locks, bridges and aqueducts.

It is hard to describe the Falkirk Wheel in words, or indeed to convey quite how strange it looks. It is like nothing else I have ever seen before or since. Dwarfing everything around it, it resembles some oversized fragment of industrial machinery, a colossal car part plonked on a hillside in a pool of water.

Huge and heavy it may be, but the Wheel has an elegance about it, the curves of its massive arms allegedly inspired by the silhouette of a Celtic double-headed axe, a ship's propeller and the ribcage of a whale. As well as being an incredible feat of engineering, it could almost pass for a monumental piece of abstract sculpture, and kinetic sculpture at that, as I was about to find out.

How it all works became clear almost immediately. It was the noise that caught my attention first, an echoey, sonorous groan as the Wheel burst into life like an awakening giant. A boat packed with tourists had already steered its way into a water tank known as a 'gondola' at the base of the arms. High above another vessel had manoeuvred into a similar tank 25 m in the air. Then it all started to turn, slowly but surely, 1,200 tonnes of steel rotating around a central axle as one boat glided upwards and the other gracefully descended.

The scale of it was truly awe inspiring and not a little terrifying, with the two 50-tonne gondolas in steady motion, each carrying a boat full of people and half a million litres of water. Within just a few minutes the ride was over. The boat which had started at the bottom was now at the top, ready to set off along an aerial channel that leads through a tunnel, passing safely under the Antonine Wall and into the Union canal. The boat which had started at the top was now drifting serenely into the basin at the foot of the Wheel, about to divest itself of its passengers.

The statistics associated with the Falkirk Wheel's planning, construction and running are amazing. Manufactured in Derbyshire, it was shipped up to Scotland piece by piece, 35 lorry loads in total, before being assembled on site. Over 1,000 staff worked on the entire construction job, many of them tightening the Wheel's 15,000 bolts into its 45,000 bolt holes by hand. Perhaps most incredible is the fact that each turn of the Wheel uses only 1.5 kWh of energy, about the same as boiling eight domestic kettles.

An idea to name it The Antonine Wheel was bandied around at the initial stages of planning, rejected I assume as too obscure, not specific enough to its exact location. Since its opening, the Falkirk Wheel has become rightly famous, and now draws crowds of visitors, even on wet summer afternoons, as the busy café testified.

I bided my time, flicking through Robertson and Keppie's *Handbook* and trying to calculate how long it would take me to reach the end of my day's walk. The torrent outside dwindled back to a wet mist, and I decided that, like it or not, I needed to head onwards. A short distance further on was Rough Castle, one of the Roman frontier's most interesting and extensive sites, a tempting thought even in this weather.

After a little bit more faffing, getting back into my cagoule, packing up my rucksack and retying my saturated boot laces, I forced myself up and out, leaving behind the state-of-the-art Falkirk Wheel and the seductive warmth of its visitor centre and heading back to my ancient Wall.

Luck was on my side again. As I powered on through the woods, guided along a complicated system of gravel footpaths by several wooden arrows marked 'Roman Fort', the rain finally lifted altogether. At last, I was able to slow my pace, pull back my hood and pay more attention to what was going on around me.

Alone again, the crowds milling around the Falkirk Wheel left far behind, I arrived at a gate bearing an unusual sign. 'Welcome to the Roman Fort of Rough Castle', it declared. The rest of its text, which comprised the kind of instructions to visitors common at such historic sites, was bilingual. Not English and Gaelic, as is often found in more northerly districts of Scotland, but English and Latin.

It's not every day that you get to read the Latin for 'Please clean up after your dog, using the bins provided in the car park' (it's *'cura ut canis excrementum in receptacula in area vehiculorum posita deponas'*, by the way – I imagine 'bins' and 'car park' presented particular challenges to the translator, but it kind of works). The warning below, *'cave paludem'*, beware waterlogged ground, seemed particularly apposite.

Through the gate, the trees thinned out. Almost immediately I arrived at another section of Roman ditch. To my left, heading west, it disappeared into the woodland, but to my right it stretched out, shallow but long, straight and true as far as the eye could see.

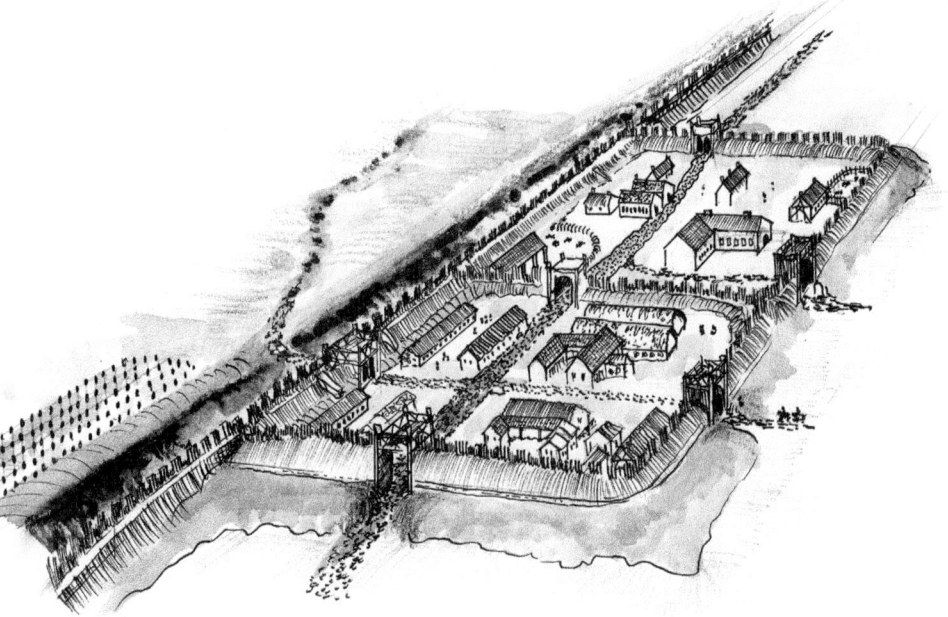

Rough Castle Roman Fort (Reconstruction)

Walking beside it, I soon noticed that much of it was sodden, pools of water collecting in its rounded base. Such flooding would no doubt have occurred in ancient times too, adding an extra layer of protection to the already formidable frontier. If there is one thing harder to clamber through than a treacherous ditch, it is surely a treacherous ditch half filled with cold, muddy water.

As I advanced, more earthworks appeared on the other side of the Antonine Wall, dips and lumps that became more pronounced the further westwards I walked. Frustratingly, I was stuck on the northern edge of the frontier, as walled-out as any ancient Caledonian, prevented from crossing by that soggy, boggy ditch. Eventually I reached an earthen causeway that took me across it and I was finally able to march into the Roman fort of Rough Castle.

With an internal area of less than half a hectare, Rough Castle may be the second smallest fort on the Antonine Wall, but it is without question the best-preserved. It is largely untouched by agriculture and lies far from any urban development. As George Macdonald poetically put it back in the 1911, 'of all the Limes forts it is the one with which the destroying influences of time have dealt most gently'. As a result, its ramparts and defensive ditches have survived to a striking degree. To the east of the fort was an annexe, a defended area slightly larger than the fort itself, the exact purpose of which remains unclear.

Standing in the north-western corner of the fort, Rough Castle's strong position becomes evident. It is perched on a natural platform, its western side plunging down into a valley at the bottom of which runs the Rowan Tree Burn. The views to the north would have been wide and far-reaching although they are now obscured by dense forest. The Antonine Wall's ditch can also be seen heading further west over the horizon, a great scar in the earth.

Rough Castle is a beautiful spot, picturesque and tranquil today, but its mighty earthworks evocative of its past importance. The edges of Falkirk may have crept closer over the past few decades, but it still feels remote, protected by a natural fence of dark trees – not lonely as such, just self-contained.

Yet again, I had the place to myself. The mystical, timeless atmosphere of Rough Castle was broken only slightly by the presence of tall metal pylons on the far side of the burn which carry power lines across the Antonine Wall from north to south. What was once a major military installation has now faded into a soft pattern of undulating earthen banks and trenches. To me, the timeworn remains of this ancient frontier fort seem indelibly carved into the Scottish landscape.

Rough Castle is a site that I know well, one that I have visited often. I always love spending time there. Along with Watling Lodge, it was the first part of the frontier that I ever visited, way back in the 1980s when I was a Roman-obsessed adolescent. The exact details of that first visit, almost ancient history itself now, are hazy. I have no idea which one of the two sites I saw first – probably Watling Lodge, given that I was coming from Edinburgh – but I do remember the excitement of finding such monumental Roman remains virtually on my doorstep.

This was the beginning of a life-long fascination with Roman Scotland, a passion that has come to shape much of my adult life. I didn't travel alone, of course. My chauffeur for the day was my long-suffering mother, a woman who, despite having little interest in history herself, was always happy to indulge my latest whim or fancy, and who facilitated countless visits to ancient ruins, stately homes, art galleries and museums throughout my childhood.

I took it all for granted back then, as youngsters are wont to do, but looking back it was these places that fired my imagination and opened up my eyes to the wonders of the past. It was those trips that made me, for better or worse, the man that I am today. It's too late to thank my mother now, so I can only hope she knew, somehow, that those afternoons spent wandering around muddy fields and echoey galleries with an often grumpy and taciturn teenager would be appreciated, eventually.

Many visitors to Rough Castle over the last three centuries have been similarly taken by its ancient grandeur. Alexander Gordon spent several hours there during his long 'antiquary peregrination' carried out in the early 1720s, carefully measuring and recording the site, later writing that the fort 'for Intireness and Magnificence, exceeds any that are to be seen on the whole Track, from Sea to Sea'.

The plan of it that he produced for his book *Itinerarium Septentrionale* features not only the ditches and ramparts of the fort and the annex, but also the outline of a building at the centre of the fort, the vestiges of a large structure that he identified as the 'Praetorium'. The word *praetorium* was used in ancient sources to describe the tents used by commanding officers on their campaigns and was later adopted by antiquarians and archaeologists to describe the administrative building at the epicentre of every Roman fort.

English antiquarian John Horsley, on the other hand, seemed underwhelmed by Rough Castle, implying that Alexander Gordon had exaggerated with his enthusiastic praise for the site and grumbling that it was too overgrown to thoroughly inspect. Perhaps he just enjoyed the opportunity to contradict Gordon. There was certainly no love lost between the two men. On hearing that Horsley was working on a new book to rival his recent *Itinerarium*, a furious Gordon wrote to their mutual acquaintances denouncing the Englishman as a plagiarist and even dismissing him as 'crasey'.

When Horsley's *Britannia Romana* was posthumously published in 1732, the Scot's criticisms only intensified. Gordon accused the late Horsley of copying an illustration of a sculpture from his own flimsy, hastily published *Additions and Corrections...to the Itinerarium Septentionale*, only for the exasperated English antiquarian Roger Gale to point out that Horsley had died several weeks before it was even released.

Jessie Mothersole encountered terrible weather when she came to Rough Castle on 28 January 1927, conditions even more hostile than those I had been enduring. Walking on the day of the infamous 'Glasgow hurricane' in which at least 26 people died, and hundreds were made homeless, she was forced to abandon her first visit due to rain blown almost horizontal by the high winds.

Returning the next day, Mothersole described the fort as 'wonderfully preserved', but also advised her readers that it was best to visit in winter, as at other times of year its remains were often hidden in bracken. Photographs of the site in George Macdonald's 1934 *The Roman Wall Scotland* show mature trees growing out of its ditches and rampart. Nowadays, the fort has been cleared of vegetation and is much easier to explore, thanks to the diligent care of Historic Environment Scotland.

The first excavations took place here in 1902-3. The stone foundations of three buildings were discovered within the fort, while a bath house was found in the neighbouring annexe. The remains were in a poor state, to the point that they were difficult to interpret but, thanks to the generic layout of such forts, the buildings could be confidently identified as a military headquarters and a commandant's house with a grain store in between.

Several other digs have taken place in the subsequent decades, adding more details to our understanding of the layout and architecture of Rough Castle. The subtle remains of wooden barrack blocks – long, low ranges where the soldiers bedded down and stored their kit, also where they ate their meals, including the bread that they had baked themselves in nearby ovens – have also been unearthed.

One find made during those early excavations would end up making an important contribution to our understanding of the terminology used by the Romans to describe their military buildings. In a stone-lined hole (probably a well or a strong-room) under the floor of the fort's central building, the headquarters that Alexander Gordon had labelled the 'Praetorium', were found three pieces of a broken stone inscription. Although fragmentary, the words carved into the sandstone panel revealed that this structure was completed by the Sixth Cohort of Nervians, a band of around 500 auxiliaries drawn from what is now Belgium who saw service on Hadrian's Wall.

The building was dedicated, as usual, to the Emperor Antonius Pius. It is the final two words of the inscription that are the most informative, or at least what is left of them: *'PRI…PIA FECIT'*. The middle letters of that first word are now lost, but epigraphists have deduced that it originally read *'PRINCIPIA FECIT'*. The phrase therefore means 'made this *principia*', as in the Nervians built it. A simple enough statement, but this inscription allowed archaeologists to correct the mistake made by Gordon and countless others in calling the fort's headquarters a *praetorium*. The proper ancient term *principia* has been adopted at forts across the Roman world ever since.

Arguably the most exciting (and definitely the most gruesome) discovery made at Rough Castle during those early twentieth-century excavations is to be found over the ditch beyond the north edge of the Antonine Wall, so I headed back across the causeway to take a look.

Over the ridge, as the ground started to slope gently downwards, I found a series of sizeable pits cut into the earth in orderly rows. The pits were full of rotting leaves and black water, their true depth impossible to gauge. Bordered by luscious green grass, they seemed harmless enough, looking not unlike a piece of contemporary land art or a curious water feature.

In fact, these regimented lines of pits were a grisly boobytrap, each hole furnished with a sharpened wooden stake, all of them then covered with branches and leaves to hide their presence. Their position in front of the Antonine Wall was intended to break the ranks of any attacking Caledonian rabble, the stakes there to impale them in the process.

By the time they constructed this Caledonian frontier, the Romans had been using such pits for generations. Julius Caesar mentioned them in his description of the conquest of Gaul, which took place in the 50s BC. While besieging the Gaulish army led by the rebellious chieftain Vercingetorix at Alesia, the Roman troops built a series of entrenchments furnished with a variety of lethal traps. Caesar's soldiers demonstrated their dark sense of humour by nominating these fearsome pits *lilia*, meaning lilies, due to their resemblance to the flower with its protruding stamen.

The *lilia* at Rough Castle were the first to be rediscovered anywhere in the Roman world, although no remains of those deadly wooden spikes were found. More defensive pits have since been identified at other sites along the Antonine Wall, including some at Callendar Park, but this is the only place where they are still exposed to view.

The Lilia Pits, Rough Castle

Innocent looking now, but once truly horrific, the *lilia* were simple but deadly. Thinking about the horrific injuries that would result from tumbling into one of them was enough to make me shudder. I tiptoed my way gingerly around them, attempting to peer into their dark depths while carefully negotiating the slippery grass, before heading back uphill to the relative safety of the fort.

Entering through the north gate again, I walked across the middle of the fort to its southern gate. Unusually, the Military Way split in two at Rough Castle, one branch climbing the steep slope up to the western gate and through the middle of the fort, the other taking a gentler detour outside its southern ramparts.

According to George Macdonald and Jessie Mothersole, who visited 25 years after Macdonald's original excavations, the paved slabs of the road that led up to the southern gate from this ring road had been worn by constant traffic into ruts like those seen today on the streets of Pompeii. None of the other entrances displayed such extreme wear and tear, suggesting to Macdonald that it was this southern offshoot of the Military Way that had been the busier or the longer used of the two branches.

Sadly, for their own preservation, the fragile foundations and paved roads inside the fort's ramparts were finally covered up several decades after their initial excavation. Extensive damage was done to them in the intervening years, due to both weathering and vandalism. Today, a bit of imagination is required to decipher the various lumps, lines and bulges in the earth at Rough Castle, tantalising clues as to what lies beneath. The task is made easier by an array of colourful interpretation panels that explain the original layout and feature digitally produced images that recreate how the fort and the surrounding terrain looked in ancient times.

The origins of the modern name of the site remain elusive. When Sir Robert Sibbald visited around the turn of the eighteenth century, he simply referred it to it as 'a great Fort' that he located 'at the Rowentree Burn-head'. Alexander Gordon was the first to call it 'Rough Castle' and, from then on, the name stuck. By the end of the eighteenth century the fort had become the permanent location of the Falkirk Trysts. Although the date of the first of these events is unknown, Lawrence Keppie believes that the name 'Rough Castle' may derive in some way from these busy, boisterous gatherings.

I left Rough Castle fort via its west gate, the northern branch of the Military Way leading me down a steep causeway over the fort's defensive ditches into the deep valley that contains the Rowan Tree Burn. And it really is deep – antiquarian John Horsley was only slightly exaggerating when he described the western side of the valley as a 'very frightful precipice'. As George Macdonald pointed out 200 years later, negotiating it on horseback, as Horsley did, would have made this dizzying descent seem even more treacherous.

Thanks to the recent downpour, the burn was babbling noisily over its rocky bed that afternoon, and I was thankful to find a small modern bridge that led me safely across it. There were, presumably, two Roman bridges here, one for each branch of the Military Way, the two routes converging on the other side of the valley. As for the turf rampart, excavations at other locations reveal that such streams would often be funnelled into culverts, stone-lined channels that led the water safely underneath.

The next 750 m stretch of the Antonine Wall is the best place to properly understand how the various elements of the structure worked together to create a (hopefully) impervious frontier. Indeed, it is still preserved here, as

Alexander Gordon described it back in the 1720s, 'in its greatest Beauty and Perfection'. Looking westwards, the modern road that brings visitors to the site follows the route of the Roman Military Way. To the right of that, the remains of the turf rampart are prominent, a grassy ridge standing up to 1.5 m tall in places. Then comes the deep ditch, beyond which the upcast mound is evident.

Much work was done on this part of the Antonine Wall by the members of the Glasgow Archaeological Society in the early 1890s. In their attempts to understand the structure and composition of the rampart they cut sections through it, also through the ramparts of Rough Castle fort, to see how both were constructed. The report on their findings, all technical stuff, written with fellow archaeologists in mind, also recorded an eccentric experiment that took place here in 1891.

James Russell, a resident of the nearby village of Longcroft, decided to reconstruct part of the rampart in an attempt to determine how tall it would have stood in Roman times. This new turf wall nicknamed a 'peat stack' by one of the workmen involved in its construction, eventually reached a height of 10 ft, with a flat top measuring 9½ ft wide. It no doubt looked splendid, but 'Mr Russell's Structural Experiment' (as the Glasgow Archaeological Society christened it) would prove to be not nearly as durable as its Roman predecessor. Severely damaged during autumn storms in 1891, in the years that followed, it slowly but steadily collapsed. No evidence of it can be seen today.

A large platform attached to the southern side of the Wall's turf rampart can still be found here, one of several along the frontier that are now referred to as 'expansions'. This expansion nearest to the fort is known as Bonnyside East. Another better-preserved one, Bonnyside West, is in the private garden of Bonnyside House nearby, while two more, Tentfield East and West, have been identified by the rampart on the other side of Rough Castle.

The eighteenth-century antiquarians noticed these mounds and spent much time considering what they might have been. Gordon assumed that they had formed the bases of 'Watch Towers' similar to the ones that he had seen on Hadrian's Wall. William Maitland referred to this one at Bonnyside East as a *'castellum'*, Latin for a little fort or tower. William Roy, who surveyed the entire wall in 1755, drew a plan of the Antonine Wall east of Rough Castle, including the square mound of Tentfield West, which he labelled 'one of the Interior CASTELLA or TURRETS'.

In 1957, the platform was finally excavated to uncover its true nature. The results, it must be said, were inconclusive. Like the rampart that it abuts, the mound was made from turf sods. Below it was a square base of stone cobbles with sides over 5 m long. Various theories have since emerged regarding the purpose of these mounds. They could, as several antiquarians claimed, have been the bases for observation towers, tall structures used to scour the lands to the north for signs of trouble. Alternatively, they may reveal the location of staircases which led up to the top of the rampart.

Evidence of burning from the ground around this Bonnyside East platform has inspired the most popular hypothesis, that these mounds were used as beacons with fires on top being used to send signals along the Antonine Wall, or even north or south to other military installations nearby.

How the Romans communicated effectively along this frontier is something that has long puzzled historians. As many over the centuries have pointed out, a mural boundary like this is difficult to garrison and control, spreading the troops out thinly across a long distance. Their training and tactics meant that the Roman army was better suited to fighting on a battlefield than defending a rampart.

One strange legend had emerged by the eighteenth century which claimed that a terracotta tube had been built into the Antonine Wall to allow communication from one command post to the next (a similar tale of a bronze tube built into Hadrian's Wall was also in circulation around this time), although quite how this worked is not explained. As an enormous trumpet or as a funnel to shout messages down? I can confidently confirm the theory is as untrue as it is implausible.

The latest research by John Poulter, a retired engineer, recently published in the scholarly journal *Britannia*, noted that, although the course of the Antonine Wall itself is sinuous and follows no obvious plan, most of the forts, fortlets and expansions along its central section are in alignment and would, therefore, have been inter-visible, at least from a height of 7.6 m.

In some cases, a fire lit at one installation could be seen not just by its closest neighbour, but also at locations much further away. The bright flames of a signal fire would certainly send a clear message to nearby garrisons: 'Help Required!' Stick a wooden tower with a brazier on top next to or inside many of the frontier's installations, and you have an effective way to communicate all along the frontier, a simple but effective alarm system.

As Poulter pointed out, such a system would call for the positions of the military sites to have been carefully plotted in advance, an idea that contradicts the theory that only six of the forts were originally planned and the rest added later as the frontier's design was adapted. All that is needed to confirm his proposals are signs of ancient post holes in the top of the one of the expansions, evidence that they supported wooden towers. Unfortunately, the fact that all the expansions that have been so far identified are extensively eroded makes that highly unlikely.

Not long after the Bonnyside East expansion, the Roman frontier headed under the garden wall of Bonnyside House and out of sight. Continuing along the road that runs parallel to it, I caught glimpses of the overgrown Roman ditch through the shadowy line of trees that surrounds this patch of private land. The course of the Roman frontier passes under the lane that I was following next to the gate into the house's grounds, the ditch reappearing on the other side as a patch of marshy ground, thick with reeds. What lay beyond was more striking – a large rocky mound that protruded dramatically from the flat ground around it. From afar, it resembled a great barrow, the resting place of some mythical warrior king. Its unusual name only adds to its air of mystery and magic. This is Elf Hill.

Despite research carried out since my walk, I have failed to find any supernatural legends linked to Elf Hill, apart from a brief footnote in the posthumous 1852 edition of Robert Stuart's *Caledonia Romana*, which states that it was reputed to be 'the favourite haunt of fairies'. It does look like the kind of place that pops up in old folk tales, in which ancient burial mounds are regularly identified as fairy dwellings or goblin lairs, to be entered at your peril.

Rather than man-made, this sizeable hillock is a completely natural feature. It clearly presented an impediment to the Romans as they constructed their frontier, since the rampart and ditch travel past its northern slope, while the Military Way loops round its southern edge.

Although I could not locate any fairy tales associated with Elf Hill, there are fantastical stories attached to the land around it, as this was long said be the site of a famous battle between Rome and Caledonia, a legend that inspired, or more likely was inspired by, the name commonly used to refer to the Antonine Wall since medieval times.

It was in the second half of the fourteenth century that John of Fordun first regaled Scots with the tale of a fearless warrior named Gryme. Fordun's Latin chronicle, *Chronica gentis Scotorum*, is packed with ripping yarns of ancient Caledonian bravery. Most of them, we can assume, are completely fictional, composed by Fordun himself or passed down to him via legends and folk tales. The purpose of history in those days was not to record facts, such as they are, but to construct an ennobling and uplifting national narrative, stories that would inspire admiration for our valiant ancestors.

In the fifth chapter of the third book of *Chronica gentis Scotorum*, Fordun recorded that Gryme was the grandfather of Eugenius, who became king of Scotland in AD 419. Fed up with being excluded from much of his kingdom by the barrier built between the Forth and Clyde by the Romans (or, as Fordun told it, by the Britons following the advice of the Romans), Eugenius and Gryme decided it was time to regain their lost lands.

The two men amassed a huge army from across the north. With Eugenius at its head, the army marched to the Antonine Wall and struck it hard: 'Having first duly ordered his engines, he broke it down to the very ground, while its guards either escaped by flight or were slain', wrote Fordun. Soon, the whole of southern Scotland was back in Eugenius' hands. The Romans, tired of repeatedly sending troops to help the feeble Britons, instructed them to retreat southwards and rebuild the southern Roman frontier (the one we call Hadrian's Wall that, confusingly, Fordun believed had originally been established by the Emperor Septimius Severus).

Fordun informed his readers that this Scottish Roman frontier now bore the name of 'Grymisdyke'. That part, as we have seen, is true, although the spelling would change over the years. The rest of his tale is pure fantasy, a hotchpotch of myth, pseudo-history and fabrication. It seems probable to me that the term Grymisdyke preceded the story, and that the legend of Gryme was inspired by the already ancient monument at some point in the early medieval period when the roots of its nickname were already long forgotten.

Still, fiction can be more exhilarating than truth, and Gryme's legendary bravery was no doubt motivating to fourteenth-century Scots, who themselves felt threatened by a malevolent force from the south, although in their case it was the rapacious kings of England rather than the Romans or southern Britons.

The eighteenth-century antiquarians who studied the Roman frontier were gradually wising up to the fact these medieval chronicles were not to be trusted, but the story of Gryme and his destruction of the Antonine Wall was still well-known at this time and is mentioned in several publications of the period. Often a note of disbelief can be detected. Alexander Gordon left it up to his readers to decide the truth, hedging his bets by suggesting that if the battle had happened at all, there was no reason to doubt that it had happened at Elf Hill. Even the pragmatic and scholarly John Horsley reported the story without a hint of scepticism.

In fact, Fordun made no specific geographical references in his account of the battle, but the fact that there are several breaks in the Roman rampart here seems to have encouraged the idea that the land around Elf Hill was the location of this great Caledonian victory. In his 1777 *General History of Stirlingshire*, local church minister turned antiquarian the Reverend William Nimmo noted those gaps in the turf rampart and areas where the ditch had been filled in but produced an altogether more convincing explanation: 'After all, this may be accounted for from the nature of the soil, which is wet and marshy'.

There is, it turns out, a small loch right behind Elf Hill. While the romantic in me loves the story of Gryme and his courageous Caledonian comrades, as a historian I am forced to admit that soggy soil is almost certainly the cause of the Antonine Wall's collapse here, and that Gryme, sad to say, probably never existed at all.

The sky was clearing up, revealing patches of blue and letting through the odd glint of sunshine. My day's journey almost at an end, I carried on into Bonnybridge, a town that exists largely as a result of the local industries that thrived here in the nineteenth and early twentieth centuries, most notably sawmills, iron foundries and brick manufacture. The locals have long been proud of their local history. Jessie Mothersole recorded that her guide during her 1927 visit to Rough Castle was an amateur antiquarian who worked in the local brickworks.

Bonnybridge is a sleepy place now, most famous in the last three decades as the 'UFO capital of Scotland'. One Scottish newspaper even described it as the UFO capital of the world a few years ago. Ever since 1992, residents and visitors have allegedly reported nearly 300 UFO sightings a year, with one local councillor even approaching four prime ministers in his (unsuccessful) attempts to open an official investigation.

My brief visit was thankfully alien free and I could not see anything that might draw intergalactic visitors to Bonnybridge. It does have a school named after the Roman frontier, which runs right under the playing fields of Antonine Primary (school motto *Nullus Murus Nos Dividit*, 'No Wall Divides Us'), the ditch surviving as a gentle hollow. Excavations in the 1930s, carried out as a new road was built, showed that the various elements of the frontier – its stone base, its ditch and its berm – were relatively well-preserved under the ground.

Close to the Antonine Wall can be found the eroded remains of a motte-and-bailey castle, a medieval timber fortress that is surely the same one mentioned in a 1542 charter, where it is referred to as 'lie Mot de Seybeggis', or the Motte of Seabegs. Like other sites I had already seen that day, the castle made use of the Roman ditch, which would have enhanced its southern defences and saved a bit of work for the medieval builders. No trace of the castle's superstructure can be detected today.

I skipped this last part of the frontier since it is all on private ground and, from the look of my map, not visible from the road. Instead, I headed down to the canal that passes the southern edge of the town. It was there that my first day of walking along the Roman frontier ended. A car was waiting by the waterside to collect me, one of the benefits of having family who live locally.

During my day's trek I had covered roughly a third of the length of the Antonine Wall, a distance of around 14 miles that had led me past some of Scotland's most fascinating heritage, but I was aware that I had plenty of miles yet to cover. It was already mid-afternoon, and although I was not exactly tired – the walking that day had been easy – now felt like a suitable time to head back to Falkirk for a warm shower, a hot meal and a good night's sleep.

I had to prepare myself for my next walk, during which I would venture northwards into the lands that lay beyond the edge of the Roman Empire, but not completely outside its influence. My next journey would lead me over the frontier as I went in search of the elusive remains of a Roman presence in the unconquered regions of Caledonia.

Chapter Three

IN SEARCH OF ARTHUR'S O'ON

It was early morning, cloudy and breezy but thankfully dry, and I was back at Watling Lodge. As we learned earlier, this was the site of a fortlet attached to the Antonine Wall that guarded an exit out of (or entrance into, depending on who you were) the Roman Empire. From here, a road led northwards into unconquered territory. Although the great turf rampart and deep ditch of the Antonine Wall marked a boundary, a dividing line between the Roman and non-Roman worlds, this was not the endpoint of Roman activity in northern Britain.

Beyond it, only a few minutes' walk from where I was standing, was a large Roman fort that was garrisoned throughout the Antonine period. In the area around this fort were other signs of Roman and Caledonian activity, including the site of one of Scotland's most enigmatic ancient (and almost definitely Roman) monuments. As a result, I had decided to briefly change direction, walking north instead of west, heading into the lands beyond the Roman frontier.

The Romans knew how to build roads that would last, and this north road out of the Watling Lodge fortlet was in use for centuries after they abandoned the Antonine Wall – it was still visible in the 1700s. Since then, it has mostly disappeared under ploughed fields and urban expansion, but as I was about to find out, it is still possible to pick up its course here and there as it heads towards Stirling.

Leaving Watling Lodge, I walked down to the Forth & Clyde Canal, crossing it by a low bridge close to the Union Inn. This led me into the town of Camelon (I pronounce it Cam-eh-lon, but there is some debate about this, many locals preferring Came-lon). Established as a small village in the eighteenth century, Camelon boomed after the opening of the canal, with ironworking, particularly the production of nails, a local speciality. While it used to boast many fine old buildings, including a Georgian mansion house just to the north of my route, most of it was demolished and rebuilt in the last century.

Carmuirs Avenue is lined with early twentieth-century social housing, those harled, semi-detached homes that are ten-a-penny in southern Scotland's ex-industrial heartland. I knew that I had to turn northwards at some point, but I wasn't sure where. Yet again, I discovered that my 1:25,000 scale Ordnance Survey map was not much help when it came to urban streets. Then, to my right, I spotted a road called Watling Street, and I knew that I was heading in the right direction.

This short street, which lies more or less on top of the line of the Roman road, took me up to the busy Glasgow Road. On the other side a petrol station and a fast-food drive-through. Next to them, a factory owned by Britain's biggest bus builder. And hidden beneath these, the remains of one of the most important and enduring Roman military installations in Scotland – Camelon Roman fort.

Sitting under a mile to the north of the Antonine Wall, the first fort at Camelon was built by Agricola sixty odd years before the construction of the Antonine frontier. It is this Agricolan fort, sometimes referred to as the 'South Camp', that lies under the bus factory and petrol station. It was severely damaged in the 1840s when a railway line was cut right through it. Because of this damage and later development of the site, little is known about the structure of the earliest fort at Camelon, which was abandoned after the Roman retreat out of Caledonia following their victory at the battle of Mons Graupius.

The Romans came back to Camelon in the early AD 140s, however, creating a new fort at the same time as they built their frontier. They obviously liked the situation. Sitting on a plateau, Camelon offers extensive views in all directions, an ideal lookout point. It is also close to the River Carron, and it has been suggested that a harbour may have been established on the river's banks, perfect for the delivery of supplies to the garrisons of both Camelon and the Antonine Wall nearby.

The Antonine fort at Camelon was built to the north of the Agricolan one, meaning that it has suffered less damage in recent centuries. Although I had often read about it, I had always assumed that there was nothing to see on the ground. During my visit to the National Museum of Scotland, however, Dr Hunter had recommended searching it out.

So it was that I left the route of the old Roman road as it disappeared under a supermarket car park, turned right along the Glasgow Road, and then left onto the Stirling Road. Past another memory of the region's Roman past – a modern street fancifully named Centurion Way – I came to Falkirk Golf Club. Dr Hunter had told me that if I asked nicely, I would be allowed onto the course to visit the site of the Roman fort, so I headed into the clubhouse bar, from where I was taken to the pro-shop. Having checked the schedule, the club professional informed me that I just had time before a junior competition began, pointing me up a steep hill to the 9-hole youth course.

It was a steepish climb, a sharp right turn at the top leading me to the southern edge of the Roman fort. Although subtle, it was possible to see the slight ridge of the fort's rampart under some hedging. Through that, the flat platform on which the Roman fort sat, its strict grid of buildings and streets now replaced with lush green grass. The railway cuts off its south-westerly corner, with the tops of its pylons sticking out of the deep cutting and the bus factory beyond. Turning round, I took in the view towards the east – the landscape may have changed beyond recognition since Roman times, but I could still see for miles, with the concrete chimney of Longannet Power Station and the hills of Fife visible in the far distance.

For centuries, the remains of Camelon Roman fort were extremely well-preserved and much admired (and sometimes misinterpreted) by early historians and antiquarians. In his 1527 *Historia gentis Scotorum* (*History of the Scottish People*), chronicler Hector Boece claimed that it had been an ancient Pictish city, founded by a certain Cruthneus Cameloun, king of the Picts. Legend relates that the high walls of this city were pierced by twelve brass gates.

In the end, according to Boece, the whole thing was cast down by the army of Kenneth MacAlpin, who some view as the first king of a unified Scotland. There is no truth in any of this, of course, but it does give us a sense that it must have still been an imposing site when Boece was alive, impressive enough to inspire such fantastical stories over 1,300 years after the Romans had left it behind.

There was still lots to see when the eighteenth-century antiquarians arrived. Sir Robert Sibbald believed Camelon to be a great Roman city, 'the chief Colony, the Seat of the Commander in chief of the Country lying upon the South-side of the Forth' and made much of its underground vaults (probably the remains of raised hypocaust floors) and the grid-like pattern of its streets. Alexander Gordon similarly called it a Roman town and wrote of 'the Tracks of Houses and Streets'. Seventy years later, however, the *Old Statistical Account* of 1797 revealed that 'there are now few vestiges remaining', and it has been all downhill since then.

Now, the only thing that can be detected by an eagle-eyed visitor is the slight rise of the fort's ramparts on the south, east and north sides, its line helpfully highlighted by a line of low trees. This at least gives an idea of its enormous scale. At 3.2 hectares, it was larger than any of the forts on the Antonine Wall. A dig in 1899-1900, led by Mungo Buchanan, uncovered its streets and the foundations of its headquarters, granaries and a luxurious commandant's house with a private bath suite.

One of the most important and unexpected discoveries at Camelon, however, was made during its partial destruction by the construction of the railway line back in 1849. A few finds were made during the digging of the cutting, the details of which are now lost. But one spectacular and unusual artefact was recorded – a splendid carved stone urn, which had been broken into pieces. It was thought to be fashioned from alabaster, and while smaller fragments ended up in private hands, the base and a substantial piece of the bowl made it into the collection of the Museum of Antiquities in Edinburgh. It was highly prized and displayed in the museum for half a century. But then, in 1901, Keeper of the Museum Joseph Anderson decided it was not Roman at all, and it was sent down into the stores where it would languish for over a hundred years.

Stone Urn, Camelon

Luckily, it was spotted there by Dr Fraser Hunter, who decided that it was worth another look. He realised that it was in fact something rare and special – a funeral urn made not from alabaster, but from Egyptian travertine. And it was Roman. Quarried in Egypt, it was likely carved in

Rome, where such things were seen as status symbols, purchased by the wealthy to hold their ashes after death. While several have been found in Italy, they seem to have been extremely rare in the outer provinces – one is known from the north of France, another from London, and then this one from the very edge of the Empire.

We will never know whose ashes it contained, although it must have been someone extremely important, perhaps a commander of the fort who had brought this urn to the frontier in case he didn't make it back alive. The reports of its discovery mention that it contained 'calcined bones', but they have long since disappeared.

Although worn and eroded by time, the fragments in the museum do retain the beautiful, striated pattern of the slightly translucent travertine, which emits a golden glow under the right light. Small areas of the original polished surface can be seen in the interior of the bowl. The stumps of a broken handle survive too, and it originally had a fancy lid surmounted by a spiky finial. Overall, it must have measured almost 40 cm in height.

It is incredible to think of the journey made by this luxury object in ancient times, across the Empire from Egypt to Rome to Caledonia. Now, thanks to Dr Hunter, its importance is once again recognised, and it has been back on display in the National Museum of Scotland. There may be more of it out there too. Maybe one day the pieces that were snapped up by Victorian collectors might be found and reunited, allowing us to restore this exotic memorial to an unidentified Roman VIP to its former glory.

Aware of the arrival of some young golfers at the far side of the fort site, I decided that it was time to leave them to it and head onwards. Back down at the clubhouse, I turned left onto the Stirling Road, which runs close to the route of the ancient Roman way.

Less than a mile further on, I reached the River Carron, here a wide waterway bordered by tall trees, mostly sycamore and ash, both riverbanks lost behind their dense canopies. The river has several associations with ancient Rome, most of them more legendary than historic. It is often proposed that a Roman harbour was located in the vicinity, an idea largely inspired by the discovery of what was believed to be a Roman anchor near here back in the 1600s (Sir Robert Sibbald wrote in 1707 that it was unearthed 'within a Century of years hence'), evidence that could be described as circumstantial at best, so more research is needed to confirm that.

Further to the west of this spot can be found the village of Dunipace. In its cemetery, a stone's throw from the river, are two mounds, known locally as the Hills of Dunipace. These hillocks, one of which is much eroded, the other still large and now covered in trees, caught the attention of the eighteenth-century antiquarians, who became convinced that they were both man-made and ancient. A story developed that they were a monument built to celebrate a peace struck with the Caledonians by the Emperor Septimius Severus following his brutal early third-century invasion of northern Britain. As the Reverend William Nimmo, minister of the nearby parish of Bothkennar, related in his 1777 book, *A General History of Stirlingshire*, some thought that the very name of the mounds provided evidence of this ancient treaty: '*Dun* signifying a hill in the ancient language of the country, and *pax*, peace in the language of Rome; the compound word Dunipace, according to this etymology, signifies the hills of peace'.

It is sometimes claimed that the mounds were fortified with a medieval wooden motte like the ones that used to stand at Watling Lodge and Seabegs, but there is no archaeological evidence for this. Robert the Bruce and William Wallace are said to have met at Dunipace for a parley in 1298, while King Edward I of England, nicknamed *malleus Scotorum* ('hammer of the Scots') due to his relentless invasions of Scotland, is also supposed to have signed a (short-lived) truce here in 1301.

Yet again, modern research has blown the romantic legends out of the water, demonstrating that the mounds are not man-made at all, but an entirely natural phenomenon, the remains of a post-glacial raised beach. Like the old tales of heroic Gryme smashing through Gryme's Dyke, it seems likely to me that the name Dunipace gave rise to these various peace-related legends, rather than the other way round.

I crossed the fast-flowing Carron using a modern road bridge, noticing to my left two earlier river crossings. Nearest to me was a late eighteenth-century stone bridge, its wide stone arch still carrying one-way traffic across to a suburb of Larbert whilst behind that was the enormous bulk of the Larbert Viaduct. Almost 200 m long and 18 m high with 14 tall spans, the viaduct was built to carry the Scottish Central Railway, which opened in 1848.

It was also the site of a terrible accident on 29 April 1867, when a train carrying meat and livestock from Perth came off the rails and several wagons tumbled over the side. The men working the train escaped with minor injuries, but many of the cattle on board perished. The viaduct still functions today, carrying trains as they head from Camelon up to Larbert, then to Dunblane and onwards up to Inverness.

There must have been a bridge here in ancient times too, built to take the Roman road over the water – men involved in dredging the river in 1773 found stone piers under the waterline at a site reported to be just beyond the viaduct, but more recent exploration has failed to identify the exact location of the Roman crossing. There is, however, evidence of multiple Roman camps at a spot called Lochlands, which lies upstream of the bridge and viaduct inside a loop of the river. Although the chronology of these camps is still not understood, they have produced signs of multiple periods of activity, suggesting that this was an important stopping-off point on the march northwards, or indeed the retreat southwards.

Next, I took a footpath which led me away from the modern road (and the line of the lost Roman road too) towards the east, skirting around the southern fringe of Stenhousemuir. To my left lay the Mill Lade, an artificial waterway that used to carry water to the enormous Carron Company Iron Works one and a half miles away. Looking rather like a mini canal, it was built in the 1760s and originally turned a water wheel, which in turn powered a pair of enormous wood and leather bellows, supplying a steady stream of air to the iron works' blast furnaces.

A waterman used to live in a cottage next to the lade, tasked with keeping it clear of weeds and debris, but nowadays it is filled with water-loving plants, as well as a fair few empty beer bottles. I spotted lots of Himalayan balsam by the side of the path, the pink flower that I had admired at Polmont before finding out that it was an unwelcome non-native species. It may look delicate and fragile, but it is certainly a more tenacious invader of these parts than the Romans ever were.

A bit further on, a fine view opened up to my right, looking south towards the Antonine Wall. Between me and the frontier was a wide plain, the river winding its way across it. It is all agriculture now, with modern houses visible in the distance, an unremarkable slice of the Central Belt, but this too is a place with a fascinating legendary past. Thanks to one of the most influential, but also one of the most contentious works of literature ever written in Scotland, it was once believed that great battles between the legions of Rome and the heroic tribes of Caledonia had taken place right here on the banks of the River Carron.

The tale of James Macpherson's and his claim to have 'rediscovered' the ancient poetry of Ossian is without doubt one my favourite episodes in Scottish history, combining the ancient past, eighteenth-century Romanticism and a vitriolic literary controversy. It all began in 1759 in the spa town of Moffat. It was there that successful playwright John Home met the ambitious young Highlander James Macpherson – brought up in Ruthven, educated at Aberdeen and Edinburgh Universities, Macpherson was working as a tutor but had dreams of becoming a poet.

Macpherson told Home about some old Gaelic poetry that he had collected in the Highlands. Home convinced him to produce English prose translations. These short texts were shared with the Edinburgh literati, who were immediately captivated by them, and then published to great acclaim in 1760 in a volume entitled *Fragments of Ancient Poetry*.

With the encouragement and financial assistance of Home and his intellectual friends, Macpherson was sent north again to find more. His mission was an immense success. He returned with not only more short poems, but also a long epic, not dissimilar in style and ambition to the great classical works of Homer and Virgil. Macpherson found them, he claimed, by speaking to old Highlanders, who had learned them by heart as the words were passed down orally from generation to generation. Other fragments supposedly survived in ancient Gaelic manuscripts.

While the previously published fragments had given no clues as to their authorship or age, these newly identified works seemed to have been composed by an ancient Caledonian bard called Ossian, son of a heroic warrior named Fingal. What is more, descriptions of historical events in the verses appeared to demonstrate that they were around 1,500 years old. When these works were printed in late 1761 under the title *Fingal, An Ancient Epic Poems in Six Books, Together with Several Other Poems Composed by Ossian*, Macpherson's fame was assured.

It is in one of the poems included in the 1761 edition of *Fingal*, entitled

'Comala', that a battle between Caledonia and Rome on the banks of the River Carron is mentioned. This poem sees Comala, a winsome maiden who has fallen in love with the dashing Fingal, sitting by the riverside. The battle has recently taken place, the waters of the Carron are running with gore, and Comala fears that her beloved Fingal is dead. 'Oh Carun of the streams,' she laments, 'why do I behold thy waters rolling in blood...Has the noise of battle been heard on thy banks.' Comala has been tricked by the jealous love rival Hidallan, (who has quite a crush on her himself) into believing that Fingal has been killed, so she is surprised and delighted when he appears before her alive and well.

The victorious Fingal then tells of the great conflict, explaining in elaborate poetical style that his enemy, a certain 'Caracul' has fled in defeat:

> Raise, ye bards of the song, the wars of the streamy Carun. Caracul has fled from my arms along the fields of his pride. He sets far distant like a meteor that incloses a spirit of night, when the wind drives it over the heath, and the dark woods are gleaming around.

Macpherson presented the poem as something of a revelation. For while the early texts that he had translated contained no events that could be securely dated, this one featured a real-life historical figure. 'This poem is valuable on account of the light it throws on the antiquity of Ossian's compositions,' he explained in a footnote: 'The Caracul mentioned here is the same with Caracalla the son of Severus, who in the year 211 commanded an expedition against the Caledonians'.

As a result of this reference to the early third-century Roman invasion of Caledonia led by Septimius Severus and his son, the poems composed by Ossian could now be dated to the third century. To Macpherson's fans, their authenticity as masterpieces of ancient literature now seemed beyond question.

Fingal was not the only Ossianic hero to come up against the Romans. In fact, the very next poem in *Fingal* contained details of another conflict between Rome and Caledonia which also seemed to have taken place in the region around the Carron. In this verse, entitled 'The War of Caros', Ossian's son, Oscar, faces up to the renegade Emperor Carausius (who according to Ossian was known to the Caledonians as 'Caros'), a Roman naval commander who seized control of Britain and northern Gaul in AD 286 and ruled this mini empire for seven years, but was ultimately assassinated by his own minister of finance.

The outcome is, predictably, a resounding victory for Caledonia. Oscar discusses his success in a conversation with a venerable bard, Ryno, who reveals that the Romans are in retreat: 'What does Caros, king of ships, said the son of the now mournful Ossian? Spreads he the wings of his pride, bard of the times of old?'. He spreads them, Oscar,' replies the bard, 'but it is behind his gathered heap. He looks over his stones with fear, and beholds thee terrible, as the ghost of night that rolls his wave to the ships'.

In his accompanying footnotes, Macpherson explained that Carausius had made repairs to 'Agricola's Wall' (by which he clearly meant the Antonine Wall) and that the 'gathered heap' mentioned by Ryno was that same Roman frontier. His disparaging description of it was surely intended as an insult to the cowardly Romans who had fled to cower behind it.

The enormous success of these poems was not restricted to Scotland – the verses attributed to Ossian became an international phenomenon. They painted a familiar picture of the indomitable Caledonians, but while even the most patriotic Scots had previously recognised their ancient ancestors as somewhat 'savage', Ossian's poems revealed them to be noble and courtly, lovers as well as fighters, their sophisticated society producing a poet to rival the greats of Greece and Rome. The poems forced southern readers to rethink their low opinions of the Highland Gaels and brought visitors flocking to the north in search of the windswept heaths and mountain streams that they had read about in Macpherson's translations.

Napoleon loved them. Goethe adored them. Over in America, Thomas Jefferson even expressed a desire to learn Gaelic so he could enjoy them in their original language. Fitting perfectly with a growing taste for the sublime, a love of high drama and the thrill of untamed wilderness, Macpherson's translations of Ossian changed perceptions of Scotland for ever.

But not everyone was won over by these literary wonders. In fact, some had severe doubts about Macpherson's story. Arran-born Gaelic scholar William Shaw was initially convinced, but later produced an essay, 'An Enquiry into the Authenticity of the Poems Ascribed to Ossian', in which he described his failed attempts find either the old Gaelic manuscripts or the aged Highlanders who could reel off lines of Ossian's poetry that Macpherson had claimed as his sources. Irish readers, meanwhile, were surprised that their own national mythical heroes Oisín and Finn MacCool had emigrated to the Highlands of Scotland.

The most famous Ossian sceptic was English literary titan Samuel Johnson, a man who has been described as 'arguably the most distinguished man of letters in English history'. Johnson dismissed the poems as childish rubbish and refused to accept that they were of ancient origin, his opinion based on a personal disdain for the Gaelic-speaking Highlanders, whom he viewed as little more than barbarians. A famous trip around the Highlands and Islands with James Boswell in the summer of 1773 did nothing to change his mind.

On his return from the north, Johnson publicly stated that Ossian was a fake, that Macpherson was nothing more than a liar who had written the poems himself and that gullible Scots who believed it all had been blinded by patriotic nostalgia: 'The Scots have something to plead for their easy reception of an improbable fiction,' he mocked, 'they are seduced by their fondness for their supposed ancestors'. A furious correspondence between the two men ensued, with Macpherson's final letter to Johnson (now sadly lost) threatening violence. Johnson was not to be cowed into silence. His defiant reply challenged the Scottish 'Ruffian' to present hard evidence that the poems were what he said they were. No evidence was forthcoming.

The Ossian controversy rolled on for years, often descending into a slanging match, with fellow Gaelic scholar John Clark accusing William Shaw of being an anti-Scottish traitor whose island upbringing meant that he could not understand proper Highland Gaelic. Macpherson promised to show his manuscript sources, but they never materialised. He claimed to be working on publishing the Gaelic originals as well, but they too were continually delayed.

From humble origins, Macpherson became a rich man, laird of the Adam-designed Belleville House near Inverness, his success as a translator of ancient poetry having led to a career in politics, during which he managed to secretly secure a lucrative parliamentary pension. He died in 1796, still swearing that Ossian was genuine, and was buried amongst Britain's literary titans in Westminster Abbey. It was only in 1809, when the supposed 'original' poems were posthumously released, that the whole scam finally collapsed – anyone with a basic understanding of the language could easily deduce that they were in fact the previously published English poems clumsily translated into Gaelic.

Today, academics tend to be sympathetic towards Macpherson. They highlight his efforts in preserving Highland culture at a time when it was under serious threat, point to the vital role that the poems of Ossian played in the evolution of the Romantic movement and find echoes of real Gaelic ballads in Macpherson's verse. Like Samuel Johnson, however, I have no qualms in naming him a fraudster. In fact, even a quick analysis of those ancient battles between the Romans and Caledonians on the banks of the Carron proves it.

The poem 'Comala' features the battle between Fingal and Marcus Aurelius Antoninus, son of Septimius Severus who took part in the early third-century Roman invasion of Caledonia and later became emperor in his own right. Ossian calls him 'Caracul', a term clearly derived from his well-known nickname Caracalla. However, as a confused Edward Gibbon noted in his iconic *The Decline and Fall of the Roman Empire* published in 1776, that nickname was first coined several years after the Romans left Caledonia and did not come into widespread use until after Caracalla's death. So how could Ossian have heard it?

Furthermore, the idea that Carausius marched up to Scotland and repaired the Antonine Wall (which Macpherson, you will remember, wrongly identifies as 'Agricola's Wall') is based on a short passage added to only two of the several manuscript copies of Nennius' *Historia Brittonum*. This was then seized on by overenthusiastic antiquarians such as Sir Robert Sibbald and elaborated into a full-scale Roman invasion of Scotland. No other evidence of this Carausian invasion has ever been found, most probably because it never happened.

Macpherson had made it all up, stealing characters from Irish myth and fragments of old Gaelic tales to create a Caledonian Golden Age, adding in a couple of recognisable historical events to his poems to 'prove' their great age. These fierce battles by the Carron were nothing more than a figment of his imagination. He was a cheat, a trickster, although you must admire the gall of someone who will stake their reputation on fake historical poetry without even bothering to thoroughly research the history of the period involved.

As for the poems, they may have moved eighteenth-century readers to tears and raptures, but nowadays they are largely forgotten. Try to read them, and I suspect you will soon discover why. Long, repetitive and opaque – without their cloak of antiquity, they quickly lose their glamour. The dastardly James Macpherson may have committed one of the greatest hoaxes of all time, but I am so glad he did. It is, I think you will agree, quite a tale.

Past the site of imaginary battles, the path by the Mill Lade eventually took me to Carron Dam nature reserve, a partially drained reservoir built as the water supply for the iron works. Today it is a Site of Special Scientific Interest that offers a haven to all sorts of flora and fauna.

Water Rail At Carron Dam Nature Reserve

Consisting of areas of wetland, fen and deciduous woodland, home to tiny water voles and the secretive water rail, it seemed almost impossible that this idyllic spot had long ago played a vital role in Scotland's industrial revolution. The adjoining ironworks that this reservoir served were founded by the Carron Company in 1759 and grew to become the biggest in Europe.

Parts for James Watt's first steam engine were produced there, as were cannons used at Waterloo and the old red telephone boxes. It is said that the glow from the giant furnaces was so bright that streetlamps were hardly needed in the vicinity. The company motto was *Esto Perpetua*, may it endure forever, but times change, and the Carron Company went into receivership in 1982. Now, all that remains is a Victorian clock tower east of Carron Dam on the old Stenhouse road.

The site that I had come to see was on the other side of the nature reserve, through an elaborate metal gateway that featured the outline of cannons, smoking chimneys and birds in flight, symbolic of the area's changing landscape. Facing me was a wide road, then a gradual rise. A side street led upwards into an estate of modern houses, a quiet corner of Stenhousemuir. Somewhere on this hillside an intriguing structure known as Arthur's O'on (sometimes Arthur's Oven) used to stand. It was a building like no other that would become the subject of enormous interest and the focus of heated debate amongst Scottish antiquarians, only to be destroyed by a penny-pinching local laird at the height of its fame.

Arthur's O'on

What Arthur's O'on was and who built it are questions that historians, antiquarians and archaeologists have been asking for centuries. A plethora of contradictory theories have been proposed. As Alexander Gordon wrote in the 1720s, 'there are various Accounts and Opinions of Authors, about Arthur's Oven, so opposite that no two have them have assigned the Work to the same Man or Use'.

Three centuries later, we are still waiting for a definitive answer, although all the evidence suggests that it was Roman. Even what it looked like is now something of a mystery, as the surviving accounts of it are often inconsistent. The most cited source is Gordon, who carefully examined it during his journeys around Scotland, later including a written account and detailed illustrations of it in his 1726 book *Itinerarium Septentrionale*.

Gordon's drawings of the O'on show a circular domed structure with a single arched door, a window above and an open oculus at the top. He described how it was built from blocks of dressed masonry; other eye-witness accounts noted that it was constructed without mortar. The skill involved in creating such a building suggests that it was designed and built by people with an impressive understanding of architecture and engineering.

Standing 22 ft tall with an external circumference at the base of 88 ft, it rested on a stone terrace on the hillside. According to earlier visitors, there was evidence of carvings on it – a figure resembling the goddess Victory and an eagle. Sir Robert Sibbald reckoned that he could see a mysterious inscription featuring the letters I.A.M.P.M.P.T. This should be treated with some suspicion, for while Roman inscriptions were almost always abbreviated, they were never so abbreviated as to make them completely incomprehensible, and Gordon's idea that this could be read as a dedication to Julius Agricola can be immediately discounted as a fantasy. Reports of a bronze finger being discovered in a crack between two of its stones in the early 1700s may indicate the presence of a cult statue although, frustratingly, the finger has since disappeared.

The origins of the building are lost in the mists of time, but it was certainly ancient. It was already famous by the early medieval period and is mentioned in Nennius' *Historia Brittonum* (he thought it was built by Carausius during that supposed invasion of Caledonia which never took place). Its popular nickname first appears in a Latin manuscript dating from the late twelfth century, in which it was referred to as *furnus Arturi*, Arthur's Oven.

Before we go any further, this curious name requires consideration. The O'on or Oven bit is straightforward – its circular shape, domed top and arched aperture look not unlike an oversized medieval bread oven. As for the Arthur part, this is a reference to the famous King Arthur. Given the similarities between the names of Camelon and the magical castle of Camelot, as well as Camlann, the location of Arthur's last battle, it was inevitable that the region would develop associations with the mythical king of the Britons. Arthur's O'on was round too, just like his celebrated table, although with an internal diameter of 19 ft 6 in, I doubt it would have held many valiant knights, never mind a sizeable piece of furniture.

The building inspired other fanciful tales over the centuries. The most imaginative is surely that recounted by fourteenth-century historian John of Fordun, who proposed that it was a mobile home used by Julius Caesar. Fordun explained that it was built without mortar so that it could be easily assembled and disassembled, carried with the legions from place to place to offer a temporary residence for the Roman general more comfortable than a tent. The fact that Julius Caesar never ventured far beyond the River Thames is not the only reason that this conjecture seems highly unlikely.

Hector Boece and others claimed that the building was almost lost in the late thirteenth century at the hands of the bellicose King Edward I of England. During one of the early invasions of the Wars of Independence, Edward set his sights on Scotland's precious antiquities. He stole the famous Stone of Scone, used for centuries in the coronations of Scotland's kings and, according to Boece, he also attacked Arthur's O'on, scratching off a valuable inscription to tarnish the precious antiquity, but sparing the building.

For Renaissance historian and poet George Buchanan, Arthur's O'on was a temple constructed to mark the further extent of Roman power in Scotland. In a 1558 Latin verse celebrating the marriage of Mary Queen of Scots to the crown prince of France, he proudly recorded the glorious Caledonian rejection of Roman oppression on this very spot:

> Here Rome was content to defend its frontiers,
> and erect walls to keep out the axe-wielding Scots.
> Here with any hope of further advance put away,
> The God Terminus symbolises the break from
> Roman rule at the River Carron.

Buchanan's idea that Arthur's O'on was a temple of the Roman god Terminus, the protector of boundaries, its position thus marking the edges of the Roman world, became popular amongst Scots. It was, after all, another welcome reminder that the Romans had tried and failed to conquer the north of Caledonia, thanks, they liked to think, to the indomitable spirit of their ancient ancestors.

Other theories were also proposed. Inspired by the hole in the roof (which we cannot say for sure was original as it may have been a later partial collapse), Sibbald thought it was a temple to the sky god Caelus. William Stukeley, who published an essay about the building in 1720 without bothering to visit it, developed the notion that it was a temple to Romulus modelled on the one in the Forum at Rome, a similarly round building which still survives today as part of the church of Santi Cosma e Damiano. Gordon imagined it a victory monument designed to hold military standards, adding that it might have served as a mausoleum to an important Roman. Some thought it was built by Agricola, some by Septimius Severus, others by Carausius.

The one thing that antiquarians agreed on was that it was constructed by the Romans. It was already old by the twelfth century, and who before that time could have created something as fine as this? The only problem is, it looks nothing like any other Roman building that either they (or indeed we) know of.

Sir John Clerk Penicuik, a gentleman antiquarian who was Gordon's main patron, understood Roman architecture better than most of his Scottish contemporaries, having taken a Grand Tour to Italy in the 1690s during which he had become completely enamoured with the classical world. He was perplexed by the O'on and its lack of identifiable Roman features, declaring in 1739 that 'nobody doubts of its being Roman, though a very plain piece of work'.

Keen to prove the O'on's classical credentials, many of the eighteenth-century commentators made an ambitious comparison with a more famous Roman building – the mighty Pantheon. Sibbald described it in 1707 as 'imitating the Pantheon at Rome', while William Stukeley went into long and convoluted detail about the similar proportions of the two buildings in his 1720 essay *An Account of a Roman Temple in Scotland*. Alexander Gordon, the only one of the three who had been to Italy, went even further, pointing out that Arthur's O'on was made from finely cut stone, while the Pantheon was only built from brick.

Others were less impressed. After he published his essay on Arthur's O'on, Stukeley wrote to Sir John Clerk that some readers had laughed at it, mocking the fact that such a fuss was being made of this bizarre building, which looked to them like nothing more than a humble doocot.

Nonetheless, many Scots were patently proud of their unique historical monument, a classical relic that attracted interest from across Britain and beyond. Since so little was known about it, it could be interpreted according to taste and political affiliation. Proud patriots viewed it as a temple of Terminus, symbolic of the apparent Roman failure to conquer the bulk of Caledonia. Devotees of classical civility saw it as proof that Roman culture had permeated their homeland.

And then, tragically, it was gone. This centuries-old marvel, recognised by the late twelfth century as one of the 'wonders' of Britain, was demolished in 1743, pulled apart stone by stone and carted down to the River Carron, where its broken masonry was used to build a dam. The culprit was its owner Sir Michael Bruce, who did not want to splash out on newly quarried stone and saw the recycling of Arthur's O'on as a cost-saving exercise.

Antiquarians were outraged, devastated even. Roger Gale nominated Bruce 'the BRUTES' and Sir John Clerk likened him to Herostratus, the ancient Greek notorious for burning down the Temple of Artemis at Ephesus, one of the Seven Wonders of the Ancient World. Stukeley went as far as to imagine a cruel revenge on Bruce, sketching a cartoon entitled 'Syr Mitchil Bruce, Stonekiller' in which the laird is shown yoked to an iron collar with stones from the O'on balanced at either end, a demon prodding him with a sharp spear towards the searing fires of Hades.

Undoubtedly the most resolute mourner was an unnamed (and clearly slightly eccentric) surveyor who, according to Edinburgh antiquarian George Paton, would later visit the site of Arthur's O'on whenever he was in the area, dragging along with him anyone he met in the vicinity and compelling them all to kneel in a circle while he loudly cursed the name of Bruce. When the dam was washed away in a storm not long after, it was recognised by some as divine retribution.

Even now, almost 280 years later, I share their pain. To think that Arthur's O'on, this peerless ancient treasure, one of Scotland's greatest historical monuments, survived for over 1,500 years only to be destroyed on a whim, to save a few pounds, still makes me angry. Standing on this hillside taking in the bland suburban surroundings, the road below me and modern houses around about, I cannot help but think how things could have been so different.

Today, even the location of Arthur's O'on is not entirely certain. Early Ordnance Survey maps marked the spot where I was standing, on the hillside above what was then the vast ironworks, as 'Site of Arthur's O'on'. This idea is based on the reports of antiquarians. William Roy, for example, the most reliable cartographer of them all, marks this spot with the words 'Here Stood Arthur's O'on', although he surveyed the region in the 1750s, years after it was destroyed. It would seem like a good place for it – looking southwards, I could make out the tower blocks of Falkirk that I had walked past the day before. The Antonine Wall runs along the grass in front of them, so if it was here on this hillside then the O'on would definitely have been visible from the Roman frontier. Depending on the level of forestation in the region in ancient times, I suppose it could have been seen from Camelon too.

Excavations carried out here in 1950 by Kenneth Steer, however, revealed absolutely nothing. It could be that, just as Sir John Clerk reported to Roger Gale after the demolition, Bruce saw to it that every single stone was removed, including the foundations. But, as Dr Hunter had pointed out when I discussed it with him at the National Museum of Scotland, a building like this would have left some trace, some disturbance in the earth, even if all the stonework were gone. Let us hope that at some point, the slight remains of this priceless relic will be uncovered somewhere else not far away.

The memory of Arthur's O'on does live on in a way, written into the geography of the place – the town of Stenhousemuir is believed to be named after the odd 'stane hoose' that used to stand hereabouts. And if you want to get an idea of what it looked like, you can always make a journey to Penicuik, ten miles south of Edinburgh. It was there in the 1760s that the late Sir John Clerk's son James replaced the old house of Newbiggin with a new Palladian mansion, Penicuik House. Next to it he placed a grand stable block, and on its roof a life-sized reconstruction of the lost monument. The measurements and illustrations in Gordon's *Itinerarium* were used as the model.

It can still be seen there today, a suitable tribute to Sir John's antiquarian pursuits and love of all things Roman. Although the stables are not open to the public (they are now the Clerk family home, converted after a fire in 1899 which left the Palladian mansion a majestic ruin), both their exterior and the O'on on top can clearly be seen from the park nearby. Visitors are welcome to explore the shell of the mansion as well as the designed landscape that surrounds it, and I thoroughly recommend making a trip to see them. The Penicuik Estate is something of an undiscovered gem right on the doorstep of the Scottish capital.

A few years ago, while I was researching the life and work of Sir John Clerk, I was lucky enough to be invited to Penicuik by the current baronet, Sir Robert Clerk, to look at some manuscripts in the immense collection of family papers. When my work was done, he generously offered to show me round, taking me into the ruined house that has recently been saved from collapse and is now in what they call 'a state of preserved ruination'.

Sir Robert took me around the converted stables – no signs of their equine origins, their interiors are now as elegant as any stately home – to view some of the family collection. He showed me a handsome portrait of the young Sir John, painted when was just back from his Grand Tour of Italy, his head filled with visions of the classical grandeur that he had encountered there. We went out into the central courtyard to inspect the replica Arthur's O'on, and finally we ascended a narrow flight of stairs into its shadowy interior.

What I found inside was a surprise. Over 800 stone boxes lined the inner walls; a tall ladder attached to a complex wooden structure stood in the centre. These are pigeonholes, in the original sense of the word. It turns out that this new Arthur's O'on was in fact a doocot, the very thing that disparaging critics had jokingly compared the ancient structure to in centuries past.

When it was first built, the doocot's boxes were filled with nesting pigeons. The ladder was designed to spin around a central column, allowing access to boxes high and low all around the interior. Pigeon was considered a great delicacy in the 1700s, and this structure would have provided a constant supply for the baronet's dinner table. The birds are no longer in residence, but this Arthur's O'on, a unique eighteenth-century memorial to one of Scotland's most tragic archaeological losses, survives; appreciated, protected (category A listed) and safe for future generations to admire.

To get back to the route of the old Roman road I had to walk west, through the town centre of Stenhousemuir. Once a sleepy backwater, Stenhousemuir was transformed by the coming of industry in the later 1700s and the arrival of the railway in the 1840s. But the new Stenhousemuir was not all sprawling, smoke-belching foundries – the famous but now defunct McCowan's toffee was invented and made here, the stuff of happy memories for me, although my childhood dentist might not agree. Today, the town carries on without the big industry or the toffee, a modern development with supermarket and library at its centre, a few small independent shops hanging on for dear life on the old main street.

I did not notice when I left Stenhousemuir and entered Larbert, as the two towns are joined, but I knew I was there when I passed Larbert railway station. Not much further on I turned right, back onto the Stirling Road that would take me north. The next part of my walk was something of a slog. My legs were tiring and the journey along the side of a noisy main road was, to be honest, pretty uneventful. I walked past the entrance to the Forth Valley Royal Hospital. Built at a cost of £300 million and opened in 2010, it sits on the site of an old Victorian psychiatric institution. On I went, across a roundabout, past the entrance of yet another golf course, and over the M876. The Roman road ran somewhere to my left, but there are no signs of it today.

As I got closer to the village of Torwood, I spotted a wooden sign by the side of the road pointing out a footpath to Torwood Castle through some woodland. The path that it marked was not on my map, but that was where I was headed, so I decided to leave the road and head into the forest.

I am glad that I did. As I soon discovered, the Tor Wood is an enchanting place. The walk was not easy, thick tree roots and large slabs of slippery bedrock pushing up out of the narrow, undulating path, but the scenery was spectacular, plenty of aged trees with gnarled trunks and the odd small glade bathed in birdsong.

This used to be a royal hunting ground, and legends tells that William Wallace hid out here in a hollow old oak tree whilst on the run. The so-called 'Wallace Oak' would later become something of a curiosity and seems to have survived right up until the nineteenth century. It was also in this forest that Robert the Bruce assembled his army in the days before Bannockburn, preparing the soldiers while keeping a watchful eye over the old Roman road that was then still the main route to Stirling.

I was uncertain as to where I was going, but I was enjoying the journey through this fairy-tale landscape. It should have been a disappointment when I emerged out of the trees onto a wider track, but at the end of the track to my left was something else to fire my imagination – a ruined castle.

Torwood Castle (sometimes referred to as Torwoodhead in older sources) is believed to have been built in 1566, the date carved onto a decorated stone that was found in the vicinity back in 1918. For many years, it was the property of the appropriately named Forrester family, who had strong links with the Crown. The lands around the castle provided wood and food for both the royal court and the garrison at the nearby fortress of Stirling.

Torwood Castle

The home that the Forresters built was stylish, a mix of medieval castle and early modern mansion. It was abandoned and crumbling as early as 1817, but it is still in remarkably decent shape for a building that has been empty for two centuries. For a while it was in the care of a charitable trust, who planned to preserve it. After the trust was dissolved in 2015, the building was left open and unprotected, and even suffered at the hands of vandals.

As I wandered around, instead of evidence of neglect and damage, I saw signs of life. The grass that surrounds the ruins was trimmed, and some benches and chairs were placed in the courtyard in front of the main entrance. Although the roofless shell of the upper storeys looked fragile, glimmers of sunlight peeking through cracks and holes in the walls, modern frames and glass had been inserted into some of the lower windows. A bright yellow traffic cone sat next to a neat pile of wooden pallets by the doorway. And was that the bark of a dog that I heard from inside the castle's thick walls?

After my visit, a quick internet search revealed that someone was living in the castle. A local man, Gary Grant, moved into the ruins in 2018 and has been protecting and restoring them ever since. The ground floor rooms have been cleared of decades of rubbish and, at the time of writing, attempts to make it waterproof are ongoing. It is a laudable project, hopefully saving Torwood for future generations. There is a certain romance to living in a tumble-down castle, but I would not envy him sleeping in there on one of Scotland's chill winter nights.

My map showed a dotted line heading north-west from the castle, marked 'ROMAN ROAD'. I assume the castle was built here for this very reason, right next to the 1,500-year-old highway that still remained more reliable than any muddy medieval track. I searched the woodland, hoping I might be able to walk a stretch of it, but there was no evidence of the road now, its route hidden under impenetrable long grass and scrub.

Instead, I walked for a couple of minutes back up the modern track towards Torwood village before I turned left into the trees, following a faint path. Coming to a large area that had recently been cleared, its dry earth dotted with splintered tree stumps, I soon lost my bearings, but I continued anyway, heading steadily upwards towards the highest point in the Tor Wood. Soon I was back in trees, high pines this time, their trunks spiky with broken branches, the ground a spongey floor of fallen needles. On I climbed, finally emerging into a clearing at the top of hill, where I reached my destination, Tappoch Broch.

When it comes to evidence of life in central Scotland before the arrival of the Romans, it doesn't get much better than Tappoch Broch. As you approach, it looks like a natural rocky outcrop, crowded with bracken and heather, but then stonework appears – a thick wall pierced by a low doorway. Clambering underneath and through, I found myself in the central courtyard of an Iron Age fortress.

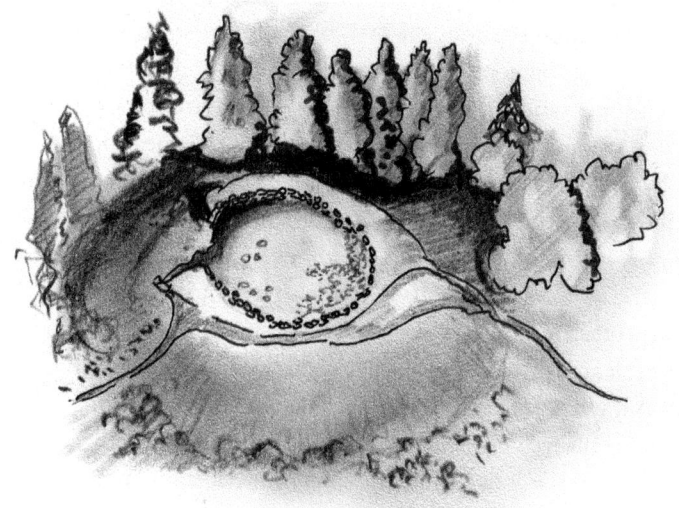

Tappoch Broch

Unique to Scotland, the tallest structures to be built in prehistoric Britain, with some still standing between 10 and 13 m high, the purpose of the stone towers that we call brochs has been debated over the years. For a long time, they were believed to be purely defensive, a place where local communities could congregate for protection in times of trouble. Now, some interpret them as grand dwellings used for various other purposes including grain storage and the manufacture of fabric and clothes.

While this approach downplays the defensive element, the tiny door and thick wall of Tappoch (over 6 m wide in places), as well as its hilltop location, suggest that the desire to keep out unwanted visitors played some part in its construction. It would not be too much of a stretch to see it as an Iron Age equivalent of a medieval castle, built by its residents both as a statement of power and a place of security, also a hive of daily activity and small-scale industry.

When I think of brochs I generally picture the very northern tip of Scotland, where most of them were situated, but there are a few in the south too. Edin's Hall Broch, for example, is near Abbey St Bathans in the Borders, Torwoodlee Broch is near Galashiels and the remains of Leckie Broch and Buchlyvie Broch (also known by the whimsical nickname of 'Fairy Knowe') can be found to the west of Stirling.

Tappoch Broch Doorway

One of the most striking features of the brochs is the passageways that were built into the thickness of their wall, with stone staircases leading to the tower's upper storeys. While the wall of Tappoch is now considerably reduced, a doorway in the central court still opens into one of these 'intramural' corridors and, incredibly, part of the staircase survives too. When the broch was first investigated in 1864 it was said to have eleven stone steps. I could only count eight. Climbing up them, I found myself on top of the broch's sturdy wall, looking down into the courtyard below.

The word 'courtyard' may not be correct, as the current thinking is that the whole interior of the tower could have been covered with a roof. We do not know for certain how such a roof would have been constructed. It might have been conical, with a wooden frame covered by thatch or turf. And yet the only broch to survive to roof level – the famous Mousa in Shetland – shows no evidence of such a structure, and no material that might have been used to cover the tower was identified during excavations. The question of how the brochs were topped comes down to what we think they were for. Was it a temporary fortress, its central area open to the elements, or elite home with a series of internal chambers, one on top of the other? In this case, the jury is still out.

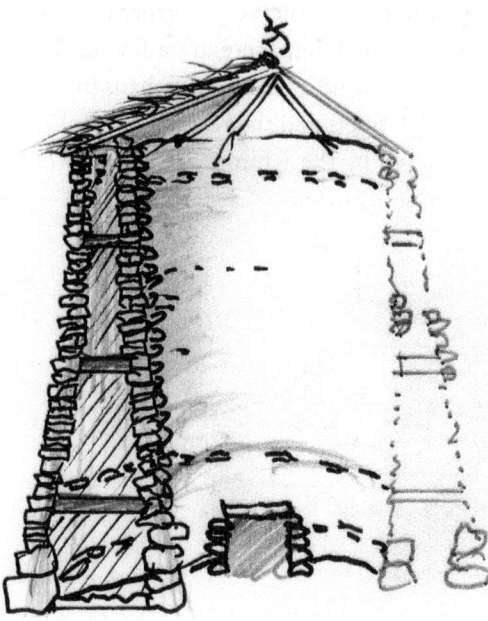
Broch – Cross-section

The archaeologists who dug at Tappoch in the 1860s did not even realise that they had found a broch, believing the almost circular central area to be a chamber sunk into a natural mound. It was found to have a rock floor. At the middle, they identified a hearth. Other discoveries included some quern stones for grinding grain, carved stone balls and fragments of pottery. Not only were the finds sparse but, unusually for brochs in this part of the world, no Roman artefacts were unearthed.

Surprising as it may sound, many of the southern brochs contain Roman objects. In fact, since these buildings are notoriously difficult to date, the presence of Roman material is a major help in proving that they were inhabited during the Roman forays into Caledonia. An examination of Torwoodlee Broch uncovered Samian ware pottery, while Roman brooches were found at Leckie and Buchlyvie near Stirling. Fragments of exquisite Roman glass vessels have also been found in Lowland brochs.

With most of them dating from the first and second centuries, these artefacts are seen as evidence of contact between Rome and the Caledonians during the Agricolan invasion and the Antonine occupation: trade, or maybe gifts given by the Roman army in return for peace and cooperation. These foreign goods, so different to local products, would surely have been highly prized by the broch dwellers.

One broch, the one at Leckie, has also provided evidence of less friendly interaction between the locals and the Roman interlopers. The remains of burnt organic material and heat-cracked stones suggest a huge conflagration, while the discovery of a stone ball of the type fired from

Roman catapults presents the alluring possibility that the broch was besieged and then destroyed by the legions as they subdued the territory in the months before the construction of the Antonine Wall.

The stone ball, about the size of a cantaloupe, is itself riven with a network of deep fissures. According to the curators of the Hunterian Museum where it is housed, these fissures might demonstrate that the ball was set alight before being fired into the broch where terrified Caledonians dowsed it in cool water, the sudden change in temperature causing the stone to split and crack. As archaeological interpretations go, this one is melodramatic and, as I quickly discovered when I posted a photo of the ball online with details of this hypothesis, it is met with a degree of scepticism amongst some archaeologists. Ultimately, it could have been an accidental fire that destroyed Leckie Broch.

The views from Tappoch Broch on this high summit would have been spectacular in the days before the tall pines were planted all around it. Fortunately, there are still a few gaps in the trees – through one of them I could see, far below me, another recently cut clearing in the woodland to the west. My map showed the line of the Roman road continuing across it, heading north-west to where it meets a dead straight modern road called, not surprisingly, Roman Road. From there it continues in an almost direct line up to the outskirts of Stirling.

Although far from conclusive, the lack of Roman material inside the broch of Torwood indicates that it was either abandoned before the Romans arrived or, less likely, built after they departed. I prefer the former theory, mainly because I love the idea that the Roman soldiers who marched along the road on their journey into deepest Caledonia spotted this high empty tower looming above them on its hilltop. These men, who hailed from across the Roman Empire, would never have seen anything like it before – dark, windowless and forbidding. They might have begun to wonder what awaited them in this strange land on the edge of the world.

The route of the old Roman Military Way becomes less clear after Stirling, lost under towns and farmland, popping up only occasionally as it heads up to the beautifully preserved Roman fort at Ardoch. It then turned eastwards at Strageath fort near Innerpeffray and on to another fort, known as Bertha, built where the River Almond meets the River Tay on the northern edge of the modern town of Perth.

Like the military installations along it (a chain of towers, fortlets and forts known as the Gask Ridge Frontier) this road was built by Agricola's men as they marched into the Highlands in the AD 70s or 80s. Then, during the second-century conquest of Caledonia, the Agricolan forts at Camelon, Ardoch, Strageath and Bertha were re-established as outposts, their garrisons tasked with keeping the peace and, if the worst came to the worst, sending word of any brewing unrest down to the Antonine Wall.

Presumably, the broch of Tappoch stood proud for generations even after its abandonment, slowly crumbling into the overgrown ruin that we see today. We do not know how tall it was when first built, but when it was excavated in 1864, an estimated 200 tons of fallen stones were removed to clear the central area. I cannot find any references to the origins of the name Torwood, but since 'tòrr' in Gaelic means a heap or a mound and 'torr' in Old English a tower, I would be willing to bet that it is derived in some way from this enormous stack of ancient masonry.

My time at Tappoch Broch was over, so I retraced my steps down the hillside back to the track which led me to Torwood village. From there I was able to rejoin the Stirling Road and begin my walk back towards Larbert. The plan was to get the train from the local station, but as I reached the entrance to the Forth Valley Royal Hospital, I felt the familiar tickle of raindrops on the back of my neck. The timing could not have been more perfect. I made a quick sprint up to the hospital's front door, where I found a waiting taxi. Within a few minutes, I was safe and dry back in Falkirk, where I would be spending the night.

Chapter Four

BONNYBRIDGE TO KIRKINTILLOCH

The Wall From Bonnybridge To Kirkintilloch

While both my walk along the Antonine Wall from Carriden to Bonnybridge and my journey north in search of the site of Arthur's O'on had proved immensely enjoyable, only slightly hampered by the unpredictable Scottish weather, the rest of my first attempt to walk the entire length of the Roman frontier turned out to be less of a success.

Things began well enough as I set off from Bonnybridge on day three, but by the time I reached the halfway mark, just as I approached Croy Hill, a light mist of rain had descended. After a brief and uncomfortable lunch, which consisted of a sandwich eaten while sitting on a boulder under the scant shelter of a tree, I headed onwards.

The weather quickly deteriorated and much of the rest of my walk was more like a march, head down, the rain pattering on my nylon hood and my glasses dripping with water. The route led me past some of my favourite parts of the Antonine Wall, but this was not a day to dawdle and explore the Roman sites or appreciate the stunning views. The final hour was a seemingly endless dash through a downpour and by the time I arrived at Kirkintilloch I was both extremely wet and very, very miserable.

I spent a relaxing night in a local hotel but woke up the following morning to the sound of yet another downpour. Pulling back the curtains to look out of the window, I discovered a dark, grey sky as far as the eye could see. I waited. And I waited. As checkout approached and the rain continued, I realised that I would have to give up and go back to Edinburgh. It was only as I got on to the train at Lenzie Station that a break finally appeared in clouds and a few patches of blue sky emerged.

As I hurtled back towards the city, I briefly wondered whether I should have been braver and carried on, but I was already tired of battling against the elements and I did not want this to be a book about walking in the rain. By the time I was back in a warm Edinburgh flat where I could remove my damp boots and peel off my soggy socks, I knew that I had made the right decision. I quickly formulated a plan to return to Scotland in the spring and complete the journey along the Antonine Wall in (hopefully) drier conditions.

Then came Covid-19. The world was shut down and travel plans cancelled. Stuck at home in London, overwhelmed at times by the constant deluge of bad news, a wave of loss and suffering, my thoughts often turned to the Antonine Wall. I remembered that feeling of freedom, of being out on my own in the Scottish landscape. Another walk became something to dream about at a time when there was not much else to look forward to, a beacon of light during the long, boring days of lockdown. I knew the Wall would wait, but I was keen to get back as soon as possible. After many weeks and months of confinement and restrictions, cooped up in a tiny city flat, I longed to stretch my legs and head off once more along the Roman frontier.

As summer progressed, the news improved: the pandemic seemed to be in retreat. By the time autumn arrived, life was becoming easier and the world more open. Feeling reckless, I booked a train to Scotland and four nights in a little cottage near Kirkintilloch for a couple of weeks later. Finally, it was time to get back to the Antonine Wall.

It was early October when I arrived in Kirkintilloch. I was raring to go, but concerned about the weather. This late in the year felt like a risky time to be walking in Scotland, but I did not want to wait until the spring, and anyway, my first attempt had proved that you can never be completely safe from the rain in central Scotland, even in the height of summer.

I chose a shorter route for the first day of my trek, from Kinneil to Watling Lodge this time. No downpours, I am relieved to report, and it proved to be a rather different experience from my first walk in other ways too. I lunched at Benny T's again, but this time the lone waitress seemed almost surprised to see me. I ate completely alone in what was usually a crowded restaurant. Callendar House was closed and had been for several months. The Antonine Wall was devoid of visitors, but then it almost always is.

My second day began by the canal at Bonnybridge. I had arrived there in a taxi from Falkirk railway station, its driver another one of those garrulous Scots who was keen to chat. I told him about my walk along the Roman frontier – he did not seem particularly interested in the Antonine Wall, but he was a keen walker and, it turns out, quite a storyteller. He kept me entertained for most of the drive with a gripping tale of a climb up Ben Nevis which almost ended with him tumbling down a mist-covered cliff.

Picking up exactly where I had finished the first leg of my walk, I headed off along the towpath which runs along the northern bank of the Forth & Clyde Canal. I was elated to be back, free again, for a couple of days at least. The weather was pleasant enough, a fresh autumn morning with a patchy sky and a bracing wind. The outskirts of Bonnybridge thinned out on the other side of the water and were soon left behind. Not much further on I spotted the first destination on my route, a well-preserved section of the Antonine Wall known as Seabegs Wood.

The only problem was that it too was on the other side of the canal. There was no bridge in sight. Instead, I turned off the towpath and skittered down a steep banking to below the water level. Down there I found an arched tunnel that passed right under the canal and the road which runs alongside it. Gloomy and dank, it was far from welcoming, but this was the only way that I could reach the Roman Wall.

This tunnel is known locally as the Pend. Walking through it was something of a challenge. It is low for a start, and extremely dark. To make matters worse, a stream pours through it, forcing me to tread slowly, carefully along a narrow, raised walkway that runs down the middle of the tunnel floor. With water gushing down either side of me, I stepped cautiously into the gloom. By the time I reached the halfway point, where visibility is at its lowest, it was just a case of keeping going and hoping for the best.

Since my visit, I have uncovered a piece of local folklore which claims that this tunnel was used back in the 1820s by a certain Charles Grindlay, a medical student and son of a local farmer, who got involved in the grisly trade of 'body snatching' made famous by Edinburgh reprobates Burke and Hare. Stolen corpses destined for the medical schools of Edinburgh and Glasgow were moved through the tunnel and stored in the neighbouring woods, although Grindlay's role in this remains unclear.

When it turned out that Burke and Hare were not only digging recently buried bodies out of the ground but also murdering vagrants and drunks to meet the demand for cadavers, Grindlay was caught up in the ensuing scandal and expelled from university. That would explain the tunnel's other nickname, 'Doctor's Pend', and possibly its rather spooky atmosphere.

Emerging safe and dry from the other side, it was only a short climb back up to the level of the road, where I found the gate leading into Seabegs Wood. The Roman ditch emerged from dense woodland and ran for around 400 m westwards, with the low ridges of the turf rampart and upcast mound perceptible in places.

The ditch may not be as immense as it is at Watling Lodge, but with sections up to 2 m deep and 12 m wide, it still makes quite an impact. Given the regular spacing of the Antonine Wall's forts, it has been proposed that there should be one at Seabegs, but several trenches dug at various spots in the vicinity between 1968 and 1978 turned up nothing.

The stand-out feature at Seabegs Wood today is, without question, the surviving stretch of the Military Way that runs along the southern edge of the Antonine Wall. A vital part of the frontier which allowed its soldiers to move from one location to another as quickly as possible, its remains, the best-preserved along the entire Wall, begin back amongst the trees which have been partially cleared to give an indication of the road's route. It carries on westwards, a subtle but visible mound in the grass 30 m to the south of the rampart.

Unlike at Hadrian's Wall, where the road along the frontier seems to have been added in the final stages of the project, as if it was something of an afterthought, this Military Way was probably constructed before the rampart itself. A small quarry which provided the gravel for its surface was discovered under one of the Rough Castle expansions, implying that the road must have been built first.

A trench cut through the Military Way at Seabegs in 1962 revealed that it was originally 7 m wide. Although the tough metalled surface that once withstood the constant pounding of Roman hobnail boots is now hidden by grass, its soft camber, which allowed rainwater to run off the road and into the drains which ran along its sides, can still be easily detected.

Antiquarian accounts of the Antonine Wall at Seabegs are varied and sometimes contradictory. It is only in recent years that the site has been cleared of the thick forest that gives it its modern name, so it must have been hard to read the lay of the land back in the seventeenth and eighteenth centuries. Sir Robert Sibbald recorded that late seventeenth-century physician and antiquarian Christopher Irvine (whose papers on the Roman frontier were acquired by Sibbald after Irvine's death in 1693) had identified not one but two forts here, one to the east of the woods (which Sibbald noted was a 'great Fort', probably the medieval motte mentioned earlier) and another to the west.

Alexander Gordon (who called it 'Sebeg-Wood') noted that the rampart was evident there, even in the woodland, but could see no sign of the Roman road which usually ran alongside it. He mentioned a mysterious 'little artificial Mount' next to the ditch to the east of Seabegs, which he believed to be a Roman foundry due to the copious amounts of iron and lead ore to be found in the vicinity – perhaps the medieval Seabegs motte again?

In his *Itinerarium Septentrionale*, Gordon recorded the distances along the Antonine Wall in paces, making it difficult to relate them to my modern map and work out exactly to what he is referring. John Horsley (who just as confusingly recorded distances along the frontier in 'chains', meaning the 66-foot-long surveying tool known as a 'Gunter Chain') contradicted Gordon, or I should say corrected him, by stating that the turf rampart, the ditch and the Military Way were all conspicuous at Seabegs, also noticing that the ditch was completely waterlogged.

What Christopher Irvine identified as a fort at the western edge of the forest was most probably the Roman fortlet that was uncovered during excavations in 1977. Similar to the fortlet found at Kinneil, this one had internal measurements of 21.8 m by 18 m. Again, as at Kinneil, there is no evidence of a permanent causeway to allow traffic to pass through the fortlet's gate and across the frontier's ditch, but it has been speculated that a wooden bridge might have been constructed for this purpose.

Only the exterior defences of the structure were examined during the dig, but small finds included pottery, hobnails from soldiers' boots and red clay gaming balls, evidence of how the men stationed there passed the long, slow hours as they guarded the Caledonian frontier. The fortlet lies right outside the protected area at Seabegs, and nothing of it can been seen above ground now.

Seabegs Wood is a lovely site, with a smattering of old trees, predominantly oak and birch, scattered across its undulating earthworks. I was alone for most of my visit, but as I was walking back along the Military Way towards the gate to make my exit another visitor appeared, not a tourist, but a dog walker whose Labrador, once let off the lead, bounded happily away across the ditch and into the distance.

It was only the second time that I had encountered other visitors (or at least human visitors) at any of the frontier's sites – a couple of dog walkers had also appeared as I was leaving Rough Castle – and it came as something as a shock. I was getting accustomed to having the Antonine Wall all to myself. Heading out of the gate, I stepped back down to the tunnel and through its dingy depths to the towpath.

The next stretch of the Forth & Clyde Canal follows the exact course of the Antonine Wall, its construction in the late 1700s wiping out much of the Roman frontier. It is no coincidence that the lines of the canal and the ancient frontier often coincide. Both were designed to take advantage of the narrow isthmus between the two estuaries, which offered the quickest route from one side of Scotland to the other. While we can assume the construction of the ancient barrier was well organised and swift, the completion of the Forth & Clyde Canal ended up being a long and slow process.

First planned and surveyed by civil engineer John Smeaton in 1763, the project was finally approved by parliament in 1768, and work began in earnest in June of that same year when the governor of the canal company dug the first spadeful of earth at the eastern end of the waterway, close to the modern town of Grangemouth. Seven years later, work ground to a halt near Glasgow as the company ran out of cash. It was only in 1785 that government money (much of it the proceeds of forfeited Jacobite estates) was provided to bring the work to completion, and the canal officially opened in 1790.

The Forth & Clyde Canal had an enormous impact on life in Scotland's central belt, becoming the main artery of commercial transport in the region. Once busy with all sorts of boats, including regular passenger services as well as cargo vessels, the canal is now quiet, with only the soft wind disturbing the sheen of its steely grey water.

I didn't see any water traffic as I walked along its towpath apart, that is, from a couple of coots and a small raft of pure white ducks with bright yellow bills (Pekin ducks I think, a domesticated breed, so presumably they had escaped from captivity) who paddled enthusiastically towards me, hoping to be fed. They quickly lost interest as I strode on past, floating despondently back towards the thick mass of reeds on the other side of the water.

I walked past three of the canal's 40 locks before I came to a bridge that allowed me to cross over and head back towards the Antonine Wall, which had now diverged southwards from the route of the canal and lay close to the B816. Turning left as I reached the road, I was able to spot another shallow stretch of the Roman ditch running through a field, only identifiable thanks to an old metal sign at the roadside which indicated its presence. After a quick look, I turned back on myself and continued westwards along the pavement, taking a left into a side road that leads to a small cluster of modern houses. It was there that I found my next port of call, one of the most important archaeological sites on the frontier, but also one of the unluckiest – the Roman fort of Castlecary.

Today, the remains of Castlecary fort can be found in an unprepossessing field, right across a dead-end lane from a Victorian schoolhouse that is now converted into a private home. This was originally one of the most impressive fortresses on the Antonine Wall. With an internal space of 1.4 hectares, it was one of only two on the frontier with a stone rampart, massive walls on all four sides that were 2.4 m thick. Excavations undertaken in the north-eastern corner of the site in 2010 revealed that the turf rampart of the Antonine Wall abuts the stone wall of the fort 10 m south of its north-east corner, which implies that the fort must have been built first, before the rampart was completed. With a large (and, so far, unexcavated) annexe attached to its east side and its high outer walls constructed from cut and squared stones, the fort would have been quite a sight in its heyday.

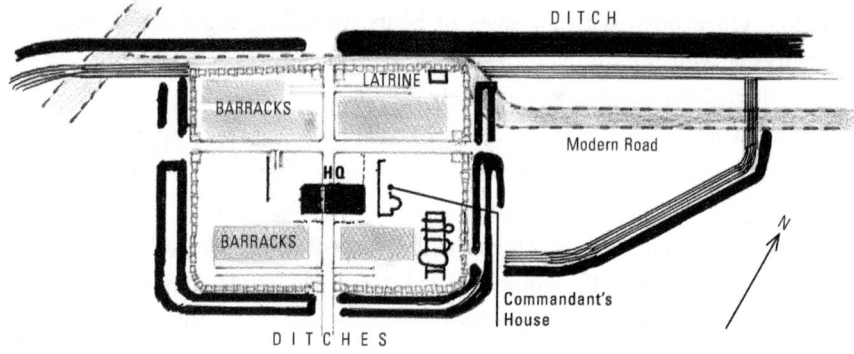

Castlecary Fort

Today, unfortunately, much has changed. Over the past six centuries, Castlecary has suffered one indignity after another, leaving it in something of a sorry state. We cannot be sure when the locals first started to pull apart the fort's ancient walls, but we do know that by the fifteenth century, builders were plundering its ruins for ready-cut stone.

Evidence of this can found hidden in the forest half a mile to the south, in the form of a sturdy little fifteenth-century tower house, called Castle Cary, which is built from recycled Roman masonry. The walls of a later two-storey wing, erected a couple of centuries after the old tower, are also made from stone taken from the Roman fort. Antiquarian William Maitland spotted men stealing stone from the site to construct outbuildings for the tower when he visited in the eighteenth century. The workers who built the Forth & Clyde Canal in the late 1760s and early 1770s came here in search of free stone, doing untold damage to the fort's remains in the process.

Things got much worse in the nineteenth century. Around 1809, a farmer blew up long sections of the fort's ramparts with gunpowder to improve the land for agriculture. But the greatest indignity to be inflicted upon Castlecary fort took place in 1841, when the Edinburgh to Glasgow railway line was built right through the middle of it.

Antiquarians were outraged at this wholesale destruction of such a significant ancient monument and one, John Buchanan, recorded his own account of the damage, describing what he saw as over 3 m of earth was removed from the site:

> This soil, if it can be so called, was in many places almost one entire mass of broken stones mingled with fragments of pottery, among which were many pieces of jars, vases and basins – some of a cream colour, and others of a lively red, elegantly ornamented with flowers and figures.

The devastation caused by the construction of Scotland's railway network was passionately and lyrically lamented in an address to the Society of Antiquaries of Scotland given by Sir James Young Simpson in 1862. An esteemed obstetrician who helped to popularise the use of chloroform as an anaesthetic, he was, like Sir Robert Sibbald and Christopher Irvine before him, a Scottish physician who was fascinated by antiquities.

Simpson's long speech, delivered soon after his election as the Society's vice-president, featured a sizeable list of historical monuments lost to the unstoppable advance of the train, an 'iron horse' that Simpson described as 'among the greatest, as well as the latest, of the agents of destruction' of our national heritage. He bemoaned the 'annihilating effect' of the railway at Castlecary and described a train journey, during which he saw from the carriage window a farmer dismantling what he believed to be 'among the last, if not the very last, remnants of Roman masonry in Scotland'. A painful sight indeed for any lover of the ancient past, although, as I would soon see, Roman masonry has happily survived at other places along the frontier.

Given all this damage over the years, we should be thankful that any traces of Castlecary fort survive at all – but survive they do. If you are determined to find a silver lining, then you could point to the fact that several interesting artefacts were found during the destruction of and construction on the site.

The men who raided it at the end of the 1760s for stones to build the nearby canal, for example, turned up animal bones, which the University of Glasgow professor John Anderson thought included boar's tusks. They also found an inscribed stone altar dedicated to the goddess Fortuna by the soldiers of the Second Legion Augusta and the Sixth Legion Victrix and a relief sculpture of the same goddess that now both reside in the collection of the Hunterian Museum in Glasgow. The altar and sculpture were dug up amongst the ruins of a building in the south-eastern corner of the fort that was thought to be a house with private bath, effusively described by William Roy as 'very elegant...in the style of [Italian Renaissance architect] Palladio'.

Goddess Fortuna, From Castlecary Fort

A detailed plan made at the time appears in Roy's hefty tome, *The Military Antiquities of the Romans in North Britain*. Unlike many of his fellow antiquarians, Roy is generally a reliable witness, at least when it comes to his maps and plans. He was born in Carluke in Lanarkshire and attended grammar school in Lanark. There are no records of where or when he trained in cartography, but in 1747 he was hired as a clerk to Lieutenant-Colonel David Watson and began work on a military survey of Scotland.

The purpose of this project was to create accurate maps of the Highlands to replace the outdated and imprecise ones used during the suppression of the 1745 Jacobite revolt. The task, later expanded to include the Lowlands, lasted until 1755, and Roy's exploration of the Scottish landscape inspired a particular interest in the nation's Roman remains. So it was that he surveyed the Antonine Wall in 1755, mapping its course and drawing plans of its largest forts. His work has proved invaluable for modern archaeologists, recording sections of the frontier long since lost to agriculture, industry, urbanisation and the elements.

The relief of Fortuna found at Castlecary is a charming little thing, showing the goddess of good luck holding her typical attributes, a long cornucopia (sometimes known as the horn of plenty) in her left hand and a rudder resting on a wheel in her right. The first attribute affirmed her position as a deity associated with bounty and fertility, the second demonstrated her role as a controller of human destiny. She wears a stylish (if crudely carved) robe that hangs off her left shoulder, her body and her arms long and sinuous. And is that a hint of a smile that can be seen on her pink sandstone lips? That may just be my imagination, but you can see why this glamourous figure was so popular amongst soldiers in the northern territories of Britannia, where good luck might have sometimes seemed in short supply.

John Buchanan, who spent time at the site as the railway was being built, managed to rescue some inscriptions as well as other smaller finds. One small (28 cm x 37 cm) stone panel was inscribed with the letters 'CHO VI ANTO ARATI', an abbreviation of *Cohortis VI Centuria Antoni Arati*', which can be translated into English as 'From the sixth cohort, the century of Antonius Aratus'. It is another centurial stone, created to record the identity of the soldiers who built part of this fort, like the lost example featuring an eagle that was much admired by the antiquarians who visited Carriden in the eighteenth century.

Although the design of the Castlecary stone is simpler than the Carriden example, it also has decorative elements, with stylised palm leaves and scrolling vine carved along the top and the text contained within an 'ansate panel', a rectangular frame with triangular handle-like wings on each side that was often placed around Roman inscriptions ('ansate' literally means to have a handle). We do not know who Antonius was, where he came from (although he shares the name Aratus with a figure from Greek mythology and an ancient Greek poet), or what kind of building he helped to construct, but it seems incredible to me that we can identify so specifically one of the men stationed here almost 2,000 years ago.

Another name has been passed down the centuries by an altar found at Castlecary in the 1850s, which bears a dedication to the water god Neptune made by the 'First Loyal Cohort of Vardullians, Roman citizens, part-mounted, a thousand strong, under the command of Trebius Verus'. The Cohort of Vardullians were an auxiliary cavalry unit who originated in northern Spain (the Roman province of Hispania Tarraconensis to be precise), but Castlecary was too small to house them all, so some must have been stationed elsewhere.

This inscription seems to be one of the earliest references to the Vardullians, but others found across Britain allow us to track their progress. They set up two altars at Lanchester in County Durham, and another at Corbridge near Hadrian's Wall. The latest signs of them so far discovered are inscribed dedications to third-century emperors Caracalla and Severus Alexander at High Rochester, a fort north of the Hadrianic frontier, which may have been their final posting.

Perhaps the most perplexing inscription from Castlecary can be found on an altar dedicated to Mercury, which was unearthed there in the 1840s. The dedication to the fleet-footed god of travellers and boundaries was made by the men of Sixth Legion who describe themselves as 'citizens of Italy and Noricum', the latter being an ancient province that equates to modern Austria and parts of Slovenia. This throws a spanner in the works when it comes to dating the Roman withdrawal from the Antonine frontier. While the most popular theory states that they left around AD 158, the men of Italy and Noricum were only drafted into the British Sixth Legion after AD 175.

Could Castlecary have served as a lone outpost after the Roman troops had withdrawn back to Hadrian's Wall? Or was the Scottish frontier in use much longer than is currently proposed? This is yet another example of the confusing, contradictory evidence that historians and archaeologists have to wrestle with as they try to figure out the history of this complex, often baffling monument.

Despite its unfortunate history, Castlecary is worth a visit – in fact, it is one of my favourite spots on the Antonine Wall. Right opposite the old schoolhouse I found two information panels at the edge of the field that contained the fort's remains. One of the panels was older, another of the traditional metal signposts that I had been spotting all along the route of the frontier. It did not contain much detail but did reveal that traces of the fort's ramparts and its north gate were still visible.

The second panel was more modern and much more informative, but also dirty and worn, a reconstruction drawing of Roman Castlecary barely legible through a layer of black mould. I stood on the quiet lane to read them both, then surveyed the site, which lay on the other side of a fence. Right beside me was a gate. The signs seemed to imply that the fort was open to the public, but the fact that the gate was tightly chained up to the gate post suggested otherwise.

I wanted to get a proper look at Castlecary – the view from across a fence was simply not enough. It was obvious that there was only one way to achieve that. Looking around me, scanning the nearby houses and the lane to make sure that nobody was looking, I carefully dropped my backpack over the other side of the gate. Then, after placing a foot on one of its lower bars, I pulled myself up and over the top, dropping ungracefully down the other side.

I was now standing in the area that was once the fort's annexe, which was protected by a rampart and ditch, although neither can be seen above ground today. Turning to my right, I could make out the low ridge in the grass which marked the eastern edge of Castlecary's platform, the earthen terrace that lifted the fort above the surrounding landscape. I walked up and onto it at around the spot where the eastern gate would have allowed the Military Way to pass into the fort interior. On the northern edge of the platform, just where it meets the modern lane, a dip indicated the site of the north gate, which led out into unconquered Caledonia. The grass was low, allowing a few squared stones to peek through, the only perceptible remnants of the fort's four heavily fortified gateways.

It is hard not to envy the eighteenth-century antiquarians who visited Castlecary before it was repeatedly wrecked and ravaged. In his *Historical*

Inquiries of 1707, Sibbald described it as 'a great Fort with much building [*sic*]' and noted the existence of an altar bearing an inscription '*MATRIBUS*', found at the fort, later moved to the collection of the Earl of Wigton at Cumbernauld less than two miles away, but now unfortunately lost.

Alexander Gordon also admired the size and state of preservation of Castlecary, calling it a 'magnificent Fort' and recording that parts of its stone outer walls were still standing. The plan of the fort in his *Itinerarium Septentrionale* shows the deep ditches that surrounded those walls, although he seems to have missed the gate on the north side that is still partially visible today. Gordon recorded the foundations of a building at the centre of the fort, its outline drawn with a dotted line, which presumably marked the location of what he called 'the Place where the General's Tent stood', actually the fort's headquarters.

Gordon listed the wealth of other antiquities discovered here, which included several inscriptions, a 'most curious Roman Lamp of Brass' and lots of broken pottery, including Samian ware 'as fine as our modern China, on some of which are divers figures raised'. John Horsley, meanwhile, included a sketch in his *Britannia Romana* of the '*MATRIBUS*' inscription described by Sibbald,

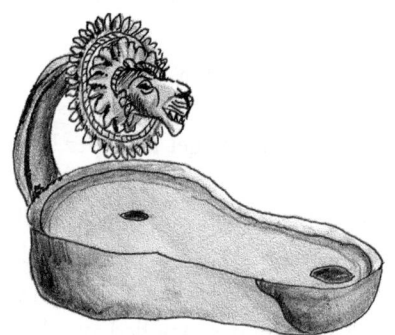

A Roman Oil Lamp

revealing it to be the top half of a broken altar. On the flat top of the altar was the focus, a shallow round hollow into which liquid offerings could be poured, below it was carved '*MATRIB MILITES VEXILL*', the final word an abbreviation of the Latin *vexillationis*. This inscription can be translated as 'To the mother goddesses, the soldiers of a detachment...'.

The cult of the three mother goddesses (*matres* in Latin) is a fascinating, if obscure phenomenon which seems to have emerged in the first century in central Gaul. It quickly spread across the northern European regions of the Roman Empire, and several inscriptions to the goddesses, as well as carved images of them, have been found in the Roman towns of Cirencester in the Cotswolds and Corbridge just south of Hadrian's Wall.

Unfortunately, we know next to nothing about the beliefs and practices attached to them. Since no written sources survive, we have only the limited archaeological evidence to go on, such as the fact that one or more of the goddesses are often shown carrying a basket of fruit, surely a symbol of fertility or abundance. The ubiquity of the mysterious Mothers is a sign of their popularity amongst Roman worshippers across Britain and beyond.

Turning back towards the railway, I headed towards a clump of trees at the foot of the enormous embankment that lifts its tracks well above the height of the Roman fort. As if on cue, a train sped past, heading from Glasgow to Edinburgh no doubt, emitting a loud electric hum as it went – modern locomotives may no longer be the smelly, smoky 'iron horses' of James Young Simpson's day, but the railway's unavoidable presence was a stark reminder of the extensive damage caused to this ancient monument in the name of progress.

Walking into the copse, I was able to get more of a sense that there was something special below my feet. In amongst the roots of the trees, poking up out of the grass, nettles and mud, were countless stones – not your common or garden rubble, but rather the meticulously cut and squared stones that were previously part of an important Roman building.

They varied in size, some not much bigger than a fist, others much larger, long and flat, perhaps the lintels of doors or windows, or maybe a step. In one patch, where the grass and soil had been worn away, it was even possible to see two courses of stones sitting neatly one of top of the other, their chiselled surfaces spotted with moss and lichen.

Elsewhere, distinct ridges in the weedy undergrowth indicated the lines of ancient walls. It may not be much, but these ridges and the muddle of half-buried masonry that lies around them give an intriguing hint of the foundations that lie under the earth. This was undoubtedly the location of the ruined building recorded on Alexander Gordon's plan, sketched way back in the early 1720s. I was standing right in the middle of the fort, on top of the remains of its headquarters, the building that we know, since the discovery of that inscription at Rough Castle, was called the *principia*.

Parts of the fort at Castlecary were excavated under the direction of the Society of Antiquaries of Scotland in 1902, around the same time that similar excavations were taking place at Rough Castle. This revived interest in ancient imperial frontiers at a time when Britain's empire was itself reaching its zenith is surely no coincidence. The archaeologists' time on the site was limited to a single season, and consequently, as George Macdonald diplomatically put it in the in 1911 edition of *The Roman Wall in Scotland*, 'the results were thus less fruitful than more time and greater thoroughness might have made them'. Many important discoveries were made, however, as the black and white photographs and the detailed fold-out plan of the site printed in Macdonald's book reveal.

The outer walls of the fort were found to be particularly strong, standing on a rubble base measuring 9 ft wide with a solid foundation of cut stones. Indeed, in the north-eastern corner, where the wall was even wider, Macdonald estimated that some of the stones must have weighed more than half a ton. Above this, the construction of the fort's ramparts changed, with dressed stones (or ashlar, to use the proper architectural term) used on the outer facings, the core consisting of concrete made from lime, sandstone gravel and boulders. Although is hard to be sure how high these great defensive walls originally stood, Macdonald hazarded an educated guess at 10 ft or more.

Investigation of the gates revealed no foundations of flanking towers or guardrooms, so it is likely that they consisted of an arch with a tower above, which is just how they are depicted on the reconstruction featured on the grubby information panel on site. The two southern corners of the fort's wall were rounded with a rectangular stone tower at each, but the northern corners, near where the fort's ramparts met the Antonine Wall, were squared.

As for the interior of Castlecary fort, the Edwardian archaeologists only had time to explore parts of it. The purpose of some of the buildings that they uncovered was obvious – the *principia* at the centre, whose broken remains I could see sticking out of the mud, a granary next to it, now reburied. Other fragmentary remains, such as a substantial wall close to the granary (which Macdonald speculated was part of the commandant's house) are harder to identify with any certainty.

The archaeologists found a latrine block in the northeast corner, a structure which was found to be in a better state than any of the other buildings uncovered during these excavations. A photo in *The Roman Wall in Scotland* shows the huge drain that led the sewage under the north wall and out of the fort. The latrine was communal, as they commonly were in the Roman world, when going to the toilet in front of, or indeed sitting right beside your fellow soldiers was very much the norm.

The supposed house with private bath first uncovered back in the eighteenth century by the men plundering the site for masonry to build the Forth & Clyde Canal was re-excavated during the 1902 dig. The long, narrow building consisting of several rooms, some with curved end walls, has now been identified as the fort's communal bath house. Although much of it had been lost to stone robbing or covered by the railway embankment, what survived matched the plan published in William Roy's *Military Antiquities* more than a century before. Like Roy, the twentieth-century excavators were impressed by the quality of the building's stonework.

While the bathhouse at the smaller fort of Rough Castle was situated in the annexe, probably due to a shortage of space, perhaps also as a safety measure to keep its blazing furnaces safely away from the other buildings, the one at Castlecary was inside the fort, right next to the stone rampart. Some of the forts had two baths, one inside the walls and one out in the annexe, although whether they were both in use at the same time is not clear. But there was certainly one benefit to placing one inside the fort – the water from the Castlecary baths was drained northwards where it could be used again to flush out the communal toilets a few metres away.

Inspecting the Roman stones that peek out of the ground at the heart of Castlecary fort, it was tempting yet again to imagine what lies beneath. That is what I love about this place, its alluring hints, its unexplored potential. A whole corner of the fort lies on the other side of the railway embankment, presumably inaccessible to visitors, although I have never actually tried to find it. Castlecary undoubtedly has much more to reveal. A geophysical survey conducted to the east of the site in 2006 identified anomalies which scholars believe could be the remains of a *vicus*, or civil settlement, right outside the ditch and rampart of the annexe.

Unfortunately, as happened at Rough Castle, the excavations carried out in 1902 were left open to the elements after the dig was hastily completed, exposing the surviving remains to the harsh Scottish weather, allowing them to degrade even further. Slowly, over the past century, they have been covered again, as the earth gradually shifted, and the grass sprouted up around them. At present, there are neither the finances nor the public interest required to dig up and consolidate such a site, to secure the fragile foundations and open it up to public view as has been done at several of the forts along Hadrian's Wall. Hopefully, one day, the ruins of Castlecary will emerge again from the damp Scottish soil and tell us more about life on the Antonine Wall.

With an eye on the time, I left the rubbly remains of the *principia* and wandered across to the western edge of the fort platform. As I progressed, the roar of distant traffic grew louder and I soon came face to face with the final insult thrown at Castlecary fort – the M80 motorway, which skims noisily past its western defences, cutting a swathe through the Antonine Wall as it goes. It could have been much worse. In 2005, plans were proposed to build a new bypass road which would have destroyed the fort altogether. Luckily, it was rejected in favour of upgrading what was then the A80 to a motorway, resulting in the tangle of lanes and slip roads that I could now see in front of me.

It was time to head off. Another ungainly jump over the gate was required, then it was back down the main road and a left turn, taking me onto a bridge which took me over the motorway. I stopped for a moment to consider this hub of transport networks. The canal running under the motorway behind me, the railway carried over it by a large sandstone viaduct ahead of me, cars and lorries roaring underneath me; two centuries of Scots making their way from east to west and vice versa, just as the Romans had done on their Military Way. Keen to escape the incessant noise and the stink of diesel, I strode onwards into the village of Castlecary.

A couple of minutes further on, I took a right turn into the car park of Castlecary House Hotel. Past a striking metal sign fashioned like a Roman shield, I was greeted by two legionaries, each bearing the skinny javelin known to the Romans as a *pilum*, their shields marked with the words *LEGIO* and *VI VIC* (the Sixth Legion Victrix). They are not real, of course, but metal cut-outs who flank the gate that leads to a path along the next section of the Antonine Wall.

The next part of my journey followed what is unquestionably the best-preserved portion of the frontier, although it is one of the least known and, if my experience is anything to go by, least visited parts of the monument. From Castlecary, it is possible to follow the ditch without significant interruption for around 5½ miles. This stretch certainly offers one of the most interesting and enjoyable walks along the Antonine Wall, although, as I was about to discover, it can also be challenging.

It started out easily enough, the black silhouettes of those Roman legionaries leaving me in no doubt that I was heading in the right direction. The line of the ditch became evident in the grass to my left as I left the village of Castlecary behind, a soft dip so shallow that it would have remained invisible to the untrained eye. To my right, a band of sheep diligently munched the grass, a few looking over as I paused to take photographs. Beyond them I could see far across the valley, with a long, low line of hills emerging in the distance.

This property used to be known as Garnhall Farm. In 1977, excavations were conducted there as plans were developed to convert the abandoned farm buildings into an Antonine Wall visitor centre. The rubble base of the turf rampart was found, showing evidence of a meeting point where two sections constructed by different teams came together, as well as signs of later repair work carried out to the rampart. In the end, the visitor centre was never built, and the farm was later demolished, another missed opportunity to raise the Antonine Wall's profile. According to Robertson and Keppie's *Handbook*, the edging stones of the rampart base can sometimes be seen sticking out of the grass around here, but despite some searching on both occasions that I walked the route, I have yet to find them.

Not much later I reached a country lane called Wyndford Road, from where the path continued across the fields. It was well signposted, suggesting that attempts had been made to improving public access to this part of the Antonine Wall, but the path itself was in a poor state. In fact, it was less of a path and more of a swamp. Some dexterity was required to leap from one tuft of grass to another to avoid drenching my boots in deep, dark puddles. Eventually, with one final jump, I made it to the kissing gate which opens onto the next length of Roman frontier.

Nearby was another of the old-fashioned metal signposts that punctuated my journey. It identified this part of the Antonine Wall as Tollpark. Featuring a concise history and description of the frontier, it informed me that 'the section of ditch running through the wood is one of the best surviving stretches on the Wall'. Strangely, the sign itself stood only a foot or so off the ground, its stunted post looking as if it had sunk into the sticky mudbath that surrounded it. The course of the Roman frontier was clear now, for although there were no remnants of the turf rampart at Tollpark, the ditch was deep, its northern bank supported by a modern farm wall, and the soft rise of the upcast mound was unmistakeable.

The next 20 minutes or so, as I marched my way along this upcast mound, was an absolute pleasure. The setting of the Antonine Wall here may not be as remote and rural as it once was, with a row of recently constructed industrial buildings (some of them sitting on the site of a Roman temporary camp) rather spoiling the view to my left, but looking in the other direction I could see open fields and a wide sky, a few pockets of sunshine breaking through the advancing ranks of cloud. The land fell away to the north of the Wall, but then rose again as it approached the slopes of the Kilsyth Hills, a volcanic ridge that merges into the Campsie Fells, this line of high ground reaching from here right across to Strathblane.

A few tiny houses could be seen in the far distance, stark white against the green, while a line of metal pylons blended more easily into the background. Apart from that, however, the landscape would not be completely unfamiliar to the soldiers who had guarded the Roman frontier all those years ago, men on sentry duty who would, like me, have scrupulously scanned this long, wide valley that runs right across central Scotland from Forth to Clyde.

The northern side of the Roman ditch at Tollpark is marked by a thin band of woodland, beech trees mostly, some very old, their trunks decorated here and there with bursts of bracket fungi. Every so often, a huge fallen tree had been allowed to rot where it lay, the wood gradually crumbling to dust but also offering a habitat to countless bugs and other tiny creatures. From time to time I had to edge along the side of the path to avoid damp ground, but I was making good progress, the relative peace broken occasionally by the buzz of the light aircraft that sailed intermittently over my head.

The row of beech trees ended, and the destination of these small aeroplanes soon became apparent. Lying to my left, close to the Antonine Wall, was the runway of Cumbernauld Airport. Originally nothing more than a grassy landing strip, it was improved in the 1980s, and is now mainly used for pilot training and charter flights in both helicopters and fixed-wing aircraft. As I passed by, yet another plane made its wobbly descent towards the tarmac, its wings tipping and bobbing in the wind before it touched down and slowed to a halt. No fan of flying at the best of times, I was glad that my feet were on solid ground.

Having said that, the ground did not remain solid for much longer. In fact, the going soon became exceptionally soft. The Roman ditch disappeared behind the airport's high fence, a necessary security measure no doubt, while the path continued along the other side, running parallel to both the ancient frontier and the modern runway.

Although the footpath was clear and easy to locate, it soon became so waterlogged that it was completely impassable. To avoid getting exceedingly wet feet, I was forced to creep along the sides of the trail, negotiating thorny bushes as I went. The fear of falling backwards and sinking into the mud, maybe even losing a shoe, was very real, as was the risk of ripping my clothes, or indeed the palms of my hands, on the rough branches. Luckily, I am fairly fit and robust. For anyone less able, this part of the walk would be virtually impossible.

Eventually, just as I reached the ruined shell of Arniebog farmhouse, the ground firmed up and I could continue more easily. The wet soil of Arniebog may have been causing me problems, but a little more than a century and a half ago it offered up two fragments of what was almost certainly a distance sculpture, discovered by the tenant farmer William Chalmers and his family as they cleared stones from a potato field to the south of the Antonine Wall.

The *Glasgow Herald* deemed the find important enough to feature a report on it on 15 June 1868, which suggested that it was Chalmers's daughter who first noticed the carved figure of a man on a flat stone that she had removed from the ground. The find spot was around 30 m south of the Antonine Wall, or 'Grim's Sheugh' as the newspaper noted it was colloquially known, 'sheugh' being a Scots word for 'ditch' or 'furrow'. The woman's discovery fitted together with another stone featuring a carved figure that, according to antiquarian John Buchanan, was found only a few feet away. The two pieces could be joined to make the left-hand side of a stone panel. The inscription had been lost, but the stone's decorative elements were like those on several of the distance slabs found along the frontier.

The 1868 *Herald* report only mentioned one of the figures carved in relief on the panel, describing it quite correctly as 'the naked figure of a Caledonian hero in captivity, bending on one knee in a suppliant attitude, with his hands tied behind his back'. When it was displayed on the Antonine Wall, this image would have made a clear statement about who was in charge – even the illiterate locals would understand this representation of their diminished status. It must have been a popular subject with the sculptors tasked with creating these distance sculptures, since three others found along the Wall feature similarly cowed and cowering 'barbarians' including, as I had seen in Edinburgh, the Bridgeness Distance Slab.

The other figure carved onto this Arniebog panel is more unusual and unexpected – a triton with a flowing beard and a powerful twisting fishtail who holds an anchor in the crook of his elbow. In ancient Greek mythology, Triton was the immortal son of sea gods Poseidon and Amphitrite who wrestled Herakles and could control the waves by blowing into a magical conch shell. The word 'triton' also came to mean a kind of merman in the Greco-Roman world, and it is just such a merman that we see on the stone from Arniebog. His presence begs the question why such a sea creature, more usually associated with maritime locations, should appear so far from any body of water – like so many of our questions regarding the history of the Antonine Wall, it is one that remains unanswered.

Despite the excitement surrounding its discovery, the ancient carving ended up being stored for several years in one of the outbuildings of Arniebog Farm. In 1871, it was seen in the farm's milking house by Christian Maclagan, a local woman (she was born in Denny near Bonnybridge in 1811) who is now recognised as one of Scotland's first female archaeologists. Maclagan later wrote a letter to the Society of Antiquaries of Scotland (who, at that time, refused to allow female fellows, making Maclagan a 'Lady Associate' instead) that described how her offer to buy the stone from the farmer on behalf of the National Museum of Antiquities in Edinburgh was refused, since the local laird was putting together a collection of such antiquities and had to be offered first refusal. Eventually, however, the broken panel was transported to the other side of the country, joining several other Roman carvings in the collection of the Hunterian Museum in Glasgow, where it can still be seen today.

Stepping over a bubbling brook and through a hedgerow, past a striking rowan tree, one half of its branches loaded with scarlet berries, the other half overwhelmed by lacy grey lichen, I found another length of Roman ditch. It ran clear and straight ahead of me, fenced in on either side, with the footpath situated yet again on top of the upcast mound.

On my previous visit, all those months before, I had encountered a small flock of sheep there. As I approached, they predictably panicked, scampering off along the lip of the ditch before slowing to a halt at what they considered a safe distance away. Only a few seconds later I had caught them up – more panic and another jittery canter further along the Antonine Wall ensued before they calmed down and came to a standstill. Again, I was upon them within the blink of an eye. And so, we continued for at least a couple of minutes before one of the sheep finally had the bright idea of trotting down into the ditch and up the other side, from where they could watch, bleating and shivering, as I passed.

There were no sheep that day, but as I came to a gate at the end of this leg of the frontier, I met some other, more exotic, local inhabitants that were sheltering in the now fading hollow of the Roman ditch – a gathering of alpacas. Beyond them was a cluster of stone buildings, the old house and outbuildings of Westerwood Farm which stands right on top of the next fort on the Antonine Wall.

Alexander Gordon was the first antiquarian to record the layout of the fort at Westerwood, and his description of it in *Itinerarium Septentrionale* makes it sound impressive. He wrote of coming across 'the distinct Vestiges of another great Roman square Fort upon the Wall, where the Praetorium [*principia*] in the middle of the Area, is very plain and distinct'. What particularly interested him was what he described as a 'Causeway which goes around this fort, on the Top of the Ramparts', by which he meant a walkway around the top of the fort's outer rampart. No signs of either the rampart or the *principia* can be seen above ground today, at least not from where I was standing on the other side of the ditch.

In the eighteenth century, the north-east corner of the fort, where the farm buildings now stand, was the location of a small village that Gordon called Westerwood Town. William Roy produced a plan of the site that was eventually published in 1793 in his *Military Antiquities*, which reveals that the main street of this village, flanked by just a handful of cottages, carried on right through the centre of the fort, following the exact route of

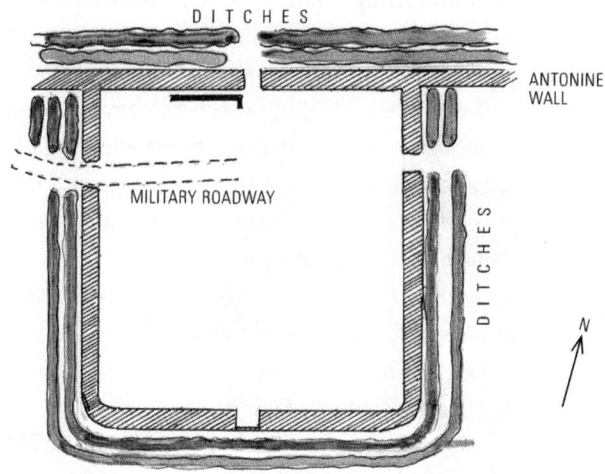

Westerwood Fort

the Roman Military Way. Today, the two entrances on either side of the farmyard lie on the same line, the eastern entrance sitting exactly where the gate into the fort stood.

When Gordon toured the Antonine Wall in 1723, he was not only making notes and plans of what he saw for publication in his book, he was also on the lookout for antiquities – not for himself, but for the collection of his patron, Sir John Clerk, who was a fervent admirer of Roman culture. It was he who lamented the loss of Arthur's O'on and whose son built a replica of it on top of his stable block. Sir John was an avid collector of ancient artefacts, with most of his treasures housed at his mansion of Newbiggin near Penicuik.

One particularly striking carving which ended up in Clerk's collection via Gordon was discovered at Westerwood, not dug up from the ground this time, but found in the wall of a cottage. This was often the way with such Roman stones – like Carriden House, where Alexander Milne displayed the carved Roman eagle on the outside of his new wing, farm cottages and barns sometimes incorporated ancient sculptures. In this humbler context, however, decorated panels and altars were appreciated more as free dressed stone, ideal for lintels and quoins, than as valuable classical antiquities.

Gordon kept an eye out for such carved or inscribed stones as he travelled along the Antonine Wall and would tempt the inhabitants with financial rewards if they would agree to hand them over. Things did not always go to plan. On one occasion he convinced a tenant to remove a Roman altar from the wall of his home, promising him payment of a crown if it featured an inscription. It did not, the payment was refused, and Gordon recounted in a letter to Clerk how the furious man and his wife had both harangued him 'like Kellwives' (a kalewife being a Scots term for a vegetable seller).

Gordon had better luck at Westerwood. The Roman carving that he found there is one that certainly stands out. He recorded its discovery in *Itinerarium Septentrionale*:

> In one of their Cottages I found a Roman stone, upon which was carved...the Figure of a Priapus, or Penis, not in the least defaced; under that Figure were the Letters EX VOTO, and above some Arithmetick Cyphers X...VI, but these were pretty much worn out.

He illustrated the stone in the book (a typically rudimentary sketch that ably demonstrates why his earlier career as a portrait painter never took off), showing the aforementioned 'Priapus, or Penis', a relief image of a male member that would be referred to by modern scholars as a 'phallus'.

Such phalluses, or *phalli*, if we are going to stick pedantically to the proper Latin plural, appear all over the Roman world. Back in classical times, the phallus was more than just something erotic, it was a magical symbol, a powerful sacred motif and good luck charm. Penises appeared on all sorts of everyday items, from oil lamps to pendants, from finger rings to wind chimes. Some of them even sported a pair of cute little wings. The Romans believed that the phallus could ward off the evil eye and prevent bad fortune. It was believed to be especially effective at protecting children and soldiers.

Plenty of Roman *phalli* have been found across Britain. Hadrian's Wall has more than its fair share, with several examples similar to the one found at Westerwood appearing at Chester's fort (one carved into the flagstone floor of its headquarters building, another on the nearby bridge over the

North Tyne, a third dug up in its bath house) as well as on the stone rampart itself, including two on the stretch of Wall that runs from Harrow Scar to Birdoswald, in Cumbria. All in all, 59 carved *phalli* have been found on Hadrian's Wall and there were no doubt many more. They tend to be located around forts and river crossings, placed there by soldiers hoping for a bit of good luck.

The words *EX VOTO* inscribed below the Westerwood phallus can be translated as 'by a vow', meaning that the item was dedicated to a god. The Latin term is still used today in the Roman Catholic church to describe offerings (often little punched-metal, wood or clay trinkets) presented to saints in return for answered prayers.

Gordon had no qualms about illustrating the Westerwood phallus in all its glory in his book. John Horsley was less bold. He had to include it in his *Britannia Romana*, in which he aimed to list all the known Roman sculptures and inscriptions in Britain, but he was clearly perturbed by the graphic subject matter. His description of the stone, which he calls a 'remarkable *Priapus* or *fallus*' offered his theory that the smaller inscription at the top (which Gordon read as 'X...VI') was an abbreviation of the phrase 'X ANNORUM', meaning 'of ten years', suggesting improbably that it could be giving thanks for the birth of a baby after ten years of infertility.

Horsley, a strict Protestant who grew up in a Nonconformist family and made a living as a Presbyterian minister, was unwilling to go into too much detail about such a heathen object. He had to illustrate it of course, otherwise his book would not be the exhaustive compendium of Roman sculptures that he intended. To solve the problem, he simply covered the offending member with a carefully drawn fig leaf. 'Decency forbids me saying any more on this subject', he wrote, 'as it obliges me to conceal the figure'. Reading his description almost three centuries later, I can still sense his blushes.

By the time Horsley saw it, the stone was in the collection of Sir John Clerk at his Penicuik estate. We already know that Clerk's son James inherited his father's love of antiquities, but later generations of the Clerk family were less interested in the late baronet's considerable collection of ancient artefacts, and in 1857 most of his Roman sculptures and inscriptions were donated to the National Museum of Antiquities, since subsumed into the National Museum of Scotland.

For some reason, however, the phallus was not part of the gift, and for years it was apparently lost, assumed destroyed in the conflagration that had consumed the interior of old Penicuik House in 1899. Then, amazingly, it was rediscovered in 1976 by scholar Iain Gordon Brown hidden in a shadowy corner of the charter room at new Penicuik House (which is, you will remember, the converted eighteenth-century stable block), where it remains to this day.

From my position on the north side of the Roman ditch, it was hard to decipher the outline of the Roman fort of Westerwood, although I could detect a raised area of long grass which was suggestive of the fort's platform. The farm buildings that stand on top of it have gone through a variety of uses. In the 1970s, when the farmland was sold, they became a short-lived youth centre, then, when the land was converted into a golf course, they were employed by the greenkeepers to store their equipment. More recently, they have been restored, with the main house now looking very smart indeed. A slight depression at the end of its garden revealed the route of the Roman frontier, while the house looked out at the wonderful view across the valley towards the Kilsyth Hills.

There have been only a few small excavations at Westerwood in modern times, often in anticipation of planned building work in the vicinity, but the most interesting discovery was made in 1963 when local teenager James Walker decided to fieldwalk across a recently ploughed field. He noticed a carved stone at the bottom of a furrow and pulled it out to reveal an inscribed altar. Made from local sandstone and bearing the deep scars of the plough blade, the altar was inscribed with a dedication 'to the *Silvanae* and *Quadriviae*'. The first are celestial wood nymphs, the second the goddesses of crossroads. Whether there was a crossroads near here is not clear, but the fact that this part of the world used to be covered in trees is clearly referenced in the fort's modern name.

It is the dedicatee of the altar that I find most intriguing. The inscription on the front reveals that it was erected by one Vibia Pacata, wife of Flavius Verecundus, a centurion with the Sixth Legion Victrix (who, as we saw earlier, left evidence of their presence on an altar at Castlecary). We don't know much about her, but her name gives us clues to her background.

The cognomen Pacata, which can be translated as 'pacified', was often found in ancient Gaul, but was most popular in North Africa, from where Vibia may have originated.

When we think of Roman frontiers, we tend to imagine them as masculine spaces, the territory of soldiers alone, but women lived there too. They often left no trace, but as we shall see further along the Antonine Wall, other evidence of the lives of these women who inhabited the very edge of the Roman world has emerged elsewhere.

James Walker, who spotted the altar and reported it to the (now defunct) Falkirk Burgh Museum, was later rewarded four pounds and ten shillings, and the farmer in whose field it was found got the same. It was only the start for Walker, who went on to become a highly respected amateur archaeologist. He has since taken part in over 30 digs on the Antonine Wall and his subsequent fieldwalks have led to the discovery of three of the frontier's fortlets.

As I left the fort of Westerwood behind, I headed yet again into the land of greens, bunkers and golf buggies as I strolled through Dullatur Golf Club. In the distance, I spotted a few players wandering down a fairway, the first humans that I had encountered since the dog walker at Seabegs Wood. It was not long before I reached what is, in my opinion at least, the most beautiful stretch of the Roman frontier, a section also known as Dullatur.

A low wooden staircase led me over a fence and into an enclosure which ran along the line of the Antonine Wall. At first, the ditch was filled with reeds, which flourished in its damp depths. Later, the reeds were replaced by a tangle of trees as the ditch got deeper. To the south of the Roman Wall lay a patch of thick conifer forest, with the route of the Military Way left unplanted to indicate its location.

Recent rain had left the ground damp and marshy in places, but the grass was lush and the trees mostly still green, clearly enjoying the mild autumn weather. It was so peaceful, so pretty, that I could not help but linger there a while. Along a few metres of the southern lip of the ditch ran a line of fallen masonry, not Roman, but a relatively recent dry-stone dyke; an old farm wall no doubt, now tumbled down and covered in moss. A wide variety of trees, including twisty-trunked oaks and smooth-barked elms, grew on the banks of the ditch, giving it the magical air of a fairy glen. My previous journey along the Antonine Wall, over a year before, had been the first time that I had visited Dullatur, and back then I could not understand why this atmospheric stretch of the frontier was not better known.

Revelling in its charms, I paused for a brief rest on the edge of the ditch and took a swig from my water bottle. As I quietly soaked up the ambiance, I suddenly got the distinct feeling that I was not alone. Turning round and looking further westwards, I came face to face with a skinny-legged deer, only a young thing, standing about 20 m away, stock still. It looked just as surprised to see me as I was to see it. Our eyes met for the briefest of moments, then it turned and fled, bouncing silently into the woods at an impressive speed. I followed its white tail as it bobbed through the trees, and then it was gone.

The Antonine Wall began a descent as it crossed a small field, before it was interrupted by the embankment of the Edinburgh to Glasgow railway. A bridge allowed a farm track to pass underneath, so I followed that. As I approached the barns of Easter Dullatur Farm, I came to a gate, not just closed but securely chained and padlocked, exactly as it had been on my previous visit. This track is supposed to be a public way giving access to the path along the Antonine Wall, but someone has obviously forgotten to tell the farmer. For the second time that morning I was compelled to pull myself up and over a locked gate, landing awkwardly with a heavy thump on the other side.

I still get irritated when I think about that locked gate. If there is a single reason this magnificent stretch of the Antonine Wall at Dullatur is both little known and largely devoid of visitors, it is surely the difficulty in getting to it. On one side I had faced waterlogged paths, on the other it was this gate. Although my morning's walk had been immensely rewarding, it had at times felt like an assault course.

So much for the recently-erected shiny green signs next to the gate that indicated the route of a public path, each one decorated with a reproduction of the galloping Roman horseman carved onto the Bridgeness Distance Slab. If getting to one of the finest sections of the Antonine Wall is this difficult, such enticements to attract more visitors become pointless. Looking on the bright side, at least the path at Easter Dullatur was in a better state than when Jessie Mothersole walked it in the late 1920s, when she described it as being 'in a terrible condition, ploughed up by the tread of many cattle into a morass of soft mud'.

Taking a second to compose myself, I plodded onwards, stopping only briefly to glance into a metal barn to my right. Scores of faces stared back at me, an enormous flock of sheep, packed tight, all of them strangely silent. Wondering what fate lay in store for them, I strode past, away from Easter Dullatur Farm and onto a single-track road that led towards the town of Kilsyth. It was narrow, and there was no pavement, so I had to walk carefully along the verge, keeping a lookout for any approaching traffic.

After a couple of minutes, the road took a sharp right turn, slicing mercilessly through the Antonine Wall. Standing at this tight corner, facing north, I could see the Roman ditch running in a straight line through the fields to my right, also heading off to my left in the direction of travel where it disappeared behind the back of Wester Dullatur Farm. My map showed the Forth & Clyde Canal straight ahead of me, right in the base of the wide valley, but it was now out of view, hidden at the bottom of a shallow slope.

The cows that churned up the road in Jessie Mothersole's day have been replaced by horses, with several of them grazing peacefully in the fields around me. Stepping on, stopping from time to time to let a car speed past, I followed the road around another sharp turn until I came to a prominent white sign: 'Antonine Wall Croy Hill'. Above it, another green arrow pointing me in the direction of 'The Antonine Walkway'.

Ahead of me lay the immense rocky mass of Croy Hill, the first proper climb that I would face on my journey. It was just past midday, so this seemed like a good time to stop for a break and some food. In fact, I ended up sitting on the same boulder which had provided a seat on my last walk, although this time there was no need to shelter from inclement weather. A rest and some sustenance were required – ahead of me were two of the best sites on the Antonine Wall, but also two sizeable hills and the most challenging walking of the entire route.

Chapter Five

CROY HILL TO KIRKINTILLOCH

Croy Hill

Croy Hill is an enormous lump of volcanic rock that was formed when molten lava cooled underground around 290 million years ago. It is also a rare patch of wilderness in this part of Scotland. As we shall see, its hard stone proved to be a huge problem for the Roman legionaries who constructed the Antonine Wall. As one of the highest points on the frontier, its slopes now present something of a challenge to the modern walker too.

The good news is that it is an area rich in Roman archaeology that offers wonderful views of the surrounding landscape, so I knew that the summit would repay the effort involved in reaching its heights.

I didn't spend much time on my lunch of a sandwich and a bar of chocolate – perching on a boulder close to a small car park was not the most comfortable place to rest and relax. Whilst being out in the open countryside had its benefits, particularly after so many months trapped in the city, I would not have minded a proper seat and a big, warm plate of fish and chips right there and then. But time was getting on, and, with two key sites coming up, I was looking forward to the rest of my afternoon on the Wall.

As I was preparing to set off, I reached into the pocket of my jacket to retrieve my all-important guidebook – the Robertson and Keppie *Handbook to the Antonine Wall*, my *vade mecum* (Latin for 'go with me') as the eighteenth-century antiquarians would have called it. It was not in my jacket pocket where I usually kept it, so I checked the other side. And then the inside pockets. I removed my backpack and rummaged through that too, looking out for its shiny red cover, getting more anxious by the second as I realised that it was nowhere to be found.

Within a minute or so it became obvious that my precious *Handbook* was gone. Casting my mind back, I remembered briefly referring to it at Dullatur, moments before my encounter with the deer. I thought back to my clumsy climb over the gate at Easter Dullatur Farm. I could only imagine that the *Handbook* had fallen out of my pocket there and was probably still lying on the ground. I was too far on to turn back and look for it, particularly since it might not even have been there that I lost it. I like to imagine that some fellow traveller might have spotted it, picked it up and adopted it, but given the fact that I had yet to meet anyone else who appeared to be walking the Roman frontier, it does seem unlikely.

As I approached Croy Hill, I came across another wide gate that was decorated with eye-catching posters. 'Hairy Coos on the Hill,' one of them announced, explaining that cows were about to be reintroduced to Croy after a long absence. Their grazing helps to create a more varied habitat for other creatures, improving biodiversity and encouraging Croy Hill's wildlife, which includes greater butterfly orchids, great crested newts, kestrels and skylarks.

The posters also featured a note of caution: 'Please leave the cattle be, and they'll do the same with you'. Next to that, a small note gave an email address for anyone who was unhappy with the reintroduction programme. I don't have anything against cows but walking through herds of them can be an intimidating experience. To my mind, their size, nervy disposition and herd mentality are not a happy combination. The smiley cartoon coo on the poster was reassuring, but it was with some trepidation that I headed through another kissing gate and onto Croy Hill.

Luckily for me, I did not need the *Handbook* to identify the route of the Antonine Wall, which is extremely well-preserved as it approaches Croy and continues up and over the hill, with the ditch clear for all to see. George Macdonald perfectly summed up the state of the ancient frontier there in the 1934 edition of *The Roman Wall in Scotland*:

> For nearly a mile onwards a descriptive account is barely required. Those who are able to visit the sector for themselves will need no guide, so conspicuous are the remains.

As I got higher, I soon found myself in an ideal position to look back and see the Roman ditch that I had missed as I walked along the road. It ran straight towards me from behind Wester Dullatur Farm, then faded into a line of reeds as it passed through wetter ground at the foot of the hill. As I turned around and looked in the direction of travel, I saw it re-emerge from a shallow pond and begin its steady climb.

The raised path that I was standing on, which runs from south to north around the base of the hill, cutting through the Roman frontier as it goes, was once the embankment of a mineral railway. Croy Hill has been heavily quarried over the years, with the sections cut out of it sometimes coming close to eating into the Roman remains, but this threat, like the quarrying itself, is now happily extinct.

Croy Hill is not exactly a lofty mountain – it is not even the highest hill on the course of the Antonine Wall – but it still felt strange to be climbing at all. Up until that point, my journey had been mostly flat, with only slight rises and falls here and there. The terrain at Croy was different to anything that I had experienced since I set off from Carriden. As I rose above the valley, the views opened up, so that for the first time in a long time, I could see southwards as well as northwards.

For so much of the walk I had been hemmed in in one direction or another, by rising ground, by trees, by embankments or by buildings. The Antonine Wall itself had generally run along the southern slope of the Forth-Clyde Valley at a level below the summit to give maximum visibility over Caledonia to the north. Now, however, I was right on top of the ridge, looking out for miles in every direction. By this point on my previous attempt to walk the Roman frontier the rain had already started. This time around, although the wind picked up as I climbed steadily higher, there were no looming dark clouds, just fresh air and a wonderful sense of freedom.

The ancient turf rampart has disappeared here, but the Roman ditch to my right, despite being clogged in places with bracken, gorse and the odd boulder, was impossible to miss as it followed me up the hillside. I had been awed by the ditch's breathtaking scale before, at Watling Lodge, where it is still over 4 m deep and 12 m wide, and at the long stretch from Castlecary to Dullatur, which seems to go on for ever.

The amount of hard physical work required to dig this huge trench by hand, as it ran for over 38 miles across the British mainland, was enormous; unthinkable today. At times, it must have been completely exhausting, hours of boring, backbreaking toil, day after day, week after week. It is no wonder that the completion of a length of Antonine Wall was publicly celebrated with elaborately carved distance markers. It was, it seems to me, the least that these tireless men deserved.

At Croy, my awe reached completely new levels, because when they arrived at this hill, the Roman legionaries found not more Caledonian mud, but hard, cold stone – volcanic basalt and dolerite to be more precise. And basalt and dolerite, igneous rocks that formed as bursts of lava cooled at different rates and different densities, are extremely hard. Yet still the legionaries continued with their ditch, swapping their spades for picks, chisels and mallets, making slow progress as they chipped, pounded and splintered their way up the hillside. You must hand it to them – such unwavering determination to get the job done, no matter what nature put in the way, is immensely admirable.

The soldiers' commitment to completing a task, even in the hardest of circumstances, when nature itself seemed to be conspiring against them, caught the imaginations of the eighteenth-century antiquarians. The 1700s were a time when the Romans were held in high regard, seen as ancient superheroes, the empire that they had built the greatest and most powerful that the world had ever known, and this rock-cut ditch only confirmed such beliefs.

For Alexander Gordon, the sight of the ditch at Croy inspired him to believe that:

> At this place...there is more of the Roman Resolution and Grandeur to be seen than on its whole Track: For it is scarcely conceivable what Pains and Expence must have been used, in cutting thro' such an amazing and rough Scene of Nature.

Such prowess suited his own patriotic agenda – after all, if the Romans were so strong, so resolute when it came to finishing a job, then what did it say about the Caledonians who successfully resisted their onslaught?

That said, even the heroic Romans had their limits when it came to cutting their ditch into rock. On average, the ditch is around 8 m wide and only 1.5 m deep on Croy Hill, significantly narrower and shallower than it is elsewhere. Most shocking for those who like to imagine that the Romans were unstoppable is the fact that the ditch completely disappears for a while, a huge mass of untouched bedrock stretching for around 25 m before the ditch appears again. To modern scholars, the obvious conclusion is that, faced with this enormous obstacle, the legionaries simply gave up and admitted defeat. After all, what difference would the absence of a few metres of ditch make to the security of the frontier, particularly up there on a hilltop?

For antiquarians, raised in a time when the Romans were revered as virtually invincible (Caledonia excepted, of course), such an idea was completely unthinkable. Gordon assumed that this uncut bedrock must have been left there on purpose, to function as a bridge across the ditch, although why such a bridge might be required on top of this wild and windy crag is not explained.

This unexpected lump of rock inspired what is surely the most bizarre antiquarian theory regarding the Antonine Wall, which appeared in William Maitland's 1757 *History and Antiquities of Scotland*. So perplexed was he by the fact that the Roman ditch was incomplete, unable to accept that it had always been that way, he proposed that the stone must have grown naturally in the centuries since the Roman retreat.

His theory is so weird, so outlandish and improbable, that his words are worth quoting in full:

> It cannot be reasonably imagined that [the Romans] would leave a rock undemolished in this part. Now as I am, for certain reasons, (too long to be inserted in this place) of opinion that rocks vegetate, the rock here, by its form, must have sprung up since the making of the said ditch.

This is not the only fantastical theory to appear in Maitland's *History and Antiquities of Scotland*. When it came to the Romans and their impact on Scottish history and culture, he was full of preposterous ideas. He proposed, for example, that several Gaelic words still in use in the north of Scotland were derived from Latin, evidence, he thought, of the widespread adoption of the classical language in ancient Caledonia. Just as unlikely was his claim that typical Highland dress, the long 'belted plaid' that was wrapped around the body and formed the famous skirt around the legs, was a direct descendant of the Roman toga. According to Maitland, the Highlanders' bonnet was a modern version of the *pileus*, a Greek felt cap that became popular in ancient Rome.

Maitland made a good living as a hair merchant, but at one point he had been the bright hope of Scottish antiquarianism. Sir John Clerk had even expressed an expectation to Roger Gale that he might end up as a 'second Camden' (as in William Camden, the great antiquarian of the Tudor age). Given his penchant for crackpot conjectures, it will come as no surprise to hear that his *History and Antiquities of Scotland* was widely criticised. The *Biographical Dictionary of Eminent Scotsmen* published in 1875 described it is as 'absolutely destitute of reputation'. Maitland would never hear the criticisms, however, as the book was published right after his death at the age of 64. It is unquestionably an entertaining read, although not in the way that its author intended.

Leaving the magical vegetating rocks behind me, I headed onwards across a scrubby plateau. It was mostly covered with long grass and bracken, as well as a few clusters of scraggly hawthorn bushes. I had reached a height of around 125 m above sea level and the outlook across the valley below was spectacular. Not much later I arrived at the site of the next fort on the Antonine Wall, marked by five tall sycamores that thrive there despite the harsh conditions.

There is nothing of Croy Hill fort to see on the ground now, although recently-installed interpretation panels indicate its position and give some details of the archaeological finds made in the area. Its remains were long hidden beneath a small village – called 'Croe-Hill Town' according to Gordon. This cluster of cottages prevented antiquarians from inspecting the Roman fort in any meaningful way, to such an extent that several of them did not even notice it.

John Horsley could not find any traces of the fort. Maitland saw no signs of it either and William Roy guessed that there must have been one hereabouts but wrote that it had been 'totally levelled'. By the time the archaeologist Sir George Macdonald visited the hill in the 1920s, most of the hamlet was in ruins, with only a single inhabited cottage surviving, but there were plenty of shaped Roman stones to be found, several of them decorated with hatching, lozenges and feather-like designs. I can understand why Croy Hill village was eventually abandoned. It must have been a difficult place to eke out a living. The Roman soldiers stationed here had no choice, of course, since the regular spacing of their forts meant that they had to build one right here, up on this blustery hill.

Although antiquarians had struggled to locate the fort on Croy Hill, excavations overseen by Macdonald in the 1920s and 1930s allow us to understand it fairly well. It only took a day or two of digging in 1920 to identify the western gate, while other digs carried out 11 and 15 years later revealed more about the fort's plan. In most respects it was a typical Antonine Wall fort, square corners where it met the Wall's turf rampart, rounded corners on the south side, a headquarters at the centre and a bath house right outside the main enclosure. A short length of cobbled road ran out of the fort's northern gate, although where it led is not clear – there were no traces of a causeway or bridge to carry it over the ditch and down the steep slope beyond.

One surprising feature that was unearthed in 1931 is a stone-lined underground chamber with steps leading down to it, at the bottom of which was a well. Macdonald was hugely struck by it, noting its 'first-rate' masonry and writing that 'no adequate conception of its impressive appearance can be conveyed in words'. News of the subterranean room attracted hundreds of curious visitors to the site at weekends, and it was even proposed that the chamber might remain open to public view after the work was concluded. Luckily, given the damage caused to other forts that were excavated in the early twentieth century and then left open to the elements, it was eventually decided to rebury it for its own protection.

Croy Hill has produced many fascinating artefacts over the years, including some fine sculptures and inscriptions. Several inscribed stones record the presence of the Sixth Legion Victrix, including an altar dedicated to the Nymphs erected by one Fabius Liberalis as well as three building inscriptions that were prominently displayed to commemorate the results of their long, hard labours up there – 'the Sixth Legion built this' is their basic message. By the time they arrived in Caledonia to construct the new frontier, the legion was already over 180 years old, having been founded in 41 BC by the man then known as Octavian, who would later become the Emperor Augustus. The Sixth had played a role in building Hadrian's Wall two decades before they arrived at Croy Hill.

One of the smaller inscriptions created by them to celebrate their work was found here in the 1720s by Alexander Gordon. He sent it to Sir John Clerk at Penicuik, and like most of Clerk's Roman stones, it can now be found in the collection of the National Museums of Scotland. Gordon spotted it in the wall of one of the cottages that used to stand on this plateau and paid the residents a small fee to retrieve it for him. It is tiny (around 25 cm x 12 cm) and simple, the letters surrounded by a clumsily carved ansate panel.

Gordon got extremely excited by this inscription, reading it incorrectly as '*LEGIO V*', or the Fifth Legion:

> *I take this to be an invaluable Rarity of its Kind, being the only stone that ever I found in the Island of Britain, with the Name of the fifth Legion impressed upon it.*

As was so often the case, it was up to John Horsley to correct him, with the English antiquarian correctly pointing out that the Fifth Legion had never been to Britain, and that this stone was carved by the Sixth (modern epigraphers have identified a faint 'I' to the right of the 'V'). Given the animosity between the two, I suspect Horsley was quietly pleased to demonstrate that Gordon's revelation was nothing of the sort.

Smaller finds were less common due, Sir George Macdonald believed, to the fact that there is so little soil for them to be buried in. Fragments of pottery were uncovered, along with some tiny pieces of glass. There was, however, what Macdonald called 'a surprisingly rich crop of ballista balls', surely the only rich crop to ever be found on this rocky hillside. Fired from a catapult-like contraption – effectively an enormous crossbow – these round stones would have done severe damage to the enemies of Rome. A bronze purse was also discovered here. Now green with age, it was worn around the arm like a bracelet and kept a soldier's coins and other small valuables safe from thieving hands.

The most important and unusual Roman antiquity to be found on Croy Hill is a carved block, now in the National Museum in Edinburgh, which probably decorated a tomb. It features the figures of three legionaries, each decked out in their military gear. The figure in the centre has a beard, his bushy facial hair implying that he had reached a greater age than his two clean-shaven companions. The men are sculpted in high relief onto a sizeable chunk of yellow sandstone. Its surface is now chipped, worn and darkened with age and the carving is rudimentary, but looking into their faces is still a strangely moving experience.

The expressions on those three faces are odd, their roughly chiselled, mask-like features almost sad, although that is certainly due more to the provincial style and the challenges presented by the material than to any attempt to convey the psychology of the subjects. Their mouths are turned down at the edges, their eyes indicated by meagre horizontal slits, while what sits on top of their heads is hard to decipher. Although I have read that they are wearing helmets, its looks to me more like they are all sporting puffy, bouffant hairdos. They stand in a row, looking fearsome in their armour and military cloaks, each holding a long throwing spear and the curved rectangular shield with a round central boss known to the Romans as the *scutum*.

No inscription survives to tell us who these legionaries were, but it has been speculated that the more mature soldier in the centre was a father, with the two younger men his children. There are examples of Roman sons dedicating funeral monuments to their fathers, so this might be the case here too. It could be that they belonged to the Sixth Legion. Given the lack of evidence of other units at Croy Hill fort, it is possible that the Sixth stayed on to garrison the Antonine Wall, although this would have been a highly unorthodox arrangement, since it was normally auxiliaries who took on this role as the frontier was completed and the legions departed.

One of the information panels at the fort site features an image of this tombstone and lines from the poem 'Roman Wall Blues' written in 1927 by W H Auden:

> Over the heather the wet wind blows,
> I've lice in my tunic and a cold in my nose.
> The rain comes pattering out of the sky,
> I'm a Wall soldier, I don't know why.

Auden was thinking of Hadrian's Wall when he composed his short verse, but his description of life on a Roman frontier could equally apply to the Antonine Wall, even more so given the Caledonian climate. I do not know if the garrison at Croy suffered from lice-infested clothes (although evidence of fleas has turned up at another fort further along the frontier), but I know very well from experience that the rain does indeed often come pattering, if not hammering out of the sky.

It is an oft-repeated joke, one much loved by modern cartoonists, that the bare-legged, shivering soldiers on duty in northern Britannia must have been horrified by the conditions that they found there, all that rain, wind and snow. The cliché relies on the idea that all Romans were from Italy, and therefore accustomed to warm air and constant sunshine, but that is a complete misunderstanding of who these men were.

Inscriptions found along the Antonine Wall reveal that many of the cohorts stationed there originally hailed from places like Belgium, northern France and the Netherlands, which are not known for their scorching temperatures. And while the original members of the First Cohort of Vardullians may have come from Spain, evidence shows that later recruits would often be found amongst the local population. Many of the men who lived on Croy Hill would probably have been born in Britannia. Some of them might even have been Caledonian.

Whoever included the poem on the information panel at Croy Hill was clearly having some fun, but it is no coincidence that this excerpt was chosen for what is undoubtedly the bleakest, most windswept spot on the Caledonian frontier. I can only imagine how tough life must have been up there. Long days, chilly nights, loneliness and boredom all adding to the difficulties. No matter where you grew up, it must have been tough. There would have been a camaraderie amongst the men, I am sure, moments of fun and friendship, but there would have been times when, looking out across the wild, empty landscape all around them, even the hardiest soldier on the Antonine Wall would have wondered exactly what they were doing there, what it was that they were supposed to be defending.

Having spent a while contemplating the lot of these rugged chaps, considering what life had been like on Croy Hill almost two millennia ago, I realised that it was time to get going. Soon I was climbing again, past the site of another fortlet (discovered during archaeological investigations in 1977) until I arrived at the highest point on Croy Hill, 140 m above sea level with exceptional views in all directions. To the south I could see the northern suburbs of Cumbernauld, smoke-dark clouds hovering above, suggestive of showers.

Down there, under that grey mist, surrounded by modern houses on an estate called Carrickstone and protected by a low metal fence, is a mysterious ancient relic – the 'Carrick Stone' after which the area was named. Although it is also known locally as the 'Standing Stone', this carved rock has the appearance of a worn and weathered Roman altar. Centuries of exposure to the elements have erased any inscription, but its rectangular form, flat sides and protruding top and base are unmistakeably classical. No one knows how it ended up in its current location, but local folklore tells that the two dents worn into its flat top mark the spots where Robert the Bruce raised his standards before the Battle of Bannockburn.

Back on Croy Hill, the rock-cut ditch continued right below the crest of the hill, even though natural crags provided the ancient rampart with ample protection from any potential Caledonian attack. To the west, the direction in which I was travelling, across a valley of trees and rolling fields, I could see the challenge that lay ahead – the steep eastern side of Bar Hill. A line of bright grass that cut a swathe through woodland marked the route of the Antonine Wall as it ascended and then disappeared over the top. Just beyond was my next destination, another Roman fort, one of the best on the frontier. It did not look too far away, but I knew that the climb up to it would severely test my increasingly weary legs.

First, I had to get down from Croy Hill, which was no easy task. The western side is much more vertiginous that the eastern approach. Alexander Gordon described it as a place of 'Rocks and frightful Precipices'. For me it was just uncomfortable, as any steep descent can be, my toes pushed into the ends of my boots and my ankles and knees finally feeling the strain of a day and a half's walk.

I have since discovered that there are two expansions on this side of the hill, square turf extensions to the back of the Antonine Wall rampart like the one I had seen at Bonnyside near Rough Castle, which may have formed the bases for signal towers. One of the Croy expansions was constructed on top of a man-made rubble base, the other was built on a platform of natural rock. Apparently, they are best viewed from below, from where, according to Robertson and Keppie's *Handbook*, they can be seen 'silhouetted against the sky'. As I no longer had my copy of the *Handbook* to alert me to their existence, I did not know to look out for them. Next time, perhaps.

As I approached the bottom of the slope, I saw two enthusiastic visitors going in the other direction – more dog walkers, as it turned out – who gave me friendly hellos. It was only as I reached the road that I realised I had completely avoided the (possibly less friendly) 'hairy coos' of Croy'. I suspect that they had not arrived yet, and I can't say that I was disappointed to have missed them.

At the bottom of Croy Hill I had to cross over a road that led into the modern village of Croy. After that, the ground began to rise again, and I started another ascent, this time onto Bar Hill. I walked along a wide farm track into some pretty woodland, my path following almost exactly the line of the Roman frontier. The trees were alive with the sounds of rustling leaves and chirping birds. It was dark and shadowy in there, but sheltered and calming too, a complete contrast to the windy hilltop that I had recently left behind.

After a while the path opened out into the long clearing that I had spied from Croy, which reached right to the top of the hill. At its centre ran a deep depression – the ditch of the Antonine Wall. At first the frontier climbed gradually and steadily, but the higher it got, the steeper it got. As I marched along its southern edge, I felt my thighs begin to burn. I stopped to take a breather and made the mistake of looking up towards the brow of the hill.

The final metres of the climb were ridiculously steep. From where I was standing, it looked almost vertical, but I had to keep going. My strategy for dealing with an abrupt incline like this is to stare at the ground directly in front of me, never looking up to see how much further I have to go, and to keep walking, one step after another. So that is exactly what I did.

The climb seemed to last forever, although it only took a few minutes. Step after step after step, each one a little bit harder than the last. As I struggled on, I wondered how it had been possible to build the turf rampart on such a steep incline. Surely the sods of turf would have simply slid down the hill. Would it have been possible to lay the all-important stone base to support it? And how would a wooden palisade have been constructed on the top? I am no engineer, but it seems to me that this hill would have presented another enormous problem to the Wall's builders.

And then, suddenly, I was at the top. I could relax for a second, sit down on the edge of the Roman ditch, and look back at the route I had just taken. I was able to see for miles, back towards Croy Hill and beyond. From this viewpoint, it is possible to appreciate how well defended the Antonine Wall was when it was fully functioning – the fort of Bar Hill is not much further on, the fortlet and expansions of Croy are on the other side of the valley, with Croy Hill fort right over the peak of the hill. If the expansions were indeed a base for signal fires, then they would have been clearly visible from here, perhaps also from military installations further to the south.

The forts attached to the Antonine Wall, of which we have securely identified 16 (or 17 if you count Carriden), are much closer to one another than those constructed along Hadrian's Wall two decades previously. David Breeze estimates that around 6,000-7,000 troops were stationed along this frontier, while Hadrian's Wall (which was almost twice as long) had about 8,000. This could imply that the builders of the Antonine Wall saw the region as particularly troublesome and felt that such a heavy concentration of soldiers was required to rebuff attacks from the north.

Were Alexander Gordon and those other patriotic antiquarians who believed that the Romans saw the Caledonians as a truly formidable foe right all along? We cannot know for sure, but the design of the frontier suggests that it is a possibility.

This view that I was enjoying, looking eastwards from the lip of Bar Hill towards Croy, is one of the most photogenic on the entire Antonine Wall, and images of it appear regularly in newspapers and on websites to illustrate stories and reports about the ancient monument. That may be partly due to its undeniable beauty, but it is probably more thanks to the fact that someone has built a wall right along the base of the Roman ditch there.

The dilapidated dry-stone dyke, a redundant farm boundary that stands less than a foot high nowadays, is not particularly old, nineteenth-century or early twentieth-century most likely, but it obviously appeals to picture editors and bloggers who want a proper bit of wall to illustrate their story about a Roman Wall. I can only wonder how many readers assume that this line of fallen stones is a fragment of ancient Roman masonry, when in fact, it is nothing of the sort.

I took a couple of minutes to recover from my recent ascent. I knew that I would need it, as my climb was not completely over. Looming above me was Castle Hill, a small plug of rock that sits on top of Bar Hill – a hill on top of a hill. Low earthen terraces run around it like contour lines, the tell-tale signs of an Iron Age hillfort. Getting to the top of it meant one last push but I was determined to do it since I had read that the views from the summit were incredible, the best on the whole walk.

Taking a deep breath, I began the final push up the steep sides of Castle Hill. By then my ankles were aching, my thighs throbbing and my lungs burning with every laboured gasp. I followed a thin, snaking path that had been worn into the grass by the feet of countless previous visitors. It was exhausting, but as soon as I reached the top, I knew that it had been worth the effort. At the summit, where numerous patches of bare rock peeked out of the dry, tufty turf, I found a white concrete trig point, the perfect spot to stand (or lean) and take in the magnificent panorama that spread out around me.

To the east, I could see a sliver of the Firth of Forth, a silvery shimmer in the far distance. Standing proud on its northern shore was the tall chimney of the Longannet Power Station, which I had spotted over the water not long after setting off from Carriden. On a clear day it is possible to see the Firth of Clyde too, but try as I might, I could not make it out. I could, however, clearly identify the city of Glasgow towards which I was headed, its distant grey sprawl sprouting tiny tower blocks.

From this spot on the top of Castle Hill, I was able to see almost the entire route of the Roman frontier and pretty much the whole distance of my walk. It looked like a long, long way. I felt pleased with myself for what I had already achieved, but also daunted by what lay ahead. This would have been the best location for the Romans to stand and admire their work once the Antonine Wall was completed. What a sight it must have been, snaking from coast to coast, an enormous cross-country barrier that marked the edge of an empire.

The existence of an Iron Age hillfort so close to the Roman Wall poses interesting questions about the relationship between the invaders and the invaded. As is so often the case with this frontier, these are questions that mostly remain unanswered, as Castle Hill fort has never been excavated. There are around 1,700 prehistoric hillforts in Scotland, of all shapes and sizes, most of them south of the Antonine frontier. Some were even built after the Roman period, but we can be certain that the fort at Castle Hill predates the arrival of the Romans as one of its lower terraces is intersected by their Wall.

Although it has long been proposed that these hillforts were permanent settlements, with embankments and possibly wooden palisades erected to protect the homes inside, modern scholarship has started to question this idea. Were they in fact temporary structures used as a last resort in times of danger? Or sacred sites created for religious ritual?

There is an assumption that Castle Hill was abandoned by the Caledonians long before the Roman invasion, but there is no actual evidence for that. The romantic antiquarian in me likes to imagine that there could have been a dramatic siege here as the embattled locals resisted Roman subjugation. The plateau at the top is small, with limited space for a settlement, which seems to suggest to me some other purpose. Whatever it was, its elevated position, steep sides and constructed ramparts would have marked it out as a place of great significance and safety.

The back of the hillfort is now lost, eaten away by modern quarrying, but hopefully at some point the surviving remains will be properly studied and reveal more about the history of this unique place. Whether or not it was still in use when the Romans arrived, the rock itself still presented a huge obstacle to the builders of the Antonine Wall – the ditch had to skirt around its northern edge, while the Military Way took a detour round its southern side. Only 180 m further on from Castle Hill, at a point where the Roman road and ditch moved back into alignment, are the remains of Bar Hill fort, the highest (150 m above sea level) and one of the finest forts on the entire frontier.

There are so many things that make Bar Hill fort exceptional. The first is its location, with the expansive view northwards across the Kelvin River towards the Kilsyth Hills and the Campsie Fells, a mighty barrier that Sir George Macdonald whimsically described as 'an imposing natural bulwark to the "northern realms of ancient Caledon"'. Unlike my previous visit, when the increasingly heavy rain had discouraged me from lingering, I was able to relax and enjoy the place. The grass had recently been mown, leaving piles of yellow hay, and the numerous trees that were scattered across the site were on the turn, their leaves brushed with hints of autumn colour.

The Roman fort was built on an escarpment, its southern half sitting much higher than the northern half. On the other side of the Antonine Wall, this decline quickly accelerates into a steep drop down into the Forth-Clyde Valley far below, a perfect natural impediment to attacks from unconquered Caledonia. Uniquely, for reasons which are not clear, the fort is not attached to the rampart of the Antonine Wall but sits about 30 m to the south of it as a completely independent entity. William Roy amongst others presented this as evidence that the fort had been built by the first-century general Agricola long before the permanent frontier was conceived, but modern scholars now reject this idea due to lack of any solid evidence of pre-Antonine activity at the site.

At Bar Hill, for the first time on this journey from east to west, it was possible to see the foundations of Roman buildings as two of the interior structures of the fort were consolidated and left open to public view following excavations that took place between 1978 and 1982. The site has produced a wealth of evidence of daily life on the Roman frontier and yielded fascinating clues as to the kind of people who lived and worked there. It was one of the first forts on the Antonine Wall to be properly excavated back in the early years of the twentieth century, and the extensive collection of artefacts discovered during the dig (most of them now on display in the Hunterian Museum) is without comparison.

The fort has been renowned for centuries. It caught the attention of the eighteenth-century antiquarians, with Sir Robert Sibbald calling it 'a great Fort, which hath had large Entrenchments'. He also mentioned the 'ruins of Buildings' and the quantity of carved and inscribed stones that had been dug up in the vicinity, noting that they had ended up 'at the Houses of the Nobility and Gentry in the Neighbourhood'.

In the *Itinerarium Septentrionale* of 1726, Alexander Gordon called Bar Hill 'a very large and well-preserved Fort upon the Wall'. He was particularly struck by the conspicuous remains of the fort's interior structures: 'There is no Roman Fort, which I know of in Scotland, where the Vestiges of the old Buildings appear so plain as here'. His plan of it showed the interior of the fort busy with enigmatic lines that indicate the position of ruined walls and what looks like an area of cobbling. Even the more reserved John Horsley enthused about it, stating that it 'deserves a particular regard and description'. The reasons that he gave still hold true today: 'Its situation and strength, and the ruins of buildings within it are very remarkable'.

Sadly, even Bar Hill fort, way up on this isolated hillside, has suffered from stone robbing. When he visited in the 1750s, William Roy noted that, although it was still possible to see the ruins of its internal buildings, their 'vestiges, however, are not now so entire as represented in the *Itinerarium*'. The *Statistical Account* of 1791 stated that the site had recently been partially dug up, revealing several 'vaults' (probably hypocaust floors), while land improvements to the Gartshore estate on which the Roman fort then stood caused more damage in the early nineteenth century. Robert Stuart wrote in his 1845 book *Caledonia Romana* that 'many of [the fort's ruined walls] have only recently been removed, to supply material for building, or to serve the purpose of enclosing the adjacent fields'.

Fortunately, the Gartshore Estate and its Roman relics passed into the hands of the Whitelaw family in the late 1870s, and the new owners proved to be more enlightened than their predecessors. In the early years of the twentieth century, Mr Alexander Whitelaw of nearby Gartshore House, a grand Scots-Baronial mansion that was demolished in 1955, paid for Bar Hill fort to be excavated under the watchful eye of estate factor Alexander Park. The results were later written up by Sir George Macdonald.

The subsequent report was Macdonald's first publication on the Roman frontier. When work began at Bar Hill in November 1902, he was employed as a lecturer in Greek at the University of Glasgow, but by the time the project ended he was working at the Scottish Education Department. In fact, although he is now recognised as one of the greatest archaeologists of his day, he was never a professional.

Some of his theories about the Antonine Wall, particularly his fixation on the idea that many of its forts were built on Agricolan foundations, are now discounted, but his approach to excavating and studying the physical remains of the Roman frontier was pioneering and has had a significant impact on the way we perceive it today.

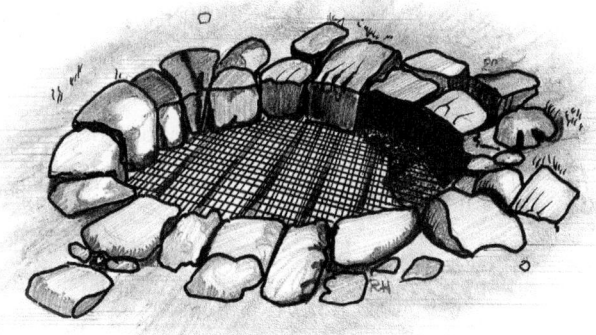

Well, Bar Hill

When the workmen arrived to excavate Bar Hill in 1902 it was a corn field. Their attention was drawn to a patch near the centre of the fort where the stubble was particularly green and the soil unusually moist. It was not long before the site began to reveal its secrets. On the very first morning of the dig an incredible discovery was made under that patch of green stubble – the fort's well, its damp and murky depths stuffed with all sorts of Roman artefacts.

I decided to begin my tour of Bar Hill at that same well. Today, it looks unexceptional – just a ring of stonework set into the grass with a modern grille over the top to prevent visitors from falling in. Glancing down into the dark, stone-lined hole, it was hard to get a sense of how important this well has been for our understanding of the history and architecture of the fort. When it was first excavated back in the winter of 1902, it proved to be an absolute treasure trove.

The initial discoveries were disappointing, consisting mostly of building stones and rubble 'piled,' as Sir George Macdonald later described it, 'in hopeless confusion'. At a depth of about 12 ft, however, a column capital appeared. After that the finds got increasingly exciting. On the third day of the job (22 November 1902), workmen pulled out five column capitals, some of them decorated with tasteful lozenge and stylised leaf patterns, as well as several column drums and a fragment of broken inscription. The deeper they got, the more complicated the job became. Two winches were set up, one to lower a workman into the narrow shaft, another to pull the heavier objects out of the well, while a running gear with two buckets was required to deal with the constantly rising water.

On 24 November, two further chunks of the broken inscription came to light alongside more column drums and pieces of oak. Two days later, an inscribed altar was discovered at a depth of 33 ft. Close by were a deer horn and a single coin which was found resting on the lip of one of the well's lining stones. Next, they discovered the remains of the pulley wheel and frame that were used to draw water from the well and the iron hoops that circled its wooden bucket. A large amphora lay at the very bottom of the shaft, resting on top of a layer of mud and gravel, which was found to contain more coins and smaller artefacts. The bottom of the well, 43 ft down, was then covered with concrete and the

Altar From Bar Hill

whole thing was allowed to fill up with water.

The fact that so many items had been thrown, apparently at random, into the well fired George Macdonald's imagination as he wrote up the results of the dig in *The Roman Forts on the Bar Hill* of 1906 (the plural 'forts' in the title referencing Macdonald's probably erroneous theory that Agricola had built a fort here six decades before the Antonine frontier was established). Was it evidence of a Caledonian attack, or were these objects discarded by the Romans themselves?

'Was the destruction wrought in sheer vindictiveness? Or was there a deliberate intention to try and render the fort untenable by a victorious foe?' he wondered. Nowadays, this jumble of broken detritus is taken as further evidence of a systematic demolition of the frontier by the retreating Romans. Everything of value was carried away to prevent it falling into the hands of the Caledonians, but anything too heavy or not worth the bother was simply buried or destroyed. In doing so, they effectively saved these artefacts, worthless to the departing army but so valuable to the modern archaeologist, for posterity.

The broken inscription and the yellow sandstone altar that loitered in the well's clammy depths for so many centuries both record the presence of the First Cohort of Baetasians at Bar Hill. The former was a record of their role in building the fort, the latter probably stood in the headquarters building in a room that was designated the regimental chapel. Originally from what is now the Netherlands, this unit of 500 infantry seems to have been based at Manchester before heading up to the Antonine Wall. Later on, as the frontier was abandoned, they relocated to Maryport near the western terminal of Hadrian's Wall, before ending up down at Reculver on the Kent coast in the fourth century.

A tombstone found at Bar Hill many centuries ago and kept at nearby Kilsyth Castle (now lost, thanks to the destruction of the castle by Cromwellian troops in 1650) was the first indication of the presence of the First Cohort of Hamians at the fort. Since then, two other inscriptions, as well as several arrowheads and fragments of bows have been unearthed. This unit of archers hailed from Hama in norther Syria. It is thought that they might have formed part of the invading force that arrived in Britain way back in AD 43 and, as far as we know, they were the only Roman bowmen to be sent to these islands.

The numerous refuse pits that were dotted all over the site of Bar Hill also turned out to be a metaphorical gold mine, containing not precious metals, but a diverse array of animal bones, pottery, a splendid wooden wagon wheel with an iron tyre and hundreds of beautifully crafted leather shoes. While shoes may at first seem slightly mundane, an everyday object that we take for granted, they reveal much about the people who used to live up on Bar Hill. Most importantly, the size of the shoes indicates that the Antonine Wall was not only the habitat of military men.

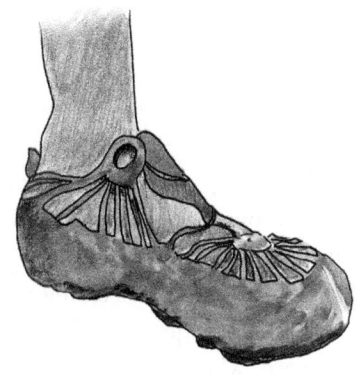

Roman Shoe From Bar Hill

The Roman shoes found on Bar Hill range from the simple and functional to the elaborate. Many of them were fashioned from a single piece of leather, often with hobnails on the soles. On some, the uppers were intricately punched to create glorious patterns, delicate frets of leather spreading out like the rays of the sun or rows of tiny perforations of various shapes and sizes that create a pleasing design. More than just practical, several of these shoes were obviously symbols of status, worn by Romans with an eye for the latest fashions.

The smaller shoes offer a valuable reminder that women and children lived on the Antonine Wall too. Some may have belonged to the wife and children of the camp commander, but their sheer quantity implies the existence of a (still undetected) settlement outside the fortress, inhabited by wives, partners and other civilians. These shoes certainly add a touch of humanity to the place – as well as echoing to the steady drum of marching hobnail boots and harsh cries of commanding officers, Bar Hill must have also rung with the laughter of children and the chatter of family life.

The Bar Hill well does not look like much today, but more interesting for modern visitors are the foundations of the headquarters building that surround it. As usual, the *principia* was situated right at the centre of the fort, in this case facing northwards. Its position reflected its role as the administrative hub of the fort, the place where meetings and assemblies took place, where the accounts were kept, and the orders posted. The fact that it was built of stone and not wood marked it out as a structure of some importance.

The layout of Bar Hill's headquarters is fairly typical. Visitors would enter it from the *via principalis*, the main street that led right across the middle of the fort from the east gate to the west. To get inside, they had to pass under a covered loggia, its sloping roof held up by the simple but unmistakeably classical columns discovered in the depths of the well. While a loggia was handy in Italy to provide shade from the scorching sunshine, we can imagine that here at Bar Hill it was more useful as a shelter from the rain. Having walked under this loggia and through the door of the headquarters, the visitors would find themselves in a spacious courtyard, where the now famous well was situated.

Next, they would step into a long indoor hall, with a raised dais in the south-west corner. In there, meetings took place, the commanding officer standing on the dais to give out orders for the day to the assembled troops. Behind this hall was a row of three smaller rooms, one of which contained a stone-lined strong box sunk into the ground.

This is where the administrative staff would have worked, the men who made sure that the soldiers got paid and that the granaries were kept full, the clerks and secretaries who looked after the daily running of this bustling military installation. The subterranean strong box (unfortunately no longer visible) held the substantial amounts of coinage needed for the soldiers' wages and other running costs. One of the rooms, probably the central one, was the regimental chapel, where the military standards were kept and offerings made, perhaps on that yellow sandstone altar found down in the well.

This once imposing building, originally the beating heart of Bar Hill fort, is now reduced to low foundations. Although the Edwardian archaeologists took great care in excavating it, they seemed less concerned with what happened to it after their job was done. As at Rough Castle and Castlecary, the ruins of the headquarters were left open to the elements for many years. When they were excavated again in the late 1970s, they were found to be severely degraded as a result. But at least it is possible to see the foundations here, giving us some impression of the *principia*'s size and layout.

Further down the escarpment, right next to the fort's northern rampart, were more foundations, this time the ruins of the soldiers' bath house. Communal bathing was a crucial part of life in the Roman world, not only a way to keep clean but a key element of the Roman way of life. To bathe was to be truly Roman. The bath house at Bar Hill was basic, consisting of a row of single rooms, each one offering a different bathing and cleansing experience, but it was a vital part of the fort, as important for morale as it was for personal hygiene.

Bathers entered from the west, walking first into a changing room where they could remove and store their clothes. They would then encounter a cold room, followed by a series of three heated rooms. The first, the *laconicum*, offered dry heat; the next, the *tepidarium*, warm steam; the last room the *caldarium*, was filled with hot steam. This *caldarium*, which resembled a modern Turkish bath, was at the eastern end of the range, right next to the roaring furnace that heated the entire building.

This small but perfectly formed bath house would have been the ideal place to relax after a long day on patrol, giving the soldiers a chance to socialise as they sweated out their aches and strains. Its warm rooms offered a brief escape from the Caledonian climate, particularly over the long winter months. A hypocaust floor, a later addition to the building, also meant toasty feet, even on the chilliest of days. On a cold, dark January evening, a visit to the baths must have been a much-anticipated treat.

Like the headquarters, the remains of Bar Hill bath house are scant (and a much better-preserved example survives further along the frontier), but a small section of the raised hypocaust survives, as do some of the foundations, all of them looking distinctly unkempt and fragile nowadays. At the eastern end of the building can be seen a prominent arched stone, the stoke hole for the furnace that heated the interior. Where the original Roman stonework has gone, concrete markers have been inserted to show the position of the lost foundations, and an information panel features a reconstruction of how the bath may have looked when it was in use.

Elsewhere can be found various other remnants of the ancient fortress. I spotted a channel of chunky stones near the north-eastern corner that formed a drain to allow excess water to escape under the fort's turf rampart and down the hill towards the frontier. In places, the subtle lines of the fort's platform and ditches can be seen. All of these, the low foundations and the time-worn earthworks, are just faint traces, hints of what used to be, but they are at least something tangible, a rare chance to see some Roman masonry on the Antonine frontier.

When asked to recommend the best site on the Antonine Wall, I often struggle to decide which is my favourite. Watling Lodge is the place to visit if you want to truly appreciate the scale of the ancient ditch, while Rough Castle, with its huge earthen banks, its gruesome *lilia* and the impressive stretch of rampart and ditch that runs next to it, is the best place to see how the various elements of the frontier worked in harmony. I love Castlecary fort too, with its overgrown jumble of Roman stones.

But when it comes to location and atmosphere, Bar Hill wins hands down. I have visited it many times, in all sorts of conditions, and it is never quite the same twice. In the sunshine, with the trees in full leaf, it is peaceful and bucolic. I once ventured up there in the depths of winter, not long after a light snowfall, to discover drifts of white that perfectly highlighted the dips and gullies of the ancient earthworks. I have even visited on a windy day when I was buffeted by gusts so strong that it felt at times like I might be lifted right off the ground.

To the Romans, this must have seemed like the ends of the earth. Today, although it is not that far from several towns and two cities, Bar Hill does retain an air of remoteness. And let's not forget the amazing view. I don't think I could ever get bored of that wide panorama, the Firth of Forth to the east, Glasgow to the west, over the valley to the hulking ridge of the Kilsyth Hills, although there were probably plenty of Roman auxiliaries who felt differently after a few months or years stationed there.

It may not have the best-preserved Roman buildings on the Wall – the aforementioned bath house further along the route wins that accolade – or even the most prominent ditches and ramparts, but as a whole, Bar Hill has something special about it. If you can only visit one site on the Antonine Wall, this is undoubtedly the one that I would recommend.

After a short sit down and a snack to prepare me for the final leg of my walk, I grudgingly pulled myself up and set off down the hillside. I was sad to leave Bar Hill, not just because I love it so much, but also because I knew that I was now facing a long, slow descent towards the village of Twechar.

Every step sent a shooting pain through my toes, up my ankles to my knees.

At the bottom of the hill I turned right, passing the Twechar Miners Welfare & Social Club, one of the last reminders of an industry that flourished here from the 1860s right up until 1968, when the last of the local coal mines was closed. Generations of Twechar's mining families were housed in lines of austere cottages known as the Barrhill Rows. Each had two rooms, paraffin lamps and no internal sanitation. Following years of petitioning from the residents, these were replaced with more comfortable homes, built by the mining company Baird & Co. in the 1920s. Council houses were built in the later twentieth century, and the Barrhill Rows and the 1920s houses, like the miners, are now largely gone.

As I got to the bottom of the hill I met yet again the Forth & Clyde Canal which was used for many years to transport the coal dug up around here. Beside it stood a shiny new billboard advertising the latest housing development to be constructed at Twechar, all part of a regeneration programme that aims to breathe life back into a region that has struggled since the closure of the mines. 'Roman Fields', they have called it, although the bland, boxy houses display no obvious references to the classical world.

From there, the Antonine Wall headed on westwards, taking a similar route to that of the modern road, the B8023. For a while, the canal towpath runs along the side of the road before the two diverge at the old farmhouse of Shirva. The first time I walked the Wall, my plan had been to carry on along the side of the road, thus staying as close to the Roman frontier as possible, but I quickly discovered that there was no pavement and no verges, but lots of fast traffic, so after a minute or two I turned back and continued alongside the canal. It leads in same direction as the Wall but lies some distance to the south of it. In the end, it did not matter that I had to leave the course of the frontier, since there is no visible evidence of it in these parts.

It was in the vicinity of Shirva that several important discoveries were made in the early 1700s. As was often the case in the days before organised archaeology, they were made by happy accident rather than by design, all thanks to the plough. The first, which took place in 1726, was a cache of inscribed Roman stones that caught the eye of the locals. Word of the finds soon spread to the antiquarian community. Alexander Gordon, who was not too far away at the time, working on a survey for a canal between the Forth and Clyde estuaries (his enthusiasm for the plan was gently mocked by Clerk, but, as we now know, Gordon was simply ahead of his time) was one of the first on the scene.

In a letter to his patron Sir John Clerk dated 24 September 1726, Gordon described what he believed to be a 'hollow mausoleum' that contained a number of carved and inscribed Roman stones. It had been uncovered about six weeks before in the 'fossa' (ditch) of the Antonine Wall. In the same letter, Gordon outlined his plans to return with the local landowner, one 'Mr Calder of Shervey', to carefully excavate the area and make a drawing of the finds.

The discovery of these antiquities aroused such excitement that it was even reported on 3 October in one of Scotland's most widely-read newspapers, *The Caledonian Mercury*, which described them as 'Evidences of the Roman Grandeur'. And while Gordon had immediately written to enthusiastic collector Clerk to report the finds, these stones eventually made their way to the ever-growing collection of ancient artefacts at the University of Glasgow. Today, they can be viewed, along with so many other objects found along the Antonine Wall, in the university's Hunterian Museum.

Gordon's plans to dig at Shirva in 1726 appear to have remained unrealised, but five years later the same spot yielded more carved panels as well as an unusual stone structure. That time Gordon was not able to see it in person, but he did get his hands on an eye-witness account and sketch made by the local church minister, James Robe. This account told of a long stone corridor with a rounded end and more carvings built into its walls, which was unearthed in the ditch of the Antonine Wall by 'some illiterate Country People digging Stones for a Park-Wall'.

Robe described the presence of pillars and empty pedestals as well as more Roman sculptures. Gordon reproduced the drawing of it in his 1732 *Additions and Corrections...to the Itineriarum Septentrionale*, a meagre and insubstantial volume that was hurriedly produced by its author to draw attention away from the imminent publication of John Horsley's far superior *Britannia Romana*. As its location is now lost (and we can assume the ancient structure destroyed) modern scholars are forced to rely on the antiquarian's questionable draughtsmanship skills as they attempt to deduce the true nature of this puzzling site.

Quite reasonably, given that it was built from Roman masonry and contained a number of Roman tombstones and assorted other classical carvings, Gordon and his contemporaries concluded that it was a 'Roman sepulchre' or 'Roman Tumulus'. Modern archaeologists, on the other hand, believe that it was a post-Roman structure known as a souterrain (from the French *sous terrain*, meaning 'under the ground'). The exact purpose of these subterranean tunnels, which are found across Scotland, has been much debated over the years. It used to be said that they were underground refuges used in times of danger, but it is now proposed that they could have been storerooms.

We can be certain that this souterrain (if that is what it was) was constructed after the Romans abandoned the Antonine Wall as it appears to have been constructed from recycled Roman masonry. Another example of this reuse of Roman stone to build a souterrain can be found at Crichton Mains, near to the village of Pathhead to the southeast of Edinburgh. There, the walls of the underground passage contain many Roman building blocks with their distinctive lozenge decoration, while a carving of a Pegasus is visible on the underside of one of the bulky lintel stones. Although the provenance of the dressed stones at Crichton is unknown, it can be assumed that those at Shirva were plundered from the ruins of Bar Hill or from Auchendavy further to the west.

The carved and inscribed stones found at Shirva are quite a collection. As many of them are tombstones or appear to come from funeral monuments, it seems likely that there must have been an (as yet undiscovered) Roman cemetery not far away. The first haul, found in 1726, included two inscribed gravestones. One bears the name of a boy called Salamanes, who, the inscription tells us, died at only 15 years of age. The stone was erected by another Salamanes, presumably the boy's father. No mention is made of a military rank, which implies that Salamanes senior, who probably hailed from the Middle East, was a civilian rather than a soldier.

Another of the Shirva stones is the grave marker of a woman named Verecunda. Like the memorial to Salamanes, it sports a carved pediment with a wreath at its centre. Only broken fragments of Verecunda's stone were found, but the simple inscription survives: *'D.M. VERECUNDAE'*, 'to the spirits of the dead and to Verecunda'. Although no more details are given, the fact that only her first name is included means that she may have been a slave, or a Caledonian who had assumed a Roman name.

The two most substantial Roman stones to be found at Shirva appeared in 1731, and although they bear no inscriptions, both feature similar carved figures, leading to speculation they were made as a pair to decorate a funeral monument. Due to extensive damage, the sex of the figures is no longer clear. While Gordon believed them both to be male, Lawrence Keppie proposed in his invaluable 1998 publication *Roman Inscribed and Sculptured Stones in Hunterian Museum* that they are in fact two women (or two carvings of the same woman) a theory that I am happy to accept.

Both figures are shown reclining, one on a couch and the other on a cart that is being pulled by mules. The larger of the two also features an odd little creature which seems to be perching on her legs. It looks like a tiny dog, perhaps the beloved companion of this unnamed woman, who must have been something of a VIP, maybe the wife of a prefect or the commandant of Bar Hill fort.

The carving on these two stones seems unsophisticated to modern eyes. As Keppie politely puts it, 'the commission has not been well executed'. The figures are confused, with strangely twisted bodies, huge heads and tiny hands, the proportions all over the place. The cart on one stone seems to have wheels at only one end, and the dog (or whatever it may be) on the other looks something like a child's drawing of their favourite pet.

The unconventional aesthetics of these sculptures certainly confused the eighteenth-century antiquarians, who had after all been brought up to admire the unsurpassed civilisation of ancient Rome and wonder at the unrivalled skill of its artists. To them, these carvings simply seemed bad. Gordon noticed the huge variation in the quality of the Shirva stones, describing some of them as 'much inferior in beauty'.

This led him to believe that the more refined sculptures found along the Roman frontier must date from the Antonine period when Roman civilisation when the Empire was in decline. In fact, such carvings, all of them produced in the mid-second century, only reveal that the sculptors working on the edge of the Roman world were unaware of the fundamentals of classical sculpture practised by their Continental counterparts and were more familiar with the Celtic-inspired Romano-British styles found in these border lands.

It is a fair distance from Shirva to Kirkintilloch, my final destination for the day, a good hour of walking at my steady pace. There are no signs of the Antonine Wall to see along the way, but it was a pleasant journey along the towpath all the same, particularly at that time of year when the trees which lined the waterway were turning gold, orange and russet, their bright leaves reflected in the still waters of the canal. This turned out to be one of the busiest parts of my route, with cyclists speeding past me from time to time, even the odd walker heading in the opposite direction, back towards Twechar.

Along the way I passed by the Roman fort of Auchendavy. Now occupied by a farmhouse and modern houses built on the site of an old steading, it is bisected by the Kirkintilloch to Kilsyth road and sits near to the canal although, thanks to a high, overgrown embankment, it is impossible to view it from the towpath.

The remains of the fort are now almost non-existent, or at least not visible above ground. Three centuries ago, the fort's triple ditches were unmistakable. William Maitland described how they still surrounded a little cluster of houses, 'in the walls of which are divers [sic] Roman stones without inscriptions'. He had heard of several ancient coins that had been unearthed there, although he had no idea of where they had ended up. According to the Revd John Skinner, an Anglican vicar from Somerset who walked the Antonine Wall over five days in September 1825, it was still then possible to see evidence of the rampart and the 'deep moat' of the fort's ditches. As is so often the case, these remains were later destroyed in the name of agriculture, filled in and levelled to make way for crops.

The towpath along which I was travelling ran right over the southern defences of Auchendavy fort. As the canal was being built in 1771, an ancient pit was found that contained five Roman altars (four complete, one broken), a stone bust, and two iron mallets. The four complete altars (and presumably the broken one too) were all dedicated by the same man, one Marcus Cocceius Firmus, centurion of the Second Legion. Either extremely devout or just hedging his bets, he had venerated a startling number of deities, including Hercules, Mars, Minerva, Victory, Jupiter and Diana. Most intriguing is his altar dedicated to the *Genio Terrae Britannicae*, the spirit of the Land of Britain, a mysterious local divinity that is, as far as I know, otherwise unattested.

The appearance of houses amongst the trees on the south bank of the canal indicated that I was approaching the town of Kirkintilloch, but it was a while before I arrived at a bridge that led me over the water and towards the town centre. Before long I reached the end of my route, the Auld Kirk Museum which, as its name suggests, is housed in an old church. It also happens to stand on top of the line of the Antonine Wall.

The first time I had arrived there I had been soaked to the skin, freezing cold and feeling very sorry for myself. I then discovered that the museum, which I had heard contained some artefacts from the Antonine Wall, was temporarily closed for the installation of a new exhibit. Instead, I had taken cover from the endless rain in the nearby William Patrick Library, where I was able to dry off, warm myself up with a hot drink and call a taxi to take me to the hotel right outside the town where I was spending the night.

This time the museum was closed again, along with pretty much every other public building in Scotland, due to the pandemic. In the grounds, however, it was possible to see one reminder of the ancient frontier in the form of some steps leading up to the museum which bore the words 'LINE OF THE ANTONINE WALL AD 140'.

To the side of these stood a large dark granite panel emblazoned with an inscription, each letter highlighted in shining gold: 'ROMAN EMPIRE NORTHERN FRONTIER'. Also recorded on the same panel was the Antonine Wall's 2008 inscription on the list of UNESCO World Heritage Sites, while at is centre was an image of a boar, the emblem of the Twentieth Legion that appears on many of the distance slabs found along the frontier. The museum would have to wait for now, but this was the ideal place to finish the day's walk.

And what a walk it had been. Covering 12 miles or so, I had seen some of the Antonine Wall's best archaeology – long lengths of the ancient ditch, some of it carved into solid bedrock, the forts at Castlecary and Bar Hill, as well as the first visible Roman buildings on the route. I had scaled the ramparts of an Iron Age fort and enjoyed the wonderful scenery along the way. It had been more arduous than my previous treks, with its muddy path and two sizeable hills to climb and then descend, and my aching calves and stinging feet were a vivid reminder of that.

It had also been a lonely walk. There were no towns on the way, no cafés to stop off for lunch and precious few humans around, apart from the dog walkers who seemed to be the only other people making use of the open spaces along the Roman frontier.

The following day I was up early and soon back at the Forth & Clyde Canal, following it westwards as I walked the last section of the Antonine Wall. I got off to a great start, with a pleasant stroll in the autumn sunshine followed by some exciting discoveries and an unexpected meeting with someone who knew the Wall extremely well, but by lunchtime the rain had started yet again.

The second half of the walk was another complete washout. By the time I arrived at the western end of the frontier, I was wet through and chilled to the bone, sick and tired of the Scottish weather. The day after, just as I was boarding the train at Glasgow to head back to London, new restrictions were put in place as the virus ran out of control. Members of the public were advised to travel only if absolutely necessary. Scotland once more went into a partial shutdown.

Back at home, I began to write up my experiences and make plans to get back as soon as possible, in the hope that I could walk the western third of the frontier in more pleasant conditions. It would be a long wait – in the end, it was almost an entire year before I could return to the Antonine Wall.

———

Chapter Six

KIRKINTILLOCH TO BEARSDEN

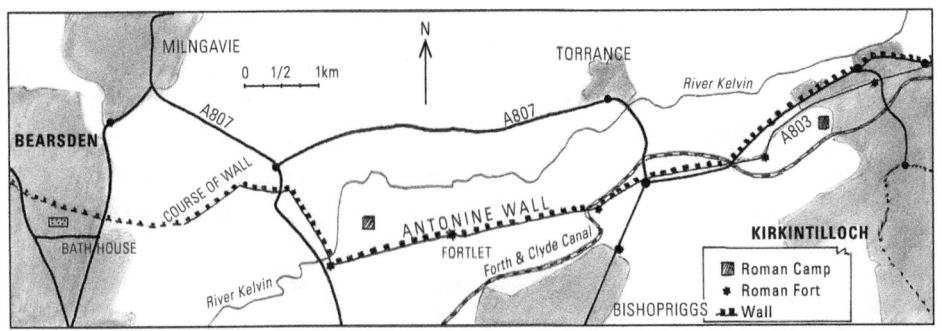

Antonine Wall From Kirkintilloch To Bearsden

It was another eleven months before I found myself back in Scotland and back on the Antonine Wall. I had hoped to complete the final leg of the journey in the summer, but more restrictions and various other impediments had forced me to keep pushing back the date until suddenly it was September. Walking so late in the year felt risky, but I realised that it was now or never, and booked myself another trip to Scotland.

The day before I set off, I was delighted to be invited for lunch in Glasgow by Professor Lawrence Keppie, a man who knows the Antonine Wall better than anyone else alive. He has spent a lifetime excavating and studying the Roman frontier and has published many books and papers on the subject, exploring not only its ancient history but also the more recent antiquarian analysis of its monumental remains.

Having studied classics at the University of Glasgow and Roman history and archaeology at Oxford and then Rome, Professor Keppie worked first as an archaeologist under the formidable Professor Anne Robertson. In 1972, he became a research assistant at the Hunterian Museum at the University of Glasgow where he would work for over 30 years, later becoming a senior curator and finally Professor of Roman History and Archaeology.

Although now officially retired, he continues to produce books and articles about all aspects of the ancient world at an enviable rate. Amongst others, he has written an extremely popular book on the Roman army as well as a helpful guide to decoding Roman inscriptions. He has edited recent editions of the invaluable Antonine Wall *Handbook*, updating and rewriting Anne Robertson's original text to such an extent that I suspect the latest volumes are more Keppie than Robertson.

As well as being great company, Professor Keppie has an incredible memory. He is able to recall names, dates and facts about the ancient history of the Antonine Wall and about his own long and distinguished career with startling ease. And while some academics can be protective of their work, he is always happy to share his ideas and encourage others to pursue their own avenues of research.

He chose an Italian restaurant in central Glasgow for our meeting which seemed appropriate – no ancient Roman delicacies like stuffed dormice or fermented fish gut sauce on the menu, but at least we were in the right part of the world. He was interested to hear about the progress of my walks, and I was keen to find out more about his long relationship with Scotland's Roman Wall.

We began by discussing the inscribed stone that Gaele had found in her garden in Nether Kinneil. It turned out that the stone had made quite a journey since I last saw it. I had sent a photograph of it to Dr Fraser Hunter at the National Museum of Scotland, who thought it merited further investigation. He organised for Falkirk archaeologist Geoff Bailey to collect it, and he then showed it to Professor Keppie, who is an expert on Scotland's Roman inscriptions.

In the end, Professor Keppie was unable to declare it a lost Roman treasure. While he agreed that there were signs of inscribed letters on the front of the stone, their poor state of preservation made it impossible to say for sure that they were carved by Roman hands. His verdict was disappointing but not entirely unexpected. The stone was now back with Gaele, who later told me that rather than being disappointed, she was pleasantly surprised that a lump of sandstone from her garden had aroused so much scholarly interest.

Next, I quizzed Professor Keppie about his own experiences of the Antonine Wall. He seemed reluctant to name a favourite site on the frontier but revealed that his first encounter with the monument was at Bar Hill fort, up on that hillside with the spectacular views along the Forth-Clyde Valley. He was only 12 at the time and had cycled six miles from his childhood home near Coatbridge. It took him three attempts to locate the fort. Back in those days there was no signposting and the hilltop was heavily wooded. The resident farmer pointed him to a path leading up to the well, which was then the only visible feature.

Bar Hill fort obviously made an impression on him for that first visit was the beginning of a lifelong relationship with the Roman frontier. Years later he would end up excavating the fort and co-authoring a book about the finds that were made there. Although he has dug at various places along the Wall and many others across Scotland, like me, he clearly has a special affection for that site.

I could talk all day about the Antonine Wall with Professor Keppie, who has a seemingly endless supply of anecdotes on the subject, but all too soon our time together came to an end. He gave me a few useful pointers for my impending journey, suggesting things to look out for as I walked before we went our separate ways. As I left the restaurant, I was full of anticipation for the journey ahead, inspired by the professor's fascinating stories, encouraged by the decent weather forecast and finally feeling that the end of my walk was in sight.

The next morning, I was yet again climbing the steps to Kirkintilloch's Auld Kirk Museum, past the granite memorial to the Antonine Wall with its inscribed boar. I had a shiny new copy of the Robertson and Keppie *Handbook* in my pocket, and I was looking forward to this second, hopefully drier attempt to reach Old Kilpatrick, the Roman frontier's western terminus. This time, the Auld Kirk was open. In fact, since it was ten in the morning, it had just opened its doors. I was the first visitor of the day.

True to its name, the Auld Kirk is one of the oldest buildings in the town. It was built in 1644 on the site of a fourteenth-century chapel dedicated to St Mary and was in use right up to the early twentieth century. After a new church was built not far away, the Auld Kirk fell into disrepair, but it was later purchased by the local council and opened as a museum over 60 years ago.

The kirk's exterior is rather dour, lifted only by the high arched window that almost fills the crow-stepped gable above its main entrance. Inside, however, it is full of colour and interest, its displays featuring a vast array of objects from the local area, artefacts both ancient and modern. The small but interesting Roman collection is right opposite the front door. Due to the tight interior of the Auld Kirk, the Roman antiquities jostle for space with other, more recent artefacts, with the result that a stone column from the *principia* of Bar Hill fort can be found standing serenely next to a bright red telephone box.

Auld Kirk Museum, Kirkintilloch

There are other items in the museum from Bar Hill, including Roman pottery, metalwork, jewellery, pieces from a board game and the leather sole of a shoe, all fascinating remnants of life on the Antonine Wall. Some disconcerting Roman medical implements can also be seen, namely a spatula and a tool known as a *ligula*, a bronze rod with a point at one end and an angled disk at the other that could be used for prodding and poking a patient in various ways.

I was surprised to spot a little Roman distance slab, featuring a dedication to the Twentieth Legion, a record of their construction of three miles and 3,304 ft of the frontier. On closer inspection, it turned out to be a very convincing plaster cast of the original at the Hunterian Museum, which was found about a mile to the east of Kirkintilloch back in 1789, buried face down in the Antonine Wall's ditch. The smallest distance marker that has so far been found, it features a carved decoration that Edwardian scholar Alexander Gibb imaginatively described as 'the figure of a lusty boar, making for a bush or tree to the right hand; emblematic no doubt of the Caledonian forest'.

Right behind the Auld Kirk is Peel Park. The Roman frontier cuts through the middle of it, so that was my next port of call. The name of the park recalls one aspect of its long history – 'peel' is the Scots word for the ground enclosed by a fence of stakes. Slap bang in the middle of Peel Park can be found the remains of one such enclosure, a high rectangular mound that was originally surmounted by a medieval castle.

Built by the Comyn family in the late twelfth or early thirteenth century, Kirkintilloch Castle consisted of a stone tower protected by ditches and a high wall. Although its modern name suggests a wooden palisade, Victorian excavations revealed that the castle was built of stone, at least in its later incarnations. Because of its location so close to Stirling, the fortress at Kirkintilloch played a major role in the Wars of Independence, when it was held by the English as they tried to supress the Scottish fight for autonomy. After the fall of the Comyns, Kirkintilloch was given by Robert the Bruce to his ally Malcolm Fleming. By then, however, the castle already appears to have been abandoned.

Given the regular spacing between the Antonine Wall's forts, eighteenth-century antiquarians calculated that there should have been one around here somewhere. The fact that there was a huge earthen platform in what is now Peel Park naturally led them to incorrectly assume that this was it. Although his writings suggest that he never made it this far west, preferring to explore the vestiges of the Antonine Wall closer to his country house at Kipps near Torphichen, Sir Robert Sibbald recorded the remains of a 'great Fort' here, 'of which the Ruins yet appear with the Vestige of a Ditch and Rampier'. Alexander Gordon nominated the mound of the Peel a Roman fort, although he seemed perplexed that he could find no reports of antiquities or inscriptions unearthed there.

Even the more diligent John Horsley got it wrong, describing the Peel as a Roman fort that was 'small but strong, and the best preserved of any'. To be fair to the antiquarians, the fact that the visible remains of the medieval castle contained recycled Roman stones may have contributed to the confusion. In the twentieth century, however, opinion started to change, and doubts began to surface regarding the Roman origins of the Peel. The renowned English archaeologist F J Haverfield even went as far as to say that there was no evidence of Roman activity there at all. Since then, excavations have revealed some Roman hearths, pottery and the postholes of narrow wooden buildings in the vicinity, items that all indicate the presence of Roman soldiers.

Most significantly, a 1979 dig in a car park on the south side of the Peel Park uncovered a long section of Roman ditch running east to west. Down in its depths were found leather shoes, pottery and a javelin head. Although the finds were limited, they confirmed beyond reasonable doubt that, while the huge mass of earth known as the Peel was not a Roman fort, there was indeed one here, all around the medieval mound in fact, the rediscovered ditch originally running along its southern edge.

Even early on a fresh September morning, Peel Park was a lively place, busy with dog walkers and families. Hidden beneath some fallen leaves I found a metal plate sunk into the ground by the path which marked the location of the Antonine Wall, its text flanked by two *peltae*, light Roman shields that were often carved as decorative elements on the frontier's distance sculptures.

More striking was a recent addition to the park – a children's playground. On a sign above its entrance were etched the words 'Peel Park Roman Fort'. Big red Roman-style shields were carved into the supporting columns. With its tall wooden towers and battlements, it looked more like a medieval castle than a Roman fort to me, but the energetic kids enjoying the various activities on offer inside did not seem to mind such glaring anachronisms.

The next part of my journey led me along the northern bank of the Forth & Clyde Canal out of Kirkintilloch as I continued towards the Antonine Wall's western end. I was expecting to see a few fragments of the Roman frontier on my way, even the masonry walls of a Roman building, but I knew that there was nothing as spectacular as the enormous ditch at Watling Lodge on this part of the journey; there would not be any long, almost uninterrupted stretches like the one between Dullatur and Bar Hill.

There are multiple reasons why the western end of the Antonine Wall is less well-preserved. The rapid growth of Glasgow in the nineteenth and twentieth centuries is one, the construction of the city's suburbs wiping out many archaeological remains. But even before that, agriculture played a major role in the destruction of the monument. As we saw at Nether Kinneil, farmers had no qualms about ploughing up or filling in ancient earthworks that got in the way of their labours.

My walk along the canal bank gave me time to ponder how attitudes towards historic monuments have changed over the centuries. Today, most of us take it for granted that preserving ancient relics is a good thing and that destroying them is most definitely bad. We do all that we can to protect these tangible reminders of our past, scheduling them, listing them, restoring them, putting fences around them. In short, we cherish and value them.

This was not always the case. Even though the eighteenth century witnessed the birth of archaeology and was a time of intense scholarly interest in the Antonine Wall and Scotland's antiquities in general, it is possible to identify Scots of that period who were positively joyful at the loss of the nation's Roman remains.

The most notable example of this is surely the Reverend William Nimmo. As already mentioned, he was a church minister at Bothkennar, by Camelon. His 1777 *General History of Stirlingshire* includes an entire chapter dedicated to a history and survey of 'The Wall of Antoninus, or Graham's Dike' as well as a map which shows the course of the frontier from Inveravon in the east to Summerston in the west. Unlike other eighteenth-century antiquarians such as Sibbald and Clerk, however, Nimmo displayed a marked dislike for the Romans and revealed himself to be completely underwhelmed with the Wall that they had built in Scotland.

'The work we have been surveying seems rather to have been originally designed as a boundary to the Roman dominion, than a defence against enemies,' he wrote dismissively. 'Unless it was always well guarded with troops, it must have been but a very feeble frontier'. Nimmo's allegiances lay with the courageous Caledonians and his language evoked the 'gathered heap' of Ossian (or rather James Macpherson) when he declared:

> *If the vanity of the Romans led them at first to imagine, that, by castles of mud, and walls of turf, they could confine the Caledonians as within another island, they were afterwards taught, by frequent experience, how much they had been mistaken.*

While similarly patriotic antiquarians such as Alexander Gordon lauded the Caledonians while also revering the remains of ancient Rome in Scotland as physical evidence of their fearless stand against conquest, Nimmo went as far as to celebrate the destruction of the Roman frontier:

> *The wall of Antoninus is now intirely demolished in many places, and the ground plowed where it stood; and, as the canal, which generally runs parallel to it, will no doubt tend to the improvement of the adjacent fields, it is probable that, twenty years hence, few remains of it will be visible: The grounds still occupied by it will be more usefully employed; and, instead of those memorials of ambition and war, succeeding generations will behold green fields and plentiful harvests, the produce of peace and industry.*

While his hope for a future filled with harmony and prosperity is undoubtedly laudable, Nimmo's idea that the erasure of Scotland's Roman heritage was something to be applauded seems odd to modern readers, particularly coming from an antiquarian. It is an attitude born, I suppose, from a healthy admiration of progress typical of the Enlightenment, combined with a patriotic disdain for anyone who would dare to attempt an invasion of indomitable Caledonia.

And while we can assume that most of the damage done to the Antonine Wall in centuries past was a result of ignorance and indifference rather than purposeful destruction, Nimmo was not alone in celebrating its loss. A similar sentiment is expressed in the anonymous *Traveller's Guide or, a Topographical Description of Scotland* of 1798, which records the loss of the Antonine Wall to the plough: 'Here we see the Caledonian trampling upon the ruins of Roman ambition, and unfettered commerce occupying the seat of imperious usurpation'.

Although William Roy found 'the tract of the wall... being every where visible' in these parts when he surveyed it in 1755, the walk from Kirkintilloch to my next stop at Cadder, a distance of just under four miles, confirmed that the destruction of the ancient frontier has been extensive in the years since.

As you leave Kirkintilloch, the line of the Antonine Wall runs westwards at a decent distance to the north of the towpath, close to the A803. Both modern road and Roman frontier cross the canal next to an old pub, originally built as a rest stop for the horses that pulled the barges, then the Wall meets the water again about 1.5 miles further on as the canal takes a sharp 90-degree turn to the south. Even when the walking route leads away from the Roman frontier, you are not missing anything as there are no remains of it to be seen above ground along here.

It is a pleasant stroll, nevertheless. I had the path to myself, bar the odd cyclist tearing past and a couple of other walkers. A smiley passer-by who was heading in the other direction alerted me to the presence of a heron that was sitting on the far bank, still as a statue, next to a discarded wheelie bin. I stopped to watch for a while. It seemed utterly indifferent, motionless and staring into space, until suddenly, with a tiny bob, it spread its long wings and lifted into flight, quickly disappearing over the trees.

Where the canal veered south, I could see on the other side of the water, nestled into the corner of the turn, the site of another Antonine Wall fort, known today as Cadder. Its presence evaded the notice of early antiquarians such as Robert Sibbald and Alexander Gordon, but John Horsley noticed 'some faint appearances of remains... near Calder church' and correctly deduced that this was the location of a fort.

Its remains must have been negligible, as the cartographer William Roy failed to include it in his (generally accurate) map of the Antonine Wall. Some evidence of a fort appeared in 1773, when workmen building the canal found the top of a Roman altar and some quern stones used for grinding grain. More ancient artefacts were turned up when the neighbouring manse's garden was landscaped in 1852, but it was only in 1929 that large-scale excavations took place.

Details of the discoveries made over the following three digging seasons, all funded by the Glasgow Archaeological Society, were released in 1933 by director of excavations John Clarke. Carefully folded inside the back cover of the published report can be found a plan of the site, drawn by Glasgow chartered surveyor Ernest Webster, printed on thin, translucent paper. It shows how the canal (surely by pure coincidence?) skirted right round the northern and western ramparts of the fort, destroying the ditch of the Antonine Wall but leaving the fort itself completely intact.

Like other early archaeologists, Clarke was extremely fired up by the idea that this might have been one of the locations originally fortified by Agricola as mentioned by Tacitus, and spent much of his report presenting evidence for this. Today, however, the deeper layers of activity that he detected are thought to date from the early Antonine occupation, perhaps belonging to a temporary camp used during the construction of the Antonine Wall.

Inside the fort's 4.7 m thick turf ramparts the archaeologists discovered the degraded remains of the fort's internal buildings, including the usual *principia* at the centre with stone granaries to the north and south of it, a wooden commandant's house with a small hypocaust floor, a bath house and several timber barrack blocks. The poor state of the structures was put down to the site being pilfered for stone during the building of the canal. Clarke himself noted that 'stones bearing obvious marks of Roman craftsmanship can be seen by the hundred among the masonry along the Canal side'.

Worse was to come in the 1940s, when, in a shocking act of vandalism, all of the ancient remains were destroyed as the plateau on which the fort stood was turned into a sand quarry. Although the location of the Roman fort still exists, the fort itself has been skimmed right off the top, its ancient foundations ripped up and dumped who knows where. If he had lived to see it, the Reverend William Nimmo would no doubt have been thrilled.

Round the bend and past the site of the lost Roman fort, I soon arrived at Cadder Church. There has been a place of worship there since at least the twelfth century. The current building, in the Neo-Gothic style, was completed in 1829. I popped into its graveyard to take a quick look at the little watchhouse and 'mortsafe', a heavy metal box that was placed over a grave for a few days after burial, both of them intended to prevent the 'bodysnatching' that was going on back at Seabegs Wood in the 1820s.

At this point, the recommended route is to continue in a south-westerly direction along the canal until you arrive at Balmore Road which leads back up to the Antonine Wall. It is quite a detour and inevitably involves missing out a long section of the ancient frontier. The first time I made this journey, back in the October of the previous year, I left the canal and entered a golf course. While both the church and neighbouring mansion and estate were formerly known as 'Calder', then more recently 'Cadder', the house and estate were confusingly renamed 'Cawder' when they were turned into a golf club in the early twentieth century.

I should point out that Cawder Golf Club is not generally open to the public (it is a health and safety thing, all those flying golf balls presenting an obvious risk to wandering visitors) but having done my research, I knew that there were Roman antiquities to see on the property. Keen to look, I contacted the club's general manager, Kevin McAleer, who immediately invited me to meet him at the clubhouse to talk about the Antonine Wall and inspect its remains as they run across the grounds.

The walk up the long, meandering driveway was wonderful, a refreshing change from a canal towpath. Signs of nineteenth-century landscaping were evident. Huge old trees were dotted around the course's fairways and a stream weaved its way through the greens and bunkers, while a belt of woodland ran around the whole place, effectively sheltering it from the outside world. I arrived early in the morning, but the course was already packed with players who were taking advantage of the fleeting early autumn sunshine. The drive led me on past a distinctive doocot, its tall round tower surmounted by a conical roof with deep overhanging eaves.

When the clubhouse finally came into view, it made quite an impression. This was the mansion now called Cawder House, its long façade fashioned from a delicious honey-coloured sandstone. Parts of it date back to the seventeenth century. I had arranged to meet Kevin in his office, a cosy, windowless room on the ground floor of the house. With its desks, computers, piles of papers and constantly ringing phones, it was clearly the nerve centre of a busy operation. After warmly welcoming me to Cawder, Kevin announced that he had invited Jim Mearns to our meeting. Jim is a leading member of the Glasgow Archaeological Society who has dug on the Antonine Wall and published his research on the Cawder section of the Roman frontier. He also happens to be a member of the golf club. Our paths had never crossed so I was excited to get the opportunity to meet him and find out more about his experiences on the Wall.

While we waited for Jim to arrive, Kevin sent me through a door in the corner of the office which led me into the juniors' locker room. It was in there, built into the wall of the old house, that I found the first of Cawder's Roman relics – a building stone of the Second Legion. It is currently protected by a sheet of shiny glass, which reflects the artificial light in the locker room, making it difficult to see and impossible to photograph. I could, nonetheless, make out a wreath held up by two winged *genii*, hovering figures with spindly legs something like cupids, the wreath framing a simple inscription:

LEG
II
AUG
FEC

This is an abbreviation of *Legio II Augusta fecit*, 'the second Legion Augusta made this'. The stone has been known to antiquarians for centuries. It is mentioned as far back as the early 1600s, around the time that it first came into the hands of the Stirlings of Keir, the family who then owned the estate. When Alexander Gordon visited in the early 1720s, he saw it built into an external wall in a courtyard. He admired both the 'beautifully cut' inscription and the opulent wreath. John Horlsey came to see it in 1728, noting that it was so high up on the wall that a ladder was required to inspect it properly. When Jessie Mothersole walked the Antonine Wall in the late 1920s, it was on the house's front façade, but it was brought inside not much later to protect it from the elements.

Its original find site is long forgotten. The stone was given to the Stirlings by John Napier of Merchiston, the mathematician who invented logarithms and dabbled in antiquities, when he married a daughter of the family in 1572. Napier owned properties in Edinburgh and Gartness, near Loch Lomond, and could have picked up the stone anywhere on his regular journeys between the two. Gordon thought it may have decorated the fort of Balmuildy a bit further to the west, presumably because it was the nearest fort of which he was aware, but a broken stone commemorating the work of the same legion from Auchendavy led Sir George Macdonald to speculate that it may have come from there.

Jim Mearns soon arrived so the three of us headed up into the main part of Cawder House. Here I was able to better appreciate its grand, elegant interiors which retain many original features. We sat down in the clubhouse bar which is housed in one of the first-floor rooms of the house. Originally an opulent drawing room, it still boasts the tall windows, high ceilings and elaborate decorative plasterwork installed in the early nineteenth century when it was redesigned by fashionable architect David Hamilton. Over a coffee and biscuits, I encouraged Kevin and Jim to share their thoughts on the Antonine Wall and endeavoured to find out more about local attitudes towards it.

We began with a chat about the carved stone in the downstairs locker room. Kevin said that, in the two years that he had worked at Cawder, I was only the third or fourth person to come to view it. We agreed that it deserved to be better known and better displayed. According to Jim, a proposal was made a few years back to move it to the foyer and arrange a small exhibition to show it off. The Hunterian Museum had even expressed an interest in getting involved, but since then no progress has been made. As Jim pointed out, the stone is currently embedded in the wall of the building and moving such a precious artefact is not an easy or inexpensive task. As with any sizeable organisation, the club's budget is always stretched one way or another, and relocating their Roman stone is understandably not an urgent priority.

In fact, Kevin suspected that few club members were aware of the presence of a Roman frontier on the course at all. One of the holes which sits close to the monument has been christened 'The Antonine Wall', but otherwise its existence is overlooked. It does cause issues, however, when it comes to carrying out work on the course. A recent plan to remodel a couple of bunkers on the second hole of the Keir course, which sits close to the Wall, had to be aborted when Historic Environment Scotland were consulted, and it turned out that the extra costs of digging on a site so close to the frontier's archaeology would be prohibitive.

Although I had enjoyed a sit down and some refreshments, I was keen to get onto the Antonine Wall with Jim as my guide. As we left the house, Jim explained that he had travelled along the frontier on foot himself, spreading the journey over three weekends. 'It's a good walk, if you know where you are going', he added, expressing disappointment that some parts of the route are still relatively inaccessible and that, as I had already found out, several sections of the path are poorly maintained.

As with Professor Lawrence Keppie, I wanted to know how Jim had first encountered the Antonine Wall. It was, he explained, while he was still a schoolboy, and thanks to an enthusiastic classics teacher who had organised a visit to Balmuildy Roman fort to the west of Cawder. Having looked at the report of excavations carried out right before the First World War, with its detailed plan of the fort's internal buildings and outer rampart, the teacher and his pupils, all members of the school history club, were expecting to find some impressive remains of Roman military architecture.

When they got there, however, they discovered an empty field. It was up to the farmer to explain that the extensive excavations had been backfilled after the dig, leaving not a single trace of the fort visible above the ground. The best that he could show them was a shallow length of Roman ditch that could be found nearby, which has, Jim informed me, since silted up and disappeared.

Fortunately, Jim was not put off by this childhood disappointment. Several years later, he took part in the excavations of the headquarters building at Bar Hill, and a photo of him in action now features on one of the site's information panels. Although he decided against a full-time career in archaeology, Jim did become president of the Glasgow Archaeological Society, an organisation that plays an active role in the study and preservation of the Roman frontier and is also responsible for the publication of Robertson and Keppie's *Handbook*.

Jim knows the Cawder section of the Antonine Wall well, and within a couple of minutes of leaving Cawder House we had ascended a steep slope where I found myself standing in front of a prominent, if overgrown, section of the Roman turf rampart which runs through woodland. Kevin had mentioned earlier that the golf club have a special arrangement with Historic Environment Scotland that they will maintain the woods with a view to protecting the archaeological remains, cutting back the trees where necessary to minimise the damage they cause to the fragile earthwork.

Amazingly, when Jim first got involved with the golf club back in the 1990s, everyone seemed to have forgotten that a well-preserved section of the ancient structure survived here amongst the trees. It was he who realised that this was not just piles of earth dumped during the landscaping of the course, but one of the highest remaining sections of the Antonine Wall's rampart, second only to the stretch that survives west of Rough Castle.

A large full section cut through the turf ridge became evident as we walked along it. Jim explained that these were the remains of one of several test trenches dug by Sir George Macdonald in 1913. Further on we could see evidence of other trenches dug by Professor Anne Robertson in the second half of the twentieth century. These cross sections helped to give an idea of how the rampart was constructed and how it might have looked when first completed in the second century.

In his 1934 edition of *The Roman Wall in Scotland*, Macdonald described what a section through the turf rampart looked like, noting the traces of several dark horizontal lines, lying parallel one above the other, mostly an inch or less deep. Between these lines, three or four inches of earth. These were the stacked turves, blocks of cut turf, the thinner dark lines the rotten remains of the heath or grass on the top of each one. While early historians suggested that this method of building a frontier was crude, inferior to the masonry wall built by Hadrian, it was in fact an effective use of the materials to hand. This turf rampart would have been just as hard to penetrate as any wall of stone.

Those dark lines are no longer visible, covered up by earth and fallen leaves, but the trenches are. Instead of repairing the inevitable damage caused to the Antonine Wall, the twentieth-century archaeologists left these cuts open, meaning that they survive today as a record of pioneering modern research into the Roman frontier. I like to think that they too will be studied by future scholars, a useful example of the archaeology of archaeology.

Out of the trees, we found ourselves back on the golf course proper. Over the eighteenth tee and past the seventeenth green, the Antonine rampart and its ditch were easy to spot. We were then at the highest point on this part of the frontier, with an incredible 270-degree vista over the Kelvin valley.

This prime location, a perfect lookout point, has led Jim to suppose that there must have been a signal tower or fortlet here, although a recent geophysical survey carried out by the Glasgow Archaeological Society proved inconclusive. The disruption caused to the remains by the construction of the golf course may have erased any evidence. On a good day, in the winter, Jim pointed out that it is sometimes possible to see Bar Hill, although on that morning the view was obscured by trees in full leaf.

We headed into more woodland. It was wild and unkempt in there, but when you spot their subtle lines, the rampart and ditch can both be made out as they head westwards through the scrub. We came across the remains of more trenches dug in the 1960s by Robertson. It took a while to locate them under all the dead leaves and nettles, but with a bit of searching we eventually tracked them down.

We emerged back onto the neat and orderly terrain of the golf course and it was time to bid farewell to my temporary guide. Before Jim returned to the clubhouse he asked where my route would take me next. I explained that I planned to head straight onwards past the boundary of Cawder estate, from where I would walk along the edge of a narrow country lane, the Balmuildy Road, which followed almost exactly the line of the Antonine Wall.

Jim seemed sceptical, but the other option was a walk back through the golf course in the opposite direction to pick up the canal towpath again, a long detour that did not appeal. I was determined to stick as close as possible to the course of the Roman frontier and I knew that this way would lead me past the site of a Roman fortlet. And so, I marched onwards, off the fairways and into more trees to find the quiet country lane. It turned out to be a big mistake.

Getting out of Cawder was the first challenge, resulting in scratchy encounters with several low-hanging branches as I breached the hedgerow on its western edge. It did not take long for me to realise that what I had believed to be a quiet country lane was in fact a busy road. Not only was there lots of traffic, it was also travelling at high speed. To make matters worse, the grassy verge was overgrown and irregular, more low tree branches forcing me to step out in the road at regular intervals, leaping into gaps between the cars and lorries that were hurtling past. Still, the thought of the alternative, that long walk back to the canal, kept me moving forward.

I reached the site of the Roman fortlet. First identified using aerial photography, it was excavated in the mid-1960s. Much of it had already been lost to ploughing, but the remains of a structure not dissimilar to the one at Kinneil was uncovered, with post holes around the gate through the Antonine Wall indicating the presence of a wooden watchtower above.

To my disappointment, there was now nothing to see, only the muddy corner of a field. My unpleasant totter along the side of the road continued. At times it felt extremely dangerous and I cursed myself for my lack of proper planning. There was a brief respite as I passed the entrance to an industrial park, the trimmed lawns in front offering a break from the long grass of the unkempt verge, as well as a chance to move away from the speeding traffic. But then, only a few metres further on, the verge petered out and disappeared completely.

I was too far on to turn back. The only option was to continue across the farmland along the south side of the road. As I soon discovered, walking over freshly ploughed earth is not easy. The farmer, working in his tractor at the other side of the field, must have wondered what I was up to as I stumbled over the churned-up earth. As I went, I started to wonder what I would find at the end of the field. Would it to be a high stone wall, or a thick hedge, cutting off my exit? Suddenly that much longer route via the canal did not seem so bad.

Luckily, the hedge at the west end of the farm had a convenient gap for me to squeeze though. I had reached the A879, the Balmore Road that led north in my direction of travel. On the far side I spotted a thin, weed-covered walkway. I don't think I have ever been so pleased to see a pavement in my entire life.

When I walked this part of the Antonine Wall for the second time, I made sure to take the longer but safer route next to the Forth & Clyde Canal. Instead of turning into the Cawder Golf Club at Cadder Church, I continued past Cadder village and on along the towpath towards the nature reserve at Possil Marsh. It took 40 minutes or so, through a strange, liminal landscape, not quite countryside, but not quite city – all around me a tangle of trees, wildflowers and bracken, the dark edges of the water dotted with lily pads, not far in the distance tall metal pylons and the high-rise blocks of outer Glasgow.

There was one benefit to taking this longer route. As the canal reached the Balmore Road, I spotted the giant head of a Roman soldier peering over at me through the long grass on top of a low ridge. Picking my way around the edge of Possil Marsh, an area of swamp and fen that is popular with migrating birds, I eventually located a path through the greenery to reach this imposing sculpture.

Up close he was a truly remarkable sight: four metres tall and moulded in a dark fibreglass, the head was sculpted by local artist Malcolm Robertson. Now called 'Aurelius' (the name was chosen by a public vote), his strong features are framed by a helmet, the Roman *galea* with its sturdy cheek guards.

Aurelius has a reproduction of one of the Antonine Wall's distance sculptures inserted into the back of his helmet. Rather appropriately for an installation that evokes the overwhelming might of the Roman military, the sculpture is a copy of an original found at Summerston a couple of miles north of here that shows a Roman cavalryman riding over two defeated Caledonians. Next to him hovers the winged goddess Victory, wreath in hand, to signify his success. On the other side of the inscription can be seen an eagle, a Capricorn (half fish, half goat; it was an emblem of the Second Legion) and yet another Caledonian with his hands tied behind his back.

Aurelius is one of a group of monuments that have recently been erected along the frontier, all part of a project named 'Rediscovering the Antonine Wall' that aims to raise awareness of this underappreciated ancient monument. As well as four reproduction stone panels, a modern sculpture in the style of the Roman carvings was also created. The one slotted neatly into Aurelius was created by stonemasons Luke Batchelor and Josephine Crossland, both trained in traditional carving techniques through apprenticeships funded by Historic Environment Scotland. The results are quite beautiful, crisper and cleaner than the Roman original, but just as powerful.

Beyond Aurelius, I came across a gap in the hedge which led me into the garden of Lambhill Stables. Erected around 1815, back in the days when barges were pulled along the canal by horses, this was a vital staging post and rest stop for the poor, hardworking creatures. Later converted into a private home, the buildings fell into disrepair before being purchased by the local community in 2007 and rebuilt four years later. They now house a social enterprise and community charity, as well as a little café, where I was able to grab a coffee and rest my aching feet.

Next, my route took me up the busy Balmore Road, past Lambhill Cemetery with its once majestic, now shabby, classical gateway, back up to the point where I had arrived the previous year after my unpleasant shortcut out of Cawder Golf Club. A bit further on, still heading north, the road cuts through the site of Balmuildy Roman fort. This was the place where Jim Mearns had first encountered the remains of the Antonine Wall, or rather failed to encounter them, as there was nothing to see but a grassy field. Since then, nothing has changed.

It was vastly different back in the eighteenth century. Cartographer William Roy described the 'many vestiges of ruinous foundations' that he found when he visited the fort in the 1750s, its size compelling him to label it 'one of the most considerable belonging to the wall'. William Maitland recorded local tales (or 'tattle', as he called them) of underground vaults and water conduits that even he thought unbelievable. Antiquarians found a cluster of around a dozen houses built within the limits of the ancient fort. It is surely noteworthy that such small farming communities popped up at fort sites all along the Wall (Croy, Auchendavy and Westerwood being other examples). It could be a result of the ready supply of building stone, or due to their situation on stable plateaus. Whatever the reason, this one did not last long, and by 1812, the little hamlet of Balmuildy had been demolished.

Balmuildy also yielded the most famous Roman inscription ever to be found in Scotland. At some point in the late 1600s, a carved stone was spotted in the wall of a nearby barn, reused as the lintel of one of its windows, and was later removed to the University of Glasgow for safekeeping. A broken piece of a stone panel with most of its words lost, it bore the following letters:

Q. LOLLIO UR
LEG AUG PR.PR

Inscription From Balmuildy

While the meaning might not be immediately obvious, the learned antiquarians quickly worked out that it was a reference to 'Quintus Lollius Urbicus, the emperor's propraetorian legate', the same man who is recorded in the *Historia Augusta* as the builder of the Antonine Wall.

Delighted with this definitive proof that our Scottish Roman Wall was the one built by Antoninus Pius (and not, say, by Septimius Severus, as had been suggested by George Buchanan and Michael Livingston amongst others), Sibbald was moved to declare it 'the most remarkable Inscription we have.' Gordon went even further, calling it 'the most invaluable Jewel of Antiquity, that ever was found in the Island of Britain, since the Time of the Romans.' Today, this highly regarded fragment can be seen in pride of place at the Hunterian Museum.

Excavations in 1912-14 revealed that Balmuildy was one of only two forts on the Antonine Wall to have a solid stone outer rampart, the other being Castlecary. Furthermore, the northern rampart of the fort has short stone 'wing walls' jutting out of each corner, perfectly placed to link up with a longer masonry rampart. The presence of these stone protrusions has been presented as evidence of an original plan to build the entire rampart of the Antonine Wall in stone, just like its Hadrianic predecessor.

For some unknown reason, it is proposed, this idea must have been dropped at the last minute and turf was used instead. Perhaps the locals were causing trouble and it was felt that the frontier needed to be constructed as quickly and as efficiently as possible. This would explain why only two of the Antonine Wall's forts have stone defences (there are signs that Castlecary also had 'wing walls'), but it does imply that the frontier was something of a rush job, an overambitious project that was never properly completed. While I am willing to consider the evidence, I do feel slightly resistant to the idea that this great frontier, the vast monument that I have affectionately (or arrogantly) come to think of as my Roman Wall, is not all that it should be.

Heading on from Balmuildy, the Antonine Wall takes a sudden turn towards the north. I followed it, or at least the road that now runs parallel to it, soon crossing over the River Kelvin. During the Second World War, large blocks of stone with crampholes were dredged up from the riverbed here, almost certainly the remains of a Roman bridge. Not much later, I arrived at Summerston Farm, which sits on the side of the Balmore Road, near the spot where the distance stone reproduced for the new monument at Lambhill Stables was originally discovered.

At this point, I needed to take a left into a narrow lane which led me into a low valley, a barren, empty kind of place dotted here and there with cottages and smallholdings. The lane led me along the foot of the valley through the yard of a derelict farm. A lonely-looking pony stood motionless in a field nearby. Otherwise, there were no signs of life. It felt very rural, not the kind of terrain that I had expected to find so close to Scotland's most populous city. The Antonine Wall, invisible here, follows the top of a ridge to the north, past the site of another fortlet discovered by aerial survey in 1977 and up to the top of Crow Hill.

I met the frontier again as I climbed out of the valley past West Millichen Farm, the track I was following joining the route of the Wall as I reached the Boclair Road. There I faced another tricky walk – a short, pavement-less stretch of this road had to be negotiated before I reached the outskirts of Bearsden.

Luckily, it was not too busy, and I was able to teeter along a narrow verge for a while before crossing onto a wider patch of grass on the other side. Eventually, facing another jog over the road as that patch of grass disappeared, I squeezed through a hedge onto yet another golf course. I shouldn't have been there, but no one was around, and I stuck close to the edge until I was finally able to re-emerge by the roadside right where a pavement appeared.

Back in the eighteenth century, this area was known as New Kilpatrick. Later, the small hamlet that grew up here was named New Kirk. With the arrival of the railway in 1863, however, it quickly developed into a wealthy suburb of Glasgow, which was christened Bearsden. The origins of the name are unclear, though there is a local tradition recounted by journalist Hugh MacDonald in his popular *Rambles Round Glasgow* of 1854 (an anthology of articles previously printed in the *Glasgow Citizen* newspaper) that the 'Bear's Den' was the site of an ancient Roman graveyard. Antiquarian John Buchanan (who, you might remember, had witnessed the damage wreaked on Castlecary by the coming of the railway) was disappointed with the choice, believing that a placename linked with the area's Roman past, like 'Chesters', would have been more appropriate.

As I arrived at Bearsden's outer limits, I came to a large modern burial ground on the north side of the road, the name of which recalled the suburb's earlier incarnation – New Kilpatrick Cemetery. The cemetery is certainly worth a quick detour, as it contains not one, but two short stretches of the Antonine Wall's stone base that have been exposed for public inspection.

The first can be found near to the entrance, running in a north-easterly direction up a gradual slope towards the top of a low ridge. From a distance, it looks like a wide strip of rubble, which is in essence exactly what it is. On the day I visited, it was looking dishevelled, with weeds and grass pushing up between the Roman stones.

I came here many years ago and clearly remember being able to see a culvert, a narrow channel built into the stone base to allow water to run under the rampart and prevent it from pooling around the bottom. Now it is lost in the thick growth. Still visible, however, was a step in the stonework, added to support the turf rampart as it climbed up the hillside.

The second stretch of the Antonine Wall's base lies further into the cemetery, running west to east this time as the frontier takes a turn back towards Crow Hill and Summerston. These two sections, which together add up to 47 m in length and are up to 4.7 m wide in places, were discovered in the early twentieth century. At one point the local council wanted to infill one of them, but thanks to the intervention of Sir George Macdonald, both are still open to view.

A culvert is more visible in the higher section, cutting an oblique line through the cobbles. Originally covered by stone slabs, its channel is now open to the sky and filled with vivid green moss. Drainage was vitally important to the survival of the Antonine Wall since turf gradually deteriorates if it becomes excessively damp. Recent scholarship suggests that the stone base played a vital role in keeping the rampart dry, allowing water to run underneath it and down out of it.

It is luckily that these bases survive at all, given the antiquarian reports that the Antonine Wall was regularly plundered for stone around New Kilpatrick. Even in their current untidy state, in which they were starting to look like neglected garden rockeries, these wide sections of the base were still potent reminders of the immense scale of the monument, evidence too that, while the turf rampart proved to be largely ephemeral, its solid stony support has turned out to be a more permanent feature. Although much of it has been lifted to make way for the plough, there must be long lengths of it that still survive underground, running under fields, gardens and, of course, golf courses, untouched and unseen for centuries.

The exposed bases at New Kilpatrick gave me a chance to appreciate the care that was expended on constructing the Roman rampart, for while most of the stone base consisted of rubble, the outer kerbstones, which were visible in ancient times, were carefully dressed and tapered. We know that these kerbstones were cut on site, since the tiny flakes that were chipped off them by masons have been found under the rampart itself. Countless hours were spent on this task alone. The flat, stable kerbs helped to contain the rougher rubble in the core of the base, but I like to think the builders were also concerned with the structure's aesthetics, creating a neat and regular outer face for the foot of the turf bulwark.

It may have been built as a strong frontier to separate and control, but the Antonine Wall needed to look good too. It made a statement about the Roman attitude to life. Despite what those medieval chroniclers may have thought, there is nothing *rusticus* or crude about it. Even in the barbaric (as they saw it) lands of Caledonia, the Romans believed that a job worth doing was worth doing properly.

On exiting New Kilpatrick Cemetery, I turned right and continued onwards along Boclair Road into Bearsden. This has long been known as one of the most genteel parts of Glasgow, and its large sandstone villas and sprawling Art Nouveau bungalows attest to many decades of prosperity. The Robertson and Keppie *Handbook* states that the dip of the ditch and slight mound of the rampart survive in private gardens along the north side of the road, but I could not spot either.

As I walked further into the city, I soon lost any sense of where the frontier ran in relation to the modern streets. Boclair Road led me down and over a crossroads with the A81. Here, yet again, I was helped by a street sign, as I stepped onto Roman Road. It took a sharp left turn, joining the route of the ancient Military Way and directing me onwards to the site of my next Roman fort, where I had the chance to inspect the finest extant Roman building in Scotland.

You could easily walk right past the Bearsden Roman bath house if you were not paying attention. Sitting at the side of the road behind a modern stone wall, surrounded by 1980s apartment blocks, it is slightly lost in this suburban setting. On closer inspection, however, it reveals itself to be a fascinating place, a site that has given us a wealth of information about the daily life of a soldier on the Antonine Wall and, also, is an important example of how aspects of classical culture penetrated the wild west of Caledonia.

Sadly, the bath house is the only part of the Bearsden fort that can be seen today. The fort was already in a poor state by the mid-eighteenth century. On Williams Roy's map of the Antonine Wall, drawn in the 1750s but not printed until 1793 in *The Military Antiquities of the Romans in North Britain*, we see a detailed plan of a Roman fort, two ditches around its west, south and east sides, the Antonine Wall along the north side and the Military Way (now underneath the modern Roman Road) running right through the middle. In the accompanying text, however, Roy noted that it was 'so much defaced by the plough' that it was almost impossible to trace its outline.

According to Hugh MacDonald, who rambled past here on his way to visit the Whangie (a dramatic ravine said to have been carved by the Devil's tail into the nearby Kilpatrick Hills), the Roman fort then known as New Kilpatrick was almost completely obliterated by the early 1850s. Hardly surprising since, as a local farmer told him, the fort's ruins had long provided 'a perfect quarry for the parish'.

MacDonald was roused by his encounter with the Roman Wall hereabouts to quote in his *Rambles Round Glasgow* a few words from a poem that, as he saw it, interpreted the ancient frontier as a mark of conquest, but also an acknowledgment of weakness:

> *The wave of Forth was joined to Clyde,*
> *When Rome's broad rampart stretched from tide to tide,*
> *With bulwarks strong, with towers sublimely crowned,*
> *While winding tubes conveyed each martial sound.*
> *To guard the legions from their painted foes,*
> *By vast unwearied toil the structure rose,*
> *When fierce in arms, the Scot, by Carron's shore,*
> *Resigned for war, the chase and mountain boar,*
> *As the chafed lion, on his homeward way*
> *Returns for vengeance, and forgets his prey.*

These lines belong to a now largely forgotten Romantic poem called 'The Clyde', written in 1764 by Lanarkshire-born poet John Wilson. Much inspired by the landscape and heritage around Glasgow (he also wrote a short ode to Crookston Castle), Wilson was forced to give up his poetry when he accepted a job at Greenock Grammar School – the ultra-Presbyterian governors saw such literary endeavours as 'profane and unprofitable', and Wilson subsequently burned most of his work.

This brief excerpt in which he considers our Roman Wall demonstrates Wilson's belief in that strange old legend of a communication tube running the length of the frontier. It shows that he was a proud pro-Caledonian patriot, while the poem's references to a battle by the River Carron in which the Romans are sent packing reveal that he had more than a passing acquaintance with the works of Ossian.

The site of the Roman fort described by Hugh MacDonald was soon to be built over as New Kilpatrick became Bearsden. The 1862 OS map shows the remains of its southern ditch in open fields. By the time the 1896 map was printed, it was mostly covered by Victorian villas sitting in walled gardens. In the early 1970s, it was decided that the area should be redeveloped, the old houses demolished to make way for flats. This provided an opportunity for an archaeological investigation, and it was during the first season of this dig in 1973 that the incredible bath house was discovered.

Delays to the construction of the new flats meant that the excavations at Bearsden could carry on for ten summer seasons in total. It was not possible to uncover the whole fort, but a complicated patchwork of pits and trenches allowed archaeologists to piece together much of its plan. What emerged was a highly uncommon layout. The fort's outer rampart followed the normal rectangular format, with a gate in the centre of each side, but at some point, as it was being constructed, the area that the rampart contained was split by another rampart running north to south.

This created an annexe that was effectively inside the fort itself, rather than to the side as is more usual. The commandant's house would normally be located near the centre, next to the *principia*, but this internal annexe left no space for it there, and so far, the residence of the fort's commander has not been found. Also unexpected for an Antonine Wall fort is the fact that all the main buildings inside (except for the granaries and bath house) were constructed from timber rather than stone.

The discovery of the well-preserved Roman bath house attracted huge public attention, with over 2,000 people turning up to see it in a single weekend during the dig. As a result, it was decided to take it into state care and consolidate it for public viewing. This was quite a task. The unearthed Roman walls were bonded with clay, all of which had to be removed and replaced with something more robust. The walls were drawn and photographed, then dismantled in short sections, with each stone numbered and cleaned. Then the stones were carefully reinserted in the same position as they had been found, this time bonded with mortar. The floor in the cold bath was covered with new flags to protect it from the feet of modern visitors, and in some areas the hypocausts were reburied under gravel to keep them safe. So it was that I was able to inspect its substantial remains.

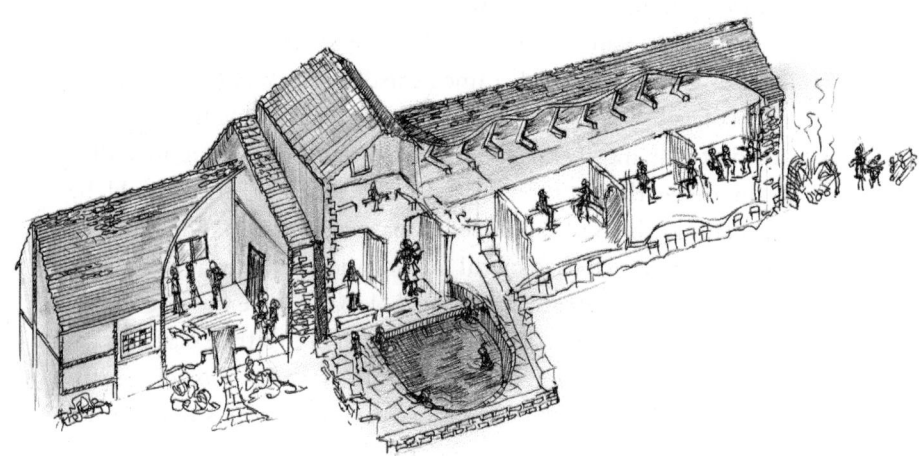

Roman Bath House, Bearsden – (Artist's Impression)

I had already viewed the foundations and fragmentary hypocaust of a relatively simple bath house at Bar Hill, where the soldiers made do with a long, thin range of three heated rooms, but the Bearsden Roman baths were built on a much larger scale. After depositing his clothes in the changing room, a soldier could relax in its seven rooms, each with a distinct atmosphere, ranging from a cold room and plunge pool near the entrance to a hot pool located next to a water tank and one of the building's two furnaces.

Underfloor heating systems, the famous hypocausts, were installed in the warm areas. Two of the rooms, namely the hot dry room (like a modern sauna) and hot steam room (like a Turkish bath) were lined with an inner 'skin' of stone slabs held in place with iron clamps, with a gap between them and the outer walls. This gap allowed warm air to circulate up from below the floor to heat the walls as well. In the steam room, several of these slim stone slabs can still be seen in position.

The interior of the bath house was finely appointed. Both the walls and floors of it rooms were decorated with painted plaster, which was specially formulated to remain waterproof. The remains of carved stone benches (more practical than wood in such damp conditions) were found in two rooms. A niche in one of the warm rooms probably held a statue, perhaps the goddess whose half life-size head was discovered in the cold bath nearby. With wide, staring eyes, pouting lips and waved hair, her sharp, linear forms remind me of the figures on the Bridgeness Distance Slab. She is traditionally identified as Fortuna but could be a local deity who was adopted into the Roman pantheon.

Head of Goddess, Bearsden Bath House

Even more magnificent was a fountain-head carved to represent a human face that was found just south of the changing room. Also featuring wide eyes and waved hair, its rounded lips surround an open hole. Placed in the wall of one of the rooms of the bath house, it would have been fed by a pipe, allowing water to pour through its gaping mouth and into a basin below.

Next to the bath house was a communal nine-seater latrine similar to the one uncovered at Castlecary in 1902. In the case of the Bearsden latrine, however, advances in archaeology have allowed more information to be extracted, not from the building itself, but from what the soldiers who used it left behind.

Decorated Fountainhead, Bearsden Bath House

Careful analysis of the material flushed out of the latrine's sewers and into the fort's ditches revealed details of the food eaten by the men who lived and worked at Bearsden Roman fort. Although we know that Roman soldiers ate some meat (mostly beef), their diet at Bearsden was mainly plant based. Wheat provided plenty of carbohydrates in the form of porridge and bread. Local wild fruit was harvested and eaten, including blackberries, raspberries and strawberries, with hazelnuts, wild turnip and radishes also identified.

Exotic foods must have been imported to the Antonine frontier, with figs, dill, coriander and poppy seeds all sent over from mainland Europe. In addition, the presence of pottery containers at Bearsden indicates that olive oil from southern Spain and wine from the south of France were consumed at the fort.

Finally, the sewage in the fort's ditch included fragments of moss, which was probably used as their version of toilet paper. As was the case at Castlecary fort, the latrine's sewers were flushed when the water was released from the baths, although how often this happened is not clear. We can imagine that, even though they display ingenious plumbing, these baths and toilets were far from hygienic by modern standards, the hot, stagnant water a simmering soup of all sorts of bacteria and bugs. And while the men enjoyed a relatively healthy and varied diet, we know from analysis of the Roman sewage that they suffered from various parasites, including roundworm, whipworm and fleas.

Frustratingly, we do not know which units the men stationed at Bearsden belonged to. An inscription records that the fort was built by the Twentieth Legion, but they would have been replaced by auxiliaries by the time the frontier was up and running. The layout of the barrack blocks found here, with eight rooms for the ordinary soldiers and a larger one at the end for the commanding decurion, is of the sort normally used by cavalry, although evidence of horses or stabling on the site has so far proved elusive.

Given the catastrophic damage that was done to the ancient site in previous centuries, the current state of the Bearsden bath house is a surprise. In places its walls stand up to eight courses, around 1.2 m tall. The various rooms, with their hypocausts, heated walls and plunge pools, are still evident, as are the stone channels that let the dirty water out of them, under the latrine and into the fort's ditches. Today the only water in these rooms might be the odd puddle on a rainy day, but visitors are nevertheless warned in more jokey bilingual signs erected by Historic Environment Scotland that running, diving and bombing are strictly forbidden (rendered into Latin as *nolite currere, urinare, desilire*).

Lunchtime was approaching, so with my own diet in mind, I headed onwards along Roman Road. Before long I arrived at a parade of shops. Round the corner I found a small café, the perfect place to stop for something to eat. The food it served was simple but tasty and the fact that, according to my OS map, it sat right on top of the course of the Antonine Wall was a bonus.

Chapter Seven

BEARSDEN TO OLD KILPATRICK

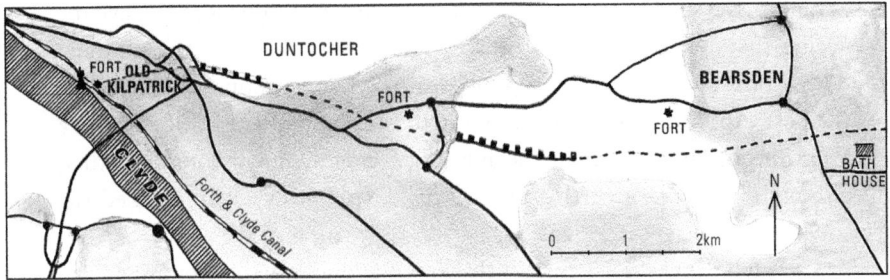

Antonine Wall West End – Bearsden To Old Kilpatrick

My final afternoon of walking the Antonine Wall began with more of Bearsden's swanky streets. According to Robertson and Keppie's *Handbook*, the Roman frontier followed the route of Thorn Road before turning northwest towards higher ground, so that too was my direction of travel. The *Handbook* also suggested that the stone base of the Roman rampart could be seen in some of the private gardens that I passed on my way. I tried to spot it, peering over high walls, down pink gravel drives and past sparkling SUVs, without any success. I soon realised that my behaviour would look rather suspicious to anyone who might be watching and gave up.

Visible remains of the Antonine Wall become scarcer the further west you go, but they do pop up from time to time. Hidden amongst Bearsden's twentieth-century streets is a short length, preserved in a hidden patch of greenery known as Roman Park. It can be accessed up a narrow path from Westbourne Crescent, which opens out into a long, thin strip of grass bordered by trees. The ditch of the Roman frontier is not obvious at first, but if you look carefully, you will spot a low camber in the lawn running parallel to the footpath as its heads westwards along the top of the ridge.

This 260 m section of the Antonine Wall was excavated in 1963 as the land was being developed and the park was later created around it. A bit further along I spotted a fenced-off area to the south of the faded ditch. Inside, my *Handbook* assured me, were a few metres of the Roman rampart's stone base. Peering in at a mass of grass and dried weeds, I could just make out a row of dressed kerb stones, but the rest was completely concealed.

On leaving the park, I struggled yet again to negotiate a modern housing estate whose streets appeared on my map as a mass of illegible lines. But, as before, the street names – Eagle Crescent and Antonine Road – gave me a clue that I was headed in the right direction. I knew that my next destination was on a hilltop, so I followed the rising ground and hoped for the best. Antonine Road took a swing to the right where I came across a long line of lawn between the houses. A metal sign pointed out that, although none of its earthworks survived, this grassy strip marked the route of the ancient frontier.

I wanted to take a left turn at that point and follow the Antonine Wall up onto the hilltop, but a conveniently placed gap in the hedge had been blocked up with the kind of high metal barrier normally used for crowd control. Instead, I had to walk to the end of the street, turn left and then left again, finally exiting Bearsden as I headed onto Castlehill.

The path that I followed was the driveway to a farm. Its buildings now lie empty and forlorn, surrounded by more crowd-control barriers bearing ominous signs warning of 'Danger!' and firmly advising me to 'Keep Out!'. This was something of a disappointment, as the day before Professor Keppie had told me about a carved stone, much worn but obviously Roman, which he had spotted in the wall of one of the farm's outbuildings. There was no chance of seeing it, hard as I tried, as the whole farmyard was securely fenced off, its buildings crumbling and roofs sagging, the walls hidden behind thick bushes. Whether the Roman stone even survives was impossible to ascertain.

Giving up, I continued up to the top of Castlehill. This was the site of the next fort on the Antonine Wall. The view from there has always been extensive. John Horsley thought it second only to that seen at Bar Hill, although it has inevitably changed significantly over the last century. I looked over rolling fields and hedges to the west, the tops of the Kilpatrick Hills appearing further north, but towards the southwest the countryside was lost under the vast housing estate of Drumchapel and the concrete towers of Blairdardie. Dark clouds hung above the city but I was not too perturbed: they were moving fast and the cloudless sky beyond suggested that any showers would be short-lived.

I was only a mile and a half from the site of Bearsden bath house. As far as we can tell, the relatively short distance between the forts of Castlehill and Bearsden was dictated by topography. Bearsden was built on a spot between two valleys, obvious routes from the north to south that would have been identified by the Romans as potential flashpoints, while Castlehill was clearly chosen for its height, almost 120 m above sea level.

Today, the top of Castlehill is crowned with a ring of aged beech trees. Known locally as the 'Witches Circle', it is romantically suggestive of an ancient druid grove, although the black marks of recent bonfires and a scattering of empty beer cans suggested that its current use was more prosaic. It certainly is a place with history, nonetheless, its modern name hinting at its important military past.

The now indiscernible Roman fort at Castlehill has never been properly excavated and its extant remains seem to have been faint even in the eighteenth century, but several antiquities relating to it have been found over the years. Two distance slabs, for example, were discovered close by. One was observed in the wall of a local cottage in the late 1600s and would later end up in the collection of the University of Glasgow (now the Hunterian Museum). Decorated with two *peltae* covered with a distinctive plumed design, it records the construction of a very precise 3666.5 paces by the Sixth Legion. Another, more simple distance sculpture was unearthed (and unintentionally damaged) by a farmer in 1847. This one celebrates the construction of 3,000 ft of the frontier by the Twentieth Legion and bears their emblem, the wild boar.

Campestres Altar Stone

In 1826, an altar was found by a ploughman a few hundred metres to the east of the fort. It was dedicated by one Quintus Pisentius Justus, prefect of the Fourth Cohort of Gauls, to both Britannia and the *campestres*, goddesses of the parade ground. Despite their Latin name, the *campestres* were in fact a Celtic cult that was spread across the empire by Gaulish cavalry. The goddesses were often associated with Epona, another Gaulish deity linked with horses and their riders who became popular in the Roman world. Both are mentioned on one of the altars dedicated by Marcus Cocceius Firmus back at Auchendavy. The fact that the *campestres* were worshipped at Castlehill strongly suggests that it was home to a cavalry unit.

Fragments of Roman pottery have been found among the roots of fallen trees around the fort site. A carved column capital decorated with chevrons and stylised leaves that was unearthed there demonstrates that at least one of Castlehill's main buildings, most probably the *principia*, was built from stone. Like Carriden at the beginning of my walk, it was aerial photography that finally confirmed the fort's exact location. Black and white shots were taken from a plane in 1947, a year that witnessed an unusually dry summer, perfect for spotting cropmarks in the parched earth. They revealed the dark lines of the fort's southern rampart and ditches, which curved towards the north just before they reached the (then still intact) farmyard.

Back in the 1720s, John Horsley noted that the eroded ramparts of Castlehill fort were topped by a hedge of thorns. That hedge is now gone, but a row of hawthorn and elder, its branches dotted with glossy red and black berries, runs down the hill. Close inspection revealed that these bushes grew in a shallow trench, the faint signs of the Antonine Wall's once formidable ditch.

On my previous visit to Castlehill, I had followed the ditch for a while down the slope before I realised that I needed to get to the other side of the hill to reach the footpath that would take me on towards Hutcheson Hill. I made the mistake of thinking that I could simply cut across the intervening field. A long and arduous traipse through damp grass that often reached over my knees ensued. Then, I found myself scrabbling through dense forest, weaving my way through a maze of trunks and sharp branches. On my second attempt, I headed back up to the Roman fort, from where it was easy to find the muddy trail which led me quickly down through Garscadden Wood (also referred to as 'Bluebell Wood' due to its colourful springtime displays) into the valley below.

The valley is called Peel Glen. The road that runs along it leads into Drumchapel, whose outskirts I now had to circumnavigate. It is hard to imagine a place more different from the casually affluent Bearsden that I had recently explored. The Drumchapel estate was constructed in the 1950s as new housing for the thousands of Glaswegians then living in crumbling inner-city tenements. Along with Castlemilk, Easterhouse and Pollok, Drumchapel was designed to be a self-contained community. Unfortunately, the promised amenities never materialised, transport links to the city were limited, and the estates soon became isolated ghettos.

When the big industries that employed the majority of Drumchapel's working-age residents started to fail, things only got worse. Conditions have improved this century with the construction of some relatively recent housing that replaced the grim, dilapidated blocks built after the Second World War, but Drumchapel is still a deprived area. Forty eight percent of its children live in poverty, life expectancy is below the Glasgow average and its unemployment rate runs at about double that of the rest of the city.

Over the Peel Glen Road, I started climbing again. I was in the western half of Garscadden Woods, a protected parcel of forest rich in native species such as silver birch, rowan and elder. A path through it forms part of the Drumchapel Way, a 4.5-mile loop that links open spaces all around the area. The Roman frontier runs along the northern edge of the forest across Hutcheson Hill. I was not able to walk along it since it cuts through farmland, but a track at the top of the woodland eventually joined it as both descended into the north-south valley cut by the Cleddans Burn.

It was not far from here that the only distance slab to be found in living memory was unearthed. During our lunch

Path To Cleddans Farm

the day before, Professor Keppie had reminisced over its discovery back in 1969, a day that he still remembers remarkably well. Still a temporary research assistant at that stage, he was working in the coin room at the Hunterian Museum, weighing the coins for one of the volumes of Professor Anne Robertson's numismatic catalogue (a task that required some dexterity and taught him how to estimate a coin's weight in a matter of seconds) when the phone rang in Professor Robertson's office.

Overhearing only one side of the conversation, Keppie soon deduced that something major had been found, an inscription of some sort, another carved Roman stone. The existence of this antiquity had come to the attention of the relevant authorities by a rather circuitous route. It had been spotted in a farmyard at Cleddans by a sales rep for an agricultural firm who was visiting the farmer. The sales rep mentioned it to his doctor, Ernest Cormack, who happened to know archaeologist Kenneth Steer. It was Steer who was now on the telephone relaying the news to Professor Robertson.

Two museum technicians were despatched in a van and the carved stone was brought back to the museum. It was a distance marker, extravagantly carved with figures and an inscription dedicated to the Twentieth Legion contained within an elaborate architectural frame. Unfortunately, during the six weeks that it had sat in the farmyard, the farmer had decided to spruce up his outbuildings with a layer of whitewash, much of which ended up on the Roman sculpture. Keppie was given the laborious task of scraping off all these drips and spots of white from the carved surface.

He obviously did a sterling job, and the sculpture is now recognised as one of the finest to be unearthed along the Antonine Wall. At its centre, under a carved arch and flanked by fluted pilaster topped by Corinthian capitals, a graceful female figure places a tiny laurel wreath over the beak of an eagle that perches atop a legionary standard. Although her identity is difficult to pin down, she may represent Britannia, seen here proclaiming the latest victory in her northern territory. Either side, kneeling below classical pediments, are two bound Caledonians, cowed witnesses to this commemoration of their defeat.

It really is a wonderful thing, carved in high relief, filled with decorative detail. Its inscription records the adjacent 3,000 ft stretch of the Antonine

Wall built by the Twentieth Legion, but it is evident that the overall design of the panel took precedence over the inscription, which is squeezed here and there into any available space. The size and style of the Wall's distance carvings varies greatly, but the Twentieth Legion certainly employed one of most ambitious sculptors, as demonstrated by this exceptional slab from Hutcheson Hill, as well as another that I encountered at the end of my journey.

Appropriately, given all the work that he put into cleaning it up, an image of the Hutcheson Hill distance slab was featured on the cover of the 2020 volume published to celebrate Professor Keppie's long and distinguished career. Entitled *The Antonine Wall: Papers in Honour of Professor Lawrence Keppie*, it is an exhaustive compendium of the recent scholarship on the history, archaeology and reception of the ancient frontier.

Over half a century on from this exciting find, we are still waiting for another distance sculpture to appear. Many will have been destroyed no doubt, smashed to pieces and recycled in farm walls or foundations, but a few might still be out there, hiding in the earth. These Scottish Roman carvings have almost always been found by chance rather than design, so we can only wait and hope that someone might stumble across one at some point in the not-too-distant future.

The sad fate of another distance sculpture found along this part of the Roman frontier is surely the most unexpected of all the Antonine Wall's antiquities. Unearthed during trenching in 1865, it too had lain forgotten in a farmyard before being purchased for £2 by James Thomson, a Glasgow lawyer. He offered it to the University of Glasgow and then to various collectors, asking only that they reimburse his costs, but his offers were all rejected.

In the end he sold it to Professor J H McChesney, the American consul at Newcastle. Attempts by the Glasgow Archaeological society to claim it back for the city went unheeded, and McChesney promptly shipped it to Chicago for display in a museum. It was there that the Roman sculpture was lost in the catastrophic fire that wiped out much of central Chicago in October 1871.

Fortunately, plaster casts of it had been made before it was destroyed, one of which is now on display in the Hunterian Museum. It reveals that the stone panel was decorated with two winged *genii*, a boar and a tree, all framed in an ansate panel. It records the same 3,000 ft of the Antonine Wall as the distance slab unearthed nearby in 1969 and was presumably displayed close to it in ancient times.

Whether all the distance sculptures would have had such a twin is not clear. Professor Keppie has proposed that they might have been displayed on either side of the Antonine Wall's turf rampart, a more elaborate example facing south, a simpler one facing north, where the potential audience would surely have been less appreciative. Intriguingly, both the slabs found on Hutcheson Hill showed signs of being intentionally buried, perhaps indicative of the organised dismantling of the frontier as the Romans retreated south.

Another short climb led me up to Cleddans Farm. The track that leads from there runs directly westwards, following the course of the Antonine Wall. The hedges on either side of it were glistening with blackberries. To my left I could see the hovering, otherworldly form of the Drumchapel Water Tower, to my right a strange looking tree with a thick grey trunk and oddly perky branches that I eventually worked out was a poorly disguised mobile phone mast. On a high point along this ridge a Roman fortlet was discovered in 1980 thanks to Professor Keppie and James Walker, who identified this as a likely site for such an installation during a fieldwalking expedition. Their intuition proved correct when a small excavation revealed the stone base of its ramparts.

Drumchapel Water Tower

Nowadays, the only physical evidence of the ancient frontier at Cleddans, besides the route of the track itself, is a slight dip along its southern side, the faint traces of the ancient ditch. Further along, as the farm track reaches the outskirts of Clydebank, a small, weather-beaten purple panel stuck high up next to a road sign commemorated the presence of the Antonine Wall. At the top, I could see an image of the merciless Roman cavalryman, who I recognised from the Bridgeness Distance Slab back in Edinburgh. This tiny, easily missed memorial to one Britain's most important historical monuments could politely be described as 'bathetic'.

Like so much of this part of the world, Clydebank was mostly rural before heavy industry arrived in the later 1800s, comprising farmland, with a cluster of small villages. Now, these villages – Duntocher, Faifley, Hardgate and others – have been subsumed into the town which became famous as a centre for shipbuilding, producing iconic vessels such as the QE2 and the Queen Mary. It was only these outskirts that I would see on my journey, the site of the old shipyard lying further south where the Clyde meets the River Cart. The shipbuilding is gone now, but the famous Clydebank Titan, a 46 m crane converted into a tourist attraction, remains down by the water, a reminder of the area's proud industrial past.

I was walking in the other direction, north along the side of the wide A8014, then turning left into a housing estate, climbing upwards through Duntocher to Goldenhill Park. As soon as I entered the park, a vast expanse of low grass, its strategic advantages became evident – my walks along the Antonine Wall had obviously given me an eye for such things. A sizeable plateau sits above the surrounding landscape. A burn runs through the valley along its northern side. This is a naturally defended spot, ideal for surveying the surrounding territory, an excellent location for a Roman fort.

The name of the place gives a clue to its ancient heritage. Duntocher is derived from the Gaelic for 'the fort on the causeway', a sign that the vestiges of the ancient frontier were evident long after the Romans abandoned it. These vestiges must have been significantly depleted by the early 1700s, as those antiquarians who visited Duntocher as they journeyed along the Antonine Wall were often confused by them.

Alexander Gordon sketched a plan of a rectangular fort, its outer ditches with the typical rounded corners, also outlining what he thought were the ruins of its slightly off-centre *principia*, but he showed the Roman frontier (which he calls 'Graham's Dyke') running right thought the interior of the fort. John Horsley's illustration features a squarer outline, with gates through its rampart on the west, south and east sides and the frontier (simply labelled 'The wall') running along its northern edge. William Roy agreed with Horsley on the relationship between the fort and the Wall (he names it 'Grime's Dyke') but marked only one gate, through the south rampart, with a road leading out of it.

Exploratory trenches dug by John Clarke on the site in 1933 revealed that the fort had a turf (rather than a stone) rampart, but it was up to Professor Anne Robertson to excavate more fully in 1948-50. What she uncovered was in many ways unexpected. The fort at Duntocher was tiny for a start, the smallest on the whole frontier, covering an area of only 0.2 hectares. Professor Keppie has since calculated that it would have held a garrison of less than a hundred men. The only stone building identified inside the fort was long and thin like a barrack block but positioned at the centre where you would expect to find the *principia*. There was a large annexe, about twice the size of the fort, although it was not investigated by Professor Robertson and her team of archaeologists.

Attached to the north-west corner of the fort was an earlier fortlet. This fortlet was originally a free-standing installation, about 18 m square, with a ditch around it and entrance gates in both the north and south ramparts. Located around 80 m above sea level, it would have been perfectly placed to take advantage of the views from the top of Golden Hill. Not long after its construction, however, the fort was built right next to it, the fort's annexe surrounding it. Finally, the Antonine Wall arrived, and its long turf rampart was incorporated into the northern side of fort and fortlet.

The Duntocher fortlet was only the second such structure to be uncovered, after the 'guard house' described by Mungo Buchanan during building work at Watling Lodge in 1894, and its discovery led to the realisation that these fortlets were a crucial element of the design of the Antonine Wall. Its reuse here as part of a fort, however, is curious. Its unusual position implies that plans changed as the Antonine Wall was being constructed. A decision may have been made that more forts needed to be added to the frontier, and a location for one of these new forts happened to coincide with an already completed fortlet. But if that was the case, why not demolish the fortlet and build the fort on top of it? Simply building around it seems an odd choice, one that must have made sense to the Romans, even if it does not to me.

Another surprise was the fact that, despite the plans made by antiquarians, the fort had no south gate. It is the only fort on the Antonine Wall not to have one. This anomaly is probably due to the sudden drop on this side of the hill, too steep for Roman traffic.

Although the stone base of the fortlet's ramparts were re-excavated in the late 1970s, with a plan mooted to leave them open to public view, in the end they were all reburied. I had read that West Dunbartonshire Council now mowed the grass to highlight the outline of the ancient structures, letting it grow longer above the ramparts of the fort, fortlet and Wall. But standing in the park, right in the middle of where the fort stood, I could not make head nor tail of it. There were areas of long grass but, hard as I tried, I couldn't relate them to the plan of the site in my *Handbook*.

Later, I took a look at the satellite view on Google Maps, a useful way to survey the Antonine Wall from the comfort of your own home, which confirmed my suspicions. Areas of longer, lighter grass do indeed follow the course of Roman ramparts, but other areas have been allowed to grow too, confusing the picture for modern visitors.

Not far away from the fort, however, were some other new developments that more clearly referenced Golden Hill's Roman heritage. A Roman themed playpark had recently been installed, next to it a life-size wooden sculpture of a heavily built Roman soldier. A wooden fingerpost had been erected pointing in the direction of Roman sites both near and far. Castlehill fort, from where I had just walked, was, it informed me,

Wooden Sculpture Of Roman Legionary, Goldenhill Park, Duntocher

0.6 leagues away. The distance to Old Kilpatrick fort, where I was headed, was 0.75 leagues. The city of Rome, to which I had no intention of walking, was 413 leagues away. For some reason, the sign makers had used the medieval English league (about three miles) instead of the Roman league (about 1.4 miles). It was, nevertheless, a light-hearted but effective reminder that, to the emperor who commanded its construction, this Roman frontier must have seemed like the back of beyond.

Next came a walk down a steep incline, following the Antonine Wall as it continued in a north-westerly direction. Halfway down this hill, the path passed a small area surrounded by a high metal fence. Inside was some of the exposed stone base of the Roman turf rampart. While previous examples I had encountered that day had been overgrown, this one was quite the opposite. It looked like it had been doused with a potent weedkiller, the rubble of the base surrounded by wilted, yellowing weeds and dusty earth. It was not a pretty sight. Staring through the bars of its tall grey cage, I could not help but feel sorry for this cheerless fragment of the Roman Wall. Still, I had a good, long look, as I knew that this would be my final encounter with a visible fragment of the ancient frontier.

Further down the hill was a war memorial dedicated to the Duntocher men who fell in both world wars. It was situated by the edge of the park close to a modern road named, yet again, Roman Road. On the other side of the road was Duntocher Burn. It was round about here that the remains of an ancient building were uncovered by chance in 1775. The first signs of it were spotted during the digging of a trench for the planting of potatoes, in which large quantities of well-made terracotta tiles of assorted sizes were found. According to bookseller John Knox who published an account of the discovery in his 1785 *View of the British Empire, More Especially Scotland*, this caused great excitement amongst the local farm workers, who proceeded to cart away these tiles for reuse.

Knox later intervened to save the ancient remains from further plundering, using, as he described it, 'threats and promises'. The discovery was mentioned in the press and aroused interest amongst the antiquarian community, with the result that a group of professors from the University of Glasgow came to inspect the remains.

Two low apertures in the base of a wall were unearthed. A local lad, John Bulloch, son of the miller at Duntocher, was persuaded to climb through one of them to see what lay inside, carrying a candle to light his way. He explored what we now know to be the area beneath a raised Roman floor, which was supported on piles of terracotta tiles. The brave boy spotted archways leading further into the hillside but, perhaps understandably, could not be convinced to venture deeper into the claustrophobic black void below Golden Hill.

Over the next three years, Edinburgh architect Charles Freebairn paid for the whole structure to be uncovered. It became clear that this was a Roman bath house, or what antiquarians often called a 'sudatory', from the Latin *sudare*, to sweat, an eighteenth-century term referencing the effects of a Roman bath's warmest rooms. Fragments of pottery that were unearthed, one featuring galloping centaurs, were sent to London to be inspected by the learned members of the Society of Antiquaries. Sketches and a plan of the building along with a map of its location were included in the 1789 edition of *Britannia*, an antiquarian tome first published in 1586 by William Camden that was updated and republished on several occasions over the next two and a half centuries.

The plan showed three rooms as well as two rounded walls known as 'apses' that are often seen in baths along the Antonine Wall. Despite the diminutive size of Duntocher fort, its bath house was around the same size as those found at the larger forts of Bar Hill, Cadder and Balmuildy. Its position on the hillside down by the burn may have required a short walk from the Roman fort above, but this was certainly a suitable location for a bathing facility that required a reliable and constant supply of fresh water.

It seems that the fragile remains of Duntocher bath house were left open to the elements after their excavation and quickly deteriorated as a result. Nineteenth-century visitors to the site described a dip in the earth and some broken tiles, but not much else. Some reported the presence of recycled Roman stones in the walls of nearby buildings, which may be where most of the bath house's ruins ended up. A short length of low wall with a drain running under it, as well as numerous fragments of tiles were, however, unearthed during digging around the war memorial in 1978.

Several smaller finds were made on the site during the late eighteenth-century excavations, including pottery and animal bones. Knox mentioned seeing 'a sooty kind of earth', evidence, no doubt, of the bath house's great furnaces. Like the bath house at Bearsden, this one must have been well-appointed. A stone sculpture of a woman was found, naked from the waist up, holding a stylised shell. A hole in the shell would have allowed water to pour through from a spout. The lines of her scraped-back hair and the folds of her skirt not only echo the ripples of water, but also clearly reference local Celtic designs.

To get across the Duntocher Burn, I had to cross a stone bridge, known for centuries as the 'Roman bridge'. There is even a Latin inscription on it which confirms its great antiquity, built into the parapet by the side of the road, not ancient but written in the style of a Roman distance marker, which can be translated as follows:

> *The Legate Quintus Lollius Urbicus ordered this bridge to be built for the Emperor Titus Aelius Antoninus Hadrianus Augustus, Father of his Country. It was restored from ruins by the Lord of Blantyre in the year of our Lord 1772*

Below that, in English, the words 'Blitzed 1941. Repaired 1943'. Such was the Roman bridge's fame in the eighteenth century that an etching of it was included in William Roy's *Military Antiquities* of 1793. It is a wonderfully romantic image, the stone arches of the two-span bridge leading over a

"Roman Bridge", Duntocher

rocky cascade, with trees and a thatched cottage in the background.

To get the best view of the bridge before crossing over it, I walked down past the Antonine Sports Centre to the side of the burn. At first sight, the structure had not changed much since the image in the *Military Antiquities* was made almost 250 years ago. The trees around it were thicker, the thatched cottage replaced by the beige walls of a modern house, but it was still incredibly picturesque. A torrent of foaming water tumbled noisily under one of its arches and on towards the Clyde.

The only problem is that the so-called 'Roman bridge' does not look very Roman at all. Antiquarian accounts which mention it tend to introduce a note of caution, if not downright incredulity as to its ancient origins. John Horsley stated that one arch of the bridge 'was supposed by some to be Roman'. William Maitland, not known for his circumspection, completely rejected this idea, suggesting that the Roman bridge would have been wooden, and this stone bridge was not Roman at all. The 1789 edition of *Britannia*, however, featured it alongside the description of the recently uncovered bath house, describing it confidently as 'the Roman bridge'.

While a delightful image of it appears in his book, even William Roy had doubts about its age, stating that it was probably rebuilt at some stage using stones from the walls of the Roman fort not far away. The illustration in Roy's *Military Antiquities* is based on a watercolour by landscape artist Joseph Farington and dated 1792, so had nothing to do with the author of the book, having been added as it was being edited for posthumous publication. As for it being built from Roman masonry, Robertson and Keppie's *Handbook* is concise in its dismissal of this notion; 'none is currently visible'.

Given the date of its eighteenth-century restoration as detailed on the inscription, the Lord Blantyre responsible must have been William Stuart, the 9th Lord who died at Erskine House on the other side of the Clyde in 1776. He may not have been the first to claim that this was a Roman bridge, but he was certainly the one that had it etched into stone for future generations to read (or at least those who could understand Latin). The locals became extremely attached to the idea that this was a Roman bridge too. In fact, in his 1854 *Rambles Round Glasgow*, Hugh MacDonald jokily warned against expressing any kind of scepticism in the presence of Duntocher residents:

> We should not like to call its antiquity into question where two or three of the Duntocher folk were gathered together. Right or wrong, they are determined to have it a Roman edifice, and would, there is reason to fear, be inclined to deal anything but gently with an obstinate incredulant.

It is worth pointing out that the bridge we see today is not the one illustrated in Roy's *Military Antiquities*, nor indeed the one traversed by Hugh MacDonald in the 1850s. As the inscription on its parapet records, that bridge was destroyed during the Clydebank Blitz of 1941. The town was targeted by the Luftwaffe due to its important role in producing ships and munitions for the Allied powers. Over two nights, 13-14 March 1941, Clydebank was laid waste and 528 of its inhabitants were killed, in proportion to its population the largest loss of civilian life in Scotland of any of the Second World War's many bombing raids. Although heavy industry was the official target, it was the residential areas that came off worse. The 'Roman bridge' was collateral damage, a victim of the thousands of bombs that rained down on Clydebank during those terrifying and devastating attacks.

In short, the bridge across the Duntocher Burn almost certainly dates from the later Middle Ages. Perhaps, in its previous form, before it was blown up and rebuilt in the 1940s, it did indeed contain Roman stones, those recycled blocks that pop up in other buildings all along the Antonine Wall, in the byre at Mumrills for example, or the medieval tower near Castlecary. Perhaps not. Although it is certainly a lovely wee bridge, I suspect its classical origins are the stuff of Romanist fantasy, invented at a time when everything Roman was held in the highest regard. Just don't tell anyone from Duntocher that I said that.

Over the bridge, I crossed over the A810 and turned into Beeches Road. This was also the route of the Antonine Wall, its rampart and ditch now lost beneath twentieth-century housing. A short length of the Military Way was, however, discovered in the grounds of St Mary's School in 1999.

The walk along Beeches Road began as a gentle climb, reaching a high point by a patch of grass. From there I could see far to the west, spotting for the first time the waters of the Clyde. A beam of sunlight burst through the clouds at just the right moment, briefly illuminating a huge mass of rock down beside the estuary. Another ancient 'dun', although not a Roman one this time, this was Dumbarton Rock.

Dumbarton Rock

The Rock was almost eight miles away from where I was standing, peeking up over the rooftops, but even from that distance, I could tell that it was enormous. In the post-Roman period, it was known as Alt Clut ('the rock on the Clyde') and served as the capital of a kingdom of the same name. It was later renamed Dun Breatann, 'fortress of the Britons', from which the modern name of Dumbarton is derived. Its high cliffs of volcanic basalt made it the ideal perch for a medieval castle, and it suffered several sieges and attacks during its long history.

In the thirteenth century Dumbarton Castle played a strategic role as a frontier fortress at a time when parts of mainland Scotland and many of its islands were Norwegian territory. Dumbarton's position by the water not far from the open sea made it a convenient escape route. Faced with violent incursions by the English, the child monarchs David II and Mary Queen of Scots both set out from there in 1334 and 1548 respectively to find safety in France. Mary's failed attempt to reach Dumbarton Rock in 1568 ultimately resulted in defeat at the Battle of Langside and her disastrous decision to flee into England.

In more recent centuries, its location by the side of the Clyde, far from the centres of power, saw its importance diminish, but it remained a garrison fortress until the eighteenth century. Although the rock is undoubtedly impressive, even from miles away, almost nothing remains of the ancient fortress or medieval castle that long ago graced its twin peaks.

Dumbarton Rock disappeared from view as Beeches Road made a sharp descent. Before long, I had reached the outer limits of Clydebank, leaving behind the tarmac road and stepping onto a track called the Thomas Wood Path, named after a local man who helped to supervise its construction. Its verges were thick with Rosebay willowherb, its pink flowers already turned to clouds of white, fluffy seeds that were waiting to be picked up and carried off by the wind.

It was in this vicinity that yet another fine distance marker was discovered. For reasons that are not clear, the short stretch of the Antonine Wall between Castlehill and Old Kilpatrick has produced many more than the eastern half. It features *peltae*, a Capricorn and a Pegasus and records the Second Legion's efforts in the construction of 3,271 ft of frontier. At some point towards the end of its conception, it seems the sculptor decided (or was perhaps instructed) to add a dedication to Antoninus Pius, which had to be awkwardly inserted into the blank spaces around the Capricorn.

First mentioned in the late seventeenth century, the distance slab was on display for many years in the wall of Cochno House a mile to the north, where it was admired by antiquarians. Alexander Gordon described it as 'executed with the best taste of any Roman Stone in Scotland'. Now, like most of the others, it can be seen in the Hunterian Museum.

The path followed exactly the course of the Antonine Wall. I was getting close to the Clyde, and close to my final destination. I had been aware of the Kilpatrick Hills for a while, a looming presence to the north of my route, but now there was no avoiding them. This expansive range extends from Dumbarton in the west to Strathblane in the east, reaching right up towards Loch Lomond. They have largely escaped the urbanisation that has covered most of the Clyde Valley and retain an air of wild ruggedness. I am sure they are quite beautiful on a sunny summer day, but as I walked past, they looked grim and gloomy, a blanket of wet cloud hanging balefully above their grey summits.

The position of this part of the Roman frontier seemed strange, extremely ineffective in terms of strategic defence. While most of the Antonine Wall ran along the southern rise of the Forth-Clyde Valley, a situation that offered extensive views over northern Caledonia, here it was at the foot of a ridge, overlooked by higher ground. This was not ideal, the hills providing cover for any attacking force. By this stage, however, its western terminus was almost in sight, down by the water, and just like me, the Wall had to get there, despite the topography.

Leaving the route of the frontier briefly to skirt the edge of a field, I walked for a while by the side of the Great Western Road. Comprising multiple lanes, it is part of the A82, which leads from central Glasgow right up to Inverness. At a noisy interchange, where it meets the A898, I was able to cut underneath it. As I headed downwards to the Clyde, another path reached upwards onto the Erskine Bridge. I had not noticed the bridge until then, and could not yet appreciate its vast scale, but I did spot a sign with a phone number for the Samaritans next to a battered old phone box, one of the few now remaining in use, both sober reminders that the bridge is one of Scotland's suicide blackspots.

A winding path took me down the side of the Dalnottar Burn through a pretty, tree-lined valley. It was at the foot of this valley that I reached the Dumbarton Road. By now, it was impossible to avoid the enormous bulk of the Erskine Bridge. I felt dwarfed by the reinforced concrete pier which towered above me, one of 14 holding up the road that allows traffic to speed high over the town of Old Kilpatrick and across the river.

The Erskine Bridge replaced a centuries-old ferry that used to perform a similar task, although at a much slower pace. Calls for a bridge began in the 1930s, but it was only in the 1960s that plans started to be formulated. It was a vast and expensive undertaking: measuring 1.3 km long and costing £10.5 million, it finally opened in 1971. Today, it carries over 35,000 vehicles per day over the river, its great height allowing boats to pass easily underneath.

To get down to sea level, I had been forced to leave the Antonine Wall behind, so next I headed northwards along the main street of Old Kilpatrick as I approached the end of the frontier. Old Kilpatrick is said by some to be the birthplace of St Patrick, although there is no hard evidence for this. Its name, nonetheless, is derived from the Gaelic 'Cille Phàdraig', meaning 'Patrick's church'.

It grew from a small village in the eighteenth and nineteenth centuries when it became a centre for the weaving industry and later shipbuilding. I walked past the nineteenth-century parish church, with its tall, pinnacled spire. A small park opposite boasted the location of St Patrick's Well, which one might assume was proof that the holy missionary did indeed hail from these parts, if the name did not appear to have been adopted as recently as the 1800s.

Within a few minutes, I had arrived at the location of the most westerly fort on the Antonine Wall. Nowadays, it is a remarkably unattractive spot, the shabby buildings of a former bus garage surrounded by a metal fence, its front yard littered with shipping containers. Even in the eighteenth century a visit to the site of Old Kilpatrick fort was something of a disappointment. Alexander Gordon guessed that a 'strong Garrison' must have been based there, but saw no signs of the Roman frontier, all of it destroyed, he concluded, by the plough. Horsley too found nothing of note but added that Roman antiquities in the area demonstrated a Roman presence thereabouts.

The reaction of antiquarians was probably not dissimilar to mine on the first occasion that I walked this leg of the Roman frontier. I arrived at Old Kilpatrick cold, wet and tired. After taking a brief look at the old bus garage, I walked around it, down Roman Crescent to Portpatrick Road. There I again met my companion for much of my journey, the Forth & Clyde Canal, which joins the Clyde not much further to the west at Bowling Harbour. While its construction caused enormous damage to the Antonine Wall, it can at least be said that its well-maintained towpath made walking the Roman frontier a much easier and more pleasurable experience.

Looking around, I could see no signs of the Wall, nor any indication that it had ended there. Then, at last, I spotted another of those tiny purple signs, halfway up a lamppost, bearing an image of the Roman horseman from the Bridgeness Distance Slab and the words 'The Antonine Wall: Frontiers of the Roman Empire World Heritage Site' As a record of the terminus of this mighty monument, it was more than a little underwhelming.

On my second visit to Old Kilpatrick, however, things had improved. By the bank of the canal, I found a new monument, a twin to the one in Harbour Road at Bridgeness. It supported a copy of a magnificent distance sculpture found nearby, which spent a few years at Mugdock Castle before the Duke of Montrose donated it to the University of Glasgow in the later 1600s. This new reproduction certainly does the original justice. Although the material is not local (the blonde sandstone, not dissimilar to that used by the Romans in Scotland, was sourced in Yorkshire) the craftsmanship was – apprentice stonemasons at the City of Glasgow College carved it with a 3D printed model as a guide, using tools not dissimilar to those used by the Romans.

The stone panel, which records the work of the Twentieth Legion, features a winged Victory. The goddess appears on other sculptures from the Antonine Wall, about to present a wreath or sometimes leaping into flight, one foot resting on a globe. This Victory, however, is more relaxed, reclining seductively, a palm frond resting on her shoulder and her robes draped over her legs. Her pose recalls that of ancient river gods, surely a reference to her location by the Clyde. Read together with the Bridgeness Distance Slab that I had seen at the beginning of the journey, this sculpture forms a powerful narrative: the Caledonians are brutally subdued, the land is cleansed during the *suovetaurilia*, then it is time to sit back and enjoy the spoils of conquest (although quite what the spoils from southern Caledonia would be is open to question).

Of all the distance markers found along the Antonine Wall, this one is perhaps the most unmistakably Roman. The reclining Victory is framed by a stylised temple façade, its pediment lifted by two fluted pilasters topped by intricate Corinthian capitals. It is probably for this reason that it was greatly admired by antiquarians. William Stukeley described it as 'a very fine Stone...with handsome Mouldings', Horsley chose it as the frontispiece to the plates in his *Britannia Romana* and it was selected as the first illustration in a set of engravings of the Roman stones at the University of Glasgow published in the late 1760s. While some of the sculptures found on the frontier, such as the gravestones from Shirva, were viewed in the eighteenth century as inferior and somewhat disappointing, there was no mistaking this sculpture's classical attributes.

As for the fort at Old Kilpatrick, which sits on a platform to the north of this new monument, it was excavated in 1923-4. With an internal area of 1.7 hectares, it predated the Antonine Wall, presumably built there to watch over the Clyde estuary and monitor its traffic. There may have been a Roman harbour here too, although no firm evidence of it has been discovered to date. The remains of the fort's *principia* and a granary, both built from stone, were found, as well as the postholes of wooden stores and barracks. Down by the Portpatrick Road, close to where I was standing, the meagre signs of a possible bath house were unearthed. Its remains seem to have been uncovered and then destroyed during the building of the canal in 1790. The baths were probably located in an annexe that lay on the south side of the fort down towards the estuary.

An eighteenth-century bascule bridge, designed to lift and allow vessels to pass underneath, leads over the canal to the crumbling ruins of a bridge-keeper's cottage, trees bursting out of its collapsed roof. The Clyde lies beyond it, although it is completely hidden by more trees. The very last plate in Sir George Macdonald's 1934 edition of *The Roman Wall in Scotland* shows a photograph of this very spot taken in 1913, although it looked rather different back then. The cottage was still inhabited for a start, there were no trees to hide the estuary and a railway line ran alongside the canal. Most importantly, a recently excavated patch of the Antonine Wall's stone base was visible by the canal edge, almost in line with the bridge.

Comparing the black and white photo in Macdonald's book to the modern landscape, I reckoned the temporarily exposed wall base would have been situated somewhere under a row of tatty wooden garages on the north side of Portpatrick Road. The railway line has gone, closed in 1964 and the tracks subsequently pulled up, but the eighteenth-century bridge, one of only two such structures to survive on this canal, is now listed and protected as a 'Scheduled Monument'.

The small exploratory dig in 1913 finally confirmed the location of the western terminus of the Roman frontier. While many had suspected that a fort stood at or near Old Kilpatrick even before its position was firmly identified, there were suggestions that the rampart of the Antonine Wall continued further along the coast. Some proposed that it reached Dunglass Castle, a much altered and now abandoned medieval fortress by the waterside a mile or so to the west. In his muddled eighth-century description of the ancient frontier, Bede even claimed that it went all the way to Dumbarton.

Thanks to George Macdonald, I could be sure that I had finally reached the end of my walk. Crossing over the canal, I continued down to the Clyde estuary. This part of Old Kilpatrick is still known as Ferrydyke, as the ferry which took passengers over the water departed from there right up until the early nineteenth century. There used to be a long quay too, named Donald's Quay after tobacco trader Robert Donald, who built himself a mansion at Mountblow not far away. The quay was demolished before the end of the nineteenth century, but Donald's Quay Light remains, a mini lighthouse, painted bright scarlet, that was installed to warn boatmen about an approaching bend in the river.

The view from the northern bank of the Clyde at Ferrydyke was glorious. The water was as dark as slate, reflecting the increasingly sombre sky. To my left, the Erskine Bridge swept over the estuary, 1,322 m from end to end, its gently curving platform supported by steel cables passing over two central pylons.

In the other direction, I could see Mar Hall, commissioned in the early 1800s by Major General Robert Walter Stuart, the 11th Lord Blantyre, a descendant of the man who rebuilt Duntocher's 'Roman Bridge' in 1772. Originally called Erskine House, it was designed by Sir Robert Smirke, best known as the architect of the British Museum, while Sir Charles Barry created its sumptuous gardens. Work began in 1828, and the enormous Elizabethan-style mansion took 17 years and over £50,000 to complete. It is now a luxury hotel surrounded by yet another of central Scotland's many golf courses.

There might not be anything Roman to see at the west end of the Antonine Wall, but it is nevertheless a wonderful spot. I stood for a minute, feeling the breeze on my face, listening to the sound of the water as it slapped listlessly against the stone wall of Ferrydyke. Finally, my journey along the Roman frontier was done. I was standing at what had been, for a brief moment, the north-western tip of the Roman Empire. I was tired, delighted, but also a little sad. The project of walking the Antonine Wall had played a huge part in my life over the previous months, giving me a purpose in difficult times and providing a huge amount of enjoyment. Now it was over. It was almost time to leave behind thoughts of ancient Caledonia, Roman garrisons and eccentric antiquarians and head back into the real world. Almost, but not quite.

Just as my journey along the Antonine Wall had begun with a visit to a museum, so it ended with another, this time to the Hunterian Museum at the University of Glasgow. It is possible to jump on a train from Old Kilpatrick Station to Glasgow Queen Street, a journey that takes less than 30 minutes, and then take the underground to Byres Road not far from the museum, but I preferred to come back another day, when I could enjoy the collection without boots and backpack.

The professors at the university, Scotland's second oldest after St Andrews, began collecting artefacts from the Antonine Wall in the late 1600s. They were particularly interested in carved stones at that time, and the collection soon grew to become the largest of its kind in the country. Along with Sir John Clerk's home at Penicuik, the university attracted a steady stream of antiquarians interested in studying the carvings and inscriptions found along the Roman frontier during the seventeenth and eighteenth centuries. In its early days, many of the stones in the collection were donated by generous aristocrats on whose estates they were found, with many of the donors being ex-students.

At first, the Roman inscribed stones and statues were housed in the library at the old university building on the High Street. They were stored in presses (cupboards) that had to be continually enlarged as the collection grew. By the late 1780s, concerns about the safety of the precious stones meant that visitors who wished to view them had to apply to one of the keyholders, the Principal or the Clerk of Faculty.

In 1810, the growing number of Roman artefacts was moved to the new Hunterian Museum in the gardens next to the university. It had been built to house an enormous collection donated by Dr William Hunter, which mostly comprised anatomical and zoological specimens.

By the later nineteenth century, the objects from the Antonine Wall seem to have become rather neglected, attracting less interest from visitors and curators. For evidence of this, look no further than the small distance sculpture found near Kirkintilloch that is decorated with a boar emerging from behind a tree, a cast of which can been seen at the Auld Kirk Museum. The original was donated by John Buchanan to the Hunterian and delivered in 1871 but ended up spending 28 years forgotten in the basement before it was rediscovered and finally put on display. By this time, the university had moved to the Gilbert Scott Building in the West End, a huge mock-medieval pile that is named for the man who designed it, a cathedral of learning that is still the main building of the institution today.

Nowadays, the Roman stones at the Hunterian are much better appreciated. In fact, the display entitled 'The Antonine Wall: Rome's Final Frontier' is the first thing you see as you step through its main entrance.

The gallery dedicated to the Roman Wall is impressive, with tall arched windows and a high vaulted ceiling, but the ranks of Roman carvings and inscriptions still hold their own in such gothic surroundings.

At the front of the exhibition stands a row of the stone columns from Bar Hill. In the middle of the gallery are glass cases containing the smaller objects found on the frontier. I saw some of the leather shoes from Bar Hill and admired their delicate decoration. Nearby I examined a chisel and hammer that were probably used in the construction of the Wall and its associated structures, the latter engraved with the name of a centurion, Ebutius, who may have supervised the building work. One fragment of terracotta tile bears the imprint of a dog's paw, capturing forever the moment that a mischievous canine ran loose around the drying yard before the clay was fired almost 2,000 years ago.

Looking at the artefacts in the Hunterian really brings the Antonine Wall to life. Little piles of hazelnut, walnut and oyster shells reminded me that the diet of the Roman frontier dwellers included many of the foodstuffs that we enjoy today, while a gaming board and dice showed how the soldiers relaxed when off duty. Also on display was the cracked stone ball from Leckie Broch, the carved waterspouts from Bearsden and Duntocher bath houses and the famous inscription bearing the name of Lollius Urbicus that Alexander Gordon nominated 'the most invaluable Jewel of Antiquity, that ever was found in the Island of Britain'.

It was great to finally get a good look at the rest of the Antonine Wall distance slabs too. There are 14 at the Hunterian, plus the plaster cast of the one lost in 'Great Chicago Fire'. The Bridgeness Distance Slab, as we know, is in the National Museum of Scotland in Edinburgh (although the Hunterian has a cast of that as well), another is in the collection of Glasgow's Kelvingrove Museum, but not currently on display.

Seeing all of them together made the variations in their size, style and content all the more noticeable. One, carved by the Sixth Legion and found near Old Kilpatrick consists of just an inscription surrounded by a simple carved moulding, but most are highly decorated. Many feature creatures both real and mythical: gods and monsters, boars and Pegasi, cupids and a triton. On others, the goddess Victory and fearless Roman cavalrymen lord it over the defeated enemy.

Despite their provincial aesthetic, the distance sculptures include decorative features that are unmistakeably classical, such as fluted pilasters, ansate panels or *peltae*. The order in which they are displayed at the Hunterian relates to the locations that they were found on the frontier, starting with the cast of the Bridgeness Slab on the right, finishing with the Old Kilpatrick on the left (or, I suppose, the other way round, depending on the direction you choose).

During my visit to the Hunterian, I was met by Dr Louisa Campbell, Lord Kelvin Adam Smith Postdoctoral Fellow at the University of Glasgow who heads up the pioneering 'Paints and Pigments in the Past' project. Since 2017, she has been studying the Roman inscribed carvings from the Antonine Wall in great depth, looking at them with fresh eyes and questioning the traditional theories about how they looked and where they were displayed. Spending so much time with the sculptures, examining them in such detail, has allowed her to appreciate them in a new light. 'Over time you develop an affinity with them and you start to see new things about them', she told me.

Dr Campbell's approach is refreshing. Archaeologists and historians (myself included) can sometimes get bogged down in old ideas and assumptions that have been passed down the generations. Questioning these assumptions often leads us in exciting new directions. Dr Campbell, for example, has proposed that the distance sculptures were not displayed on the turf rampart of the Antonine Wall, but rather by the Military Way, where they could be seen by the passing troops and others moving along the roadway. 'These things served an important purpose', she pointed out. 'They would have been in a prominent position to serve that purpose.'

Her study of the pigments used on the carvings that decorated the Roman frontier has produced some fascinating results. Innovative (and non-invasive) technologies such as portable X-ray fluorescence analysers and comparisons with sculptures from other parts of the Roman Empire have allowed Dr Campbell to pinpoint the colours used on the carved distance markers, identifying the elemental and mineral composition of the pigments to recreate their original hues and tones. While the natural elements contained within the sandstone combined with centuries of cleaning presented challenges, her discoveries were nevertheless ground-breaking.

I asked if any stone had provided particularly clear results, and Dr Campbell immediately led me over to the sculpture that was found at

Summerston Farm, which has also been reproduced at Lambhill Stables. It features dynamic scenes of conquest, with a Roman rider galloping over two bound Caledonians, a figure of the goddess Victory standing close by. On the other side, an eagle and Capricorn surmount another Caledonian captive. Dr Campbell found traces of the compound minium (a lead oxide) spotted across the bodies of the Caledonians and on the beak of the eagle: its vibrant red tones would have evoked the splatters of blood. The presence of orpiment (an arsenic sulphide) on Victory's dress demonstrate that it was once yellow, while white lead around its edges suggest an elegant white trim. The letters of the all-important inscription were highlighted with bright madder red.

While previous attempts to replicate the pigments on Scotland's Roman sculptures have featured inauthentic bright primary colours, Dr Campbell's findings revealed previously undiscovered depth to these frontier works. Just like the artists who painted the marbles in Rome, the painters working on the Antonine Wall layered and mixed their pigments to create soft and subtle shades. These sculptures and inscriptions must have looked magnificent when they were in position on or by the frontier. They still look magnificent today, ranked one beside the other, although we are inevitably less enamoured with their images of bloody conquest and merciless subjugation than their intended audience.

Dr Campbell clearly has a close connection with these sculptures. She feels that the way we talk about them does not always do them justice. She dislikes, for instance, the term 'slab', which is perhaps more reminiscent of a concrete patio than a complex work of art. She prefers to refer to them as 'distance sculptures', and I am minded to do the same in future.

My discussion with Dr Campbell, the final meeting of my walk, gave me much food for thought. While antiquarians were perplexed by some of the carved reliefs that they found on the Wall, judging some to be better (by which they meant more recognisably Roman) than others, we must move on from these reductive attitudes. The collection of sculptures created to adorn the Antonine Wall is unique – as far as we know, nothing like it existed anywhere else in the Roman world. Far from being inferior to the graceful marbles housed in the great museums of the world, they are a remarkable memorial to one of the most dramatic and intriguing chapters in the long story of Scotland, a short-lived conquest which has, as I had discovered on my journey, left an ineradicable imprint on the Scottish landscape and the Scottish psyche.

Standing before the distance sculptures was a humbling experience. Hearing about Dr Campbell's research made me realise that, although we may think we understand such ancient artefacts, there are always new discoveries to be made, new avenues of research to follow and new theories to be formulated.

The same is true of the Antonine Wall. On reaching the end of my walk along it, I felt that I knew it better than ever before. I had seen how the frontier interacted with the landscape as it made its way across the narrowest part of the British Isles, and now had a better sense of the ways in which the Roman builders and engineers had taken advantage of the topography and battled against the geology as they went. Exploring the remains of the Wall and examining the many artefacts and sculptures found along its length had provided me with a new insight into why it was constructed and what it was like to live and work on or near it.

Walking all along the ancient frontier had allowed me to appreciate how, even after its abandonment, the Antonine Wall has survived against the odds, dug into the soil and carved into the bedrock, influencing the routes of modern boundaries and roads. Its stones had been recycled and its ditch repurposed and in places it had succumbed to the elements and the forces of human progress, but even there the names of the streets and places that it crossed bore its memory.

Scots down the centuries struggled to understand who built it, what it was for, how it worked and why it was abandoned, inventing improbable tales and fanciful theories that reveal a great deal about their own beliefs, prejudices and expectations. Slowly but surely, particularly in the last century or so, we have made discoveries that help us understand it more fully.

There is still much to learn, mysteries to be solved, finds to be made. Future archaeologists will have plenty of work to do as they re-examine the Roman frontier, fieldwalking, reassessing old finds, scanning and perhaps even digging previously unexcavated sites. In the end, some aspects of its story may evade us for ever. To a certain extent, the Antonine Wall will always remain somewhat unknowable. That, I suspect, is all part of its enduring allure.

EPILOGUE

When I first planned my journey on foot along the Antonine Wall, I had hoped to complete it in a single trip: three days to get from Carriden to Old Kilpatrick and then an afternoon to walk up to Tappoch Broch and the site of Arthur's O'on. In the end, it took me a little over two years. Inevitably, a few things changed during that time and also in the months since I completed this book.

The sculpture based on the Roman harness is now in place by the entrance to Kinneil Estate. Created by sculptor Phil Neal from brass sheet, it sits on top of a 10 ft high column of sandstone and is known as the 'Kinneil Gate Guardian'. The Longannet Chimney, which acted as a landmark at various points on my walk is now gone, demolished in a cloud of concrete dust. The Falkirk Distillery that sits close to the Antonine Wall is finally up and running 12 years after it was begun and has recently been granted a licence to sell its Lowland malt.

More new monuments have also appeared along the Antonine Wall thanks to the (now award-winning) Rediscovering the Antonine Wall project. During a recent trip to Scotland, I made a pilgrimage to visit two of them.

My first stop was Croy Hill. It was a grey and misty early summer morning, with high winds and rain forecast for the afternoon, just the kind of conditions that I had become accustomed to as I journeyed along the Wall. I took the train to Croy railway station, then walked the short distance through the village to the foot of the hill.

This time, I was travelling in the other direction from my previous journey, west to east, and it took me a while to get my bearings. After a couple of false starts, I found the path onto the hill and began my climb. On the way up, I was able to make out the subtle humps of the expansions that I had missed on my first visit. Over the summit, I passed the site of the fortlet and then the Roman fort, stopping for a while to admire the view, or at least what was visible between the clouds. Heading on, I continued towards Dullatur, walking along the side of the rock-cut ditch, pausing briefly to inspect William Maitland's 'vegetating' rocks before I made my descent.

At the bottom of the slope, I came face to face with the most recent arrival on the hill – the enormous head of a Roman centurion fashioned from weathered steel. He has a powerful presence, seven metres tall, the crest of his helmet reaching towards the sky like a great metal sunburst, gazing over towards Camelon and the site of Arthur's O'on. The surface of the metal was lightly oxidised, its velvety patina a rich, rusty red, but he still felt solid, unmovable, a force to be reckoned with.

The sculpture was conceived by Svetlana Kondakova, who trained at Edinburgh College of Art, and built by Gordon Simpson of Big Red Blacksmiths, based in West Lothian. Kondakova has created several pieces of public art, including sculptures, mosaics and a mural, but when I contacted her about the Croy Hill centurion, she told me that it had been a particularly challenging commission, her biggest to date.

She began with a small and flimsy card maquette, which then had to be scaled up to create the giant sculpture. The original plan was that the sculptor would work together with the blacksmith to construct the final piece, but pandemic restrictions meant that Simpson more or less made it on his own. Its hillside location meant that the enormous head (which Kondakova and Simpson nicknamed 'Big Jim') needed to be made and transported in segments and reconstructed piece by piece on site, like a huge 3D jigsaw.

As with Aurelius, the Roman head at Lambhill Stables, a final name for the steel centurion was selected by a public vote. The winning suggestion was 'Silvanus', the Roman god associated with woodland and wild countryside. Altars dedicated to Silvanus have been discovered all over Britannia, from Somerset to Hadrian's Wall, and three have been found on the Antonine Wall, two at Bar Hill and one at Auchendavy. There are only a few trees on Croy Hill nowadays, but Silvanus was later linked with fields and boundaries, so perhaps the name is not entirely inappropriate for a soldier who sits on the edge of the Empire.

I love this sculpture, not only its stunning design, but also the way that it dominates everything around it, just as the Antonine Wall would have done in its heyday. It manages to be both beautiful and intimidating at the same time. Stern-featured and determined, Silvanus looks like he is made to last. I have no doubt he will remain on Croy Hill much longer than the flesh and blood Romans who used to patrol this very same spot.

Next, it was back over Croy Hill and a short train journey (which was, it turned out, perfectly timed to avoid a torrential downpour) to Falkirk. There, I searched out Cow Wynd. The unusual name of this street predates the great Falkirk cattle trysts, apparently relating to the fact that farmers would bring their cows along there on the way to the common grazing grounds to the south of the town. It is also right next to the site of the Antonine Wall fort that now lies under the bowling green and Scout hall.

To the side of the road on Cow Wynd, another carving has been erected. Its design is clearly inspired by the Roman distance sculptures found along the frontier, but this is not a reproduction. Its inscription is in English, for a start. Its bears the date 2020 and celebrates not the efforts of ancient legionaries, but the achievements of the many people who are now working hard to protect and promote the Roman Wall, a group designated 'the 21st Century Legion': 'FOR REDISCOVERING THE ANTONINE WALL PROJECT 21ST CENTURY LEGION MADE THIS MMXX'.

The figural scenes around the inscription show the other side of the Roman invasion, telling the story from the Caledonian point of view. On the left-hand side, a battle, but on this occasion, rather than the indigenous people being cut down and slaughtered, a chariot-driving Caledonian brandishes his sword over a fallen Roman soldier. A carnyx, the animal-headed Iron Age battle horn, frames the scene. The piece of stone chosen by sculptors Josephine Crossland and Luke Batchelor is a golden Cop Crag sandstone from Northumberland that is naturally flecked with patches of vivid purple. When I got in touch to ask her about the commission, Crossland explained that they had chosen it on purpose, as it reminded them of splashes of blood.

On the other side of the inscription, a Caledonian couple stand before a broch (Tappoch perhaps?) as they meet with two kneeling Romans. A vase is changing hands, a gift maybe, or a trade. In contrast with the ancient distance sculptures, with their unmistakable messages of Roman victory, conquest and subjugation, this stone presents a more nuanced vision of ancient Caledonia, in which the locals fought back, but also interacted with the new arrivals.

There is much more to be discovered about how the Caledonians reacted to the Roman invasion and the construction of the Antonine Wall, how it impacted on their way of life and how they resisted or accepted it. Both Dr Fraser Hunter and Dr Louisa Campbell told me that they saw further research on this subject as an important factor in understanding this complex frontier. The modern carving in Falkirk also recognises that there is more to this story than the ruthless Roman cavalrymen and the gloating winged Victories of the ancient stones, opening our eyes to the many other tales that the Wall has to tell.

These new installations will surely bring more visitors to the Antonine Wall, shining a light on this long overlooked national treasure and attracting a whole new audience to it. They may introduce the monument to local inhabitants too, those who have previously been unaware of its importance, or even of its very existence. The work of the '21st Century Legion' carries on, with more exciting plans in the pipeline. I look forward to seeing how things develop, and I strongly suspect that the journeys described in this book will not be the last of my walks along the Roman frontier.

Just like the landscape that it runs through, the Antonine Wall has changed since I first set off from Carriden, not the ancient monument itself perhaps, but the way in which it is presented to visitors. It will ever be so. Even today, over 1,800 years since the Romans abandoned it, the story of the frontier is far from over. Thanks to initiatives such as the Rediscovering the Antonine Wall project, new funds have helped to make it more visible, attracting new audiences of all ages and backgrounds. Scotland's Roman Wall is finally emerging from the long shadow of Hadrian's Wall and getting its own moment in the spotlight. Hopefully, this renewed interest in its history and archaeology will only continue to blossom and grow.

A monument of this scale and this importance is never frozen in time, like a specimen pickled in formaldehyde or a dish preserved in aspic. If you decide to walk along the Roman frontier, or maybe just visit a few of its individual sites, the experiences you have will no doubt be subtly different to mine. The Antonine Wall exposes different aspects of itself in different weather and different times of day. It changes with the seasons. As we have seen, it has constantly evolved over the centuries – fading in places, ruthlessly destroyed in others, but also revealing itself to the archaeologist's trowel or the aerial photographer's camera, allowing us glimpses into its enigmatic past.

Nowadays, there is little digging going on, none of the large-scale excavations like those directed by Sir George Macdonald or Mungo Buchanan. The current policy is to leave its fragile remains alone, safely underground, unless building work, the laying of drains say, or a new road, threaten to damage the archaeology. Then, small rescue digs might take place. This may change too, as attitudes alter, although I doubt it will be any time soon.

Our analyses of the Antonine Wall, of how it was built, how it worked and what it was for, will inevitably develop too. New findings may completely contradict current thinking. Just as we raise an eyebrow at the idea of a terracotta communication tube or smile at fanciful notions of vegetating rocks and heroic Caledonian princes, so future generations might look back in amusement at some of our theories about the history and function of the Roman frontier. Whoever coined the phrase 'you can't rewrite history' obviously had no idea of how history works. The future is unpredictable, often surprising. But then, as I discovered on my walks along the Antonine Wall, so is the past.

SELECT BIBLIOGRAPHY

Antiquarian Books

Fordun, John of, *Chronicle of the Scottish Nation*, Volume IV (Edinburgh: Edmonston and Douglas, 1872) (Available on archive.org)

Gordon, Alexander, *Itinerarium Septentrionale; or, a Journey Thro' Most of the Counties in Scotland, and Those in the North of England* (London: 1726) (Available on books.google.co.uk)

Horsley, John, *Britannia Romana; or, the Roman Antiquities of Britain* (London: 1732) (Available on archive.org)

MacDonald, Hugh, *Rambles Round Glasgow: Descriptive, Historical, and Traditional* (Glasgow: Thomas Murray & Son, 1856) (Available on books.google.co.uk)

Macpherson, James, *Fingal, An Ancient Epic Poem, in Six Books: Together with Several Other Poems, Composed by Ossian the Son of Fingal* (London: 1762) (Available on books.google.co.uk)

Nimmo, William, *A General History of Stirlingshire* (Edinburgh: 1777) (Available on books.google.co.uk)

Roy, William, *The Military Antiquities of the Romans in Britain* (London: 1793) (Available on maps.nls.uk)

Sibbald, Robert, *Historical Inquiries, Concerning the Roman Monuments and Antiquities in the North-Part of Britain Called Scotland* (Edinburgh: 1707) (Available on books.google.co.uk)

Stukeley, William, *An Account of a Roman Temple and Other Antiquities near Graham's Dike in Scotland* (London: 1720) (Available on books.google.co.uk)

Modern Publications

Breeze, David, *Bearsden: A Roman Fort on the Antonine Wall* (Edinburgh: Society of Antiquaries of Scotland, 2016) (Available as a free download on www.socantscot.org)

Breeze, David, *The Antonine Wall* (Edinburgh: John Donald, 2006)

Breeze, David and William Hanson (eds), *The Antonine Wall: Papers in Honour of Professor Lawrence Keppie* (Oxford: Archaeopress Publishing, 2020)

Keppie, Lawrence, *Roman Inscribed and Sculptured Stones in the Hunterian Museum, University of Glasgow* (London: Society for the Promotion of Roman Studies, 1998)

Keppie, Lawrence, *The Antiquarian Rediscovery of the Antonine Wall* (Edinburgh: Society of Antiquaries of Scotland, 2012)

Macdonald, George, *The Roman Wall in Scotland* (Glasgow: James MacLehose and Sons, 1911 and Oxford: The Clarendon Press, 1934)

Mothersole, Jessie, *In Roman Scotland* (London: The Bodley Head, 1927)

Robertson, Anne and Lawrence Keppie, *The Antonine Wall: A Handbook to Scotland's Roman Frontier* (Glasgow: Glasgow Archaeological Society, 2015)

Online Resources

Canmore: National Record of the Historic Environment: www.canmore.org.uk

Falkirk Local History Society: www.falkirklocalhistory.club

Historic Environment Scotland, Antonine Wall. Statements of Significance: https://www.historicenvironment.scot/archives-and-research/publications

The Antonine Wall: Frontiers of the Roman Empire: www.antoninewall.org

OTHER TITLES BY TIPPERMUIR BOOKS

Spanish Thermopylae (2009)

Battleground Perthshire (2009)

Perth: Street by Street (2012)

Born in Perthshire (2012)

In Spain with Orwell (2013)

Trust (2014)

Perth: As Others Saw Us (2014)

Love All (2015)

A Chocolate Soldier (2016)

The Early Photographers of Perthshire (2016)

Taking Detective Novels Seriously: The Collected Crime Reviews of Dorothy L Sayers (2017)

Walking with Ghosts (2017)

No Fair City: Dark Tales from Perth's Past (2017)

The Tale o the Wee Mowdie that wantit tae ken wha keeched on his heid (2017)

Hunters: Wee Stories from the Crescent: A Reminiscence of Perth's Hunter Crescent (2017)

A Little Book of Carol's (2018)

Flipstones (2018)

Perth: Scott's Fair City: The Fair Maid of Perth & Sir Walter Scott – A Celebration & Guided Tour (2018)

God, Hitler, and Lord Peter Wimsey: Selected Essays, Speeches and Articles by Dorothy L Sayers (2019)

Perth & Kinross: A Pocket Miscellany: A Companion for Visitors and Residents (2019)

The Piper of Tobruk: Pipe Major Robert Roy, MBE, DCM (2019)

The 'Gig Docter o Athole': Dr William Irvine & The Irvine Memorial Hospital (2019)

Afore the Highlands: The Jacobites in Perth, 1715-16 (2019)

'Where Sky and Summit Meet': Flight Over Perthshire – A History: Tales of Pilots, Airfields, Aeronautical Feats, & War (2019)

Diverted Traffic (2020)

Authentic Democracy: An Ethical Justification of Anarchism (2020)

'If Rivers Could Sing': A Scottish River Wildlife Journey. A Year in the Life of the River Devon as it flows through the Counties of Perthshire, Kinross-shire & Clackmannanshire (2020)

A Squatter o Bairnrhymes (2020)

In a Sma Room Songbook: From the Poems by William Soutar (2020)

The Nicht Afore Christmas: the much-loved yuletide tale in Scots (2020)

Ice Cold Blood (2021)

The Perth Riverside Nursery & Beyond: A Spirit of Enterprise and Improvement (2021)

Fatal Duty: The Scottish Police Force to 1952: Cop Killers, Killer Cops & More (2021)

The Shanter Legacy: The Search for the Grey Mare's Tail (2021)

'Dying to Live': The Story of Grant McIntyre, Covid's Sickest Patient (2021)

The Black Watch and the Great War (2021)

Beyond the Swelkie: A Collection of Poems & Writings to Mark the Centenary of George Mackay Brown (2021)

Sweet F.A. (2022)

A War of Two Halves (2022)

A Scottish Wildlife Odyssey (2022)

In the Shadow of Piper Alpha (2022)

Mind the Links: Golf Memories (2022)

Perthshire 101: A Poetic Gazetteer of the Big County (Andy Jackson (editor), 2022)

The Banes o the Turas: An Owersettin in Scots o the Poems bi Pino Mereu scrievit in Tribute tae Hamish Henderson (Jim Mackintosh, 2022)

FORTHCOMING

The Whole Damn Town (Hannah Ballantyne, 2022)

Fat Girl, Best Friend (Sarah Grant, 2022)

Balkan Rhapsody (Maria Kassimova-Moisset, translated by Iliyana Nedkova Byrne, 2022)

Families of Spies (David Miller, 2022)

William Soutar: Collected Poetry, Volume I (Published Work) (Kirsteen McCue, Philippa Osmond-Williams and Paul S Philippou (editors), 2022)

William Soutar: Collected Poetry, Volume II (Published Work) (Kirsteen McCue, Philippa Osmond-Williams and Paul S Philippou (editors), 2022)

William Soutar: Collected Poetry, Volume III (Unpublished Work) (Kirsteen McCue, Philippa Osmond-Williams and Paul S Philippou (editors), 2023)

The Black Watch from the Crimean War to the Second Boer War (Derek Patrick and Fraser Brown, 2023)

A British Wildlife Journey (Keith Broomfield, 2023)

The Japan Lights (Iain Maloney, 2023)

All Tippermuir Books titles are available from bookshops and online booksellers. They can also be purchased directly (with free postage & packing (UK only) – minimum charges for overseas delivery) from www.tippermuirbooks.co.uk. Tippermuir Books Ltd can be contacted at mail@tippermuirbooks.co.uk